Profiles in Success

Profiles in Success

Inspiration from Executive Leaders

Volume 16

GORDON J. BERNHARDT, CFP®, AIF®

ISBN: 978-0-9972483-5-7 (paperback)

First edition

Gordon Bernhardt conducts interviews of business leaders primarily in the Washington D.C. area who come recommended by their peers. The profiles included in this volume are a result of these interviews. As a result of these additional insights Mr. Bernhardt has published these profiles. Gordon Bernhardt is the President and CEO of Bernhardt Wealth Management, a registered investment adviser with the Securities and Exchange Commission. Registration is mandatory for all persons meeting the definition of investment adviser and does not imply a certain level of skill or training. The business leaders may or may not be clients of Bernhardt Wealth Management. These interviews are independent of investment advisory services and do not imply any endorsement of Gordon Bernhardt or Bernhardt Wealth Management by the business leaders.

This book exists because of all the inspirational individuals who so graciously shared their stories with me. I am thankful for the opportunity to get to know each and every one of you. I feel like a better person thanks to what I learned from you and your story.

To my team at Bernhardt Wealth Management—Tim Koehl, Solon Vlasto, Bonnie Maingault, Evan McCullers, Kent Davis, Ben Madtes, and Carol Dreistadt. I would never have been able to do this without your efforts and support throughout the process. Thank you for all you do for each other and for our clients.

I am deeply grateful to Peter Schwartz, Master Chair of Vistage Worldwide, for your help and encouragement on this project.

And lastly, this book would not have been possible without the guidance and creative support of Karen Embry.

Table of Contents

Foreword

Vistage is the world's largest CEO coaching and peer advisory organization for small and medium sized businesses. For more than 60 years we've been helping CEO's, business owners and key executives solve their greatest challenges. As a Vistage chair, I facilitate six peer advisory groups for the purpose of helping senior executives become better leaders, make better decisions and produce better results. We meet in a confidential setting without any competitors in the room. This creates an environment in which everyone is free to be honest and in return receive unvarnished advice and insight from peers to a degree they simply couldn't get anywhere else. This environment of raw honesty, genuine caring and commitment toward each other, produces extraordinary results.

In the past 16 years, I have worked with 279 CEOs and business owners. During that time, I have witnessed countless heroics on the part of these individuals as they have taken their companies thru the Great Recession, three government shutdowns and a global pandemic. I believe the greatest untold story is that of our country's small- and mid-size business owner. The privilege of my professional life is working with these individuals as they deal with VUCA (volatile, uncertain, complex, ambiguous) environments. They bravely face all the disruption, continual technical and adaptive challenges in an effort to grow the business, and keep their people employed. Unfortunately, the story of the small business owner seldom appears in the *Wall Street Journal.* These stories are about the triumph of spirit over circumstance in that many of these individuals have come from, or have been through, very challenging conditions and situations. As a Vistage Chair the privilege of my professional life is to be a "participatory companion" working closely with these heroes of the American economy and for their Vistage Group to bear "witness" to these amazing journeys.

Two Cs of Leadership

I was once a business owner. I was a start-up guy who took a couple of early-stage concepts to maturity. This is where I learned the "technical skills" or "competency" side of being a leader–the tactics, processes and how to execute. Competency is certainly necessary, but it turns out there is an even more important component of leadership and that is "consciousness" or "adaptive skill." Consciousness or the "adaptive skill" is what is going on internally–the individual's personal operating software–that we may not even be aware is running. It is the "habits of thinking," subconsciously, that shape how we perform in a certain context. For example, a person who grew up under difficult circumstances makes meaning out of that experience which shows up in the way they lead. For some, it empowers them, and for others, it inhibits them. The small business of the future that is purpose-led, customer-centric, experience-driven, and technology-scaled requires new mindsets far more than new toolsets or skillsets.

As a CEO coach, I work to help surface "habits of thinking" (mindsets). Through our conversations my clients begin reframe "how to see the problem" and they ask themselves, "Is the mindset that got me here the one I need to get there?" CEOs who join my Vistage groups not only pay attention to the technical aspects of growing the business, they pay attention to their own personal growth as leaders. How a CEO is experienced as a leader by their employees determines their leadership impact, which determines organizational effectiveness.

Certainly, every leader needs to develop a "technical "skill-set in order to execute at a high level. More important than that, today's leader must grow their mind (adaptive skill) in order to handle the ever-increasing complexity of the modern business environment. To effectively deal with todays' VUVA environments, it is essential that today's leaders develop VUCA mind (Vision, Understanding, Clarity, Adaptability).

A Trajectory of Success

Typically, individuals enter into adulthood with a success strategy. That is, in order to be "safe, secure and worthwhile in this world" I must be as seen in the eyes of others. Imagine a young person who grows up in a supportive environment, gets involved in athletics and turns out to be really good. They receive standing ovations for their accomplishments on the field or court and learn through that experience that in order to be seen as worthwhile they must achieve. That is a healthy message that they take into adulthood with a determination to work hard and achieve. Because they achieve, they get promoted into a role where they now manage others. For the first time, a shift in consciousness is required. They discover that it is no longer just about their achievements but it is through the achievements of others that determine successful outcomes. "I need to value the efforts of others and start helping others to succeed because it's not about me, it's about us." This very significant shift can be very difficult for many people because it means they have to let go of strategies that had previously worked for them and find new strategies. Almost everyone struggles through this stage before accepting that "what got me here won't get me there."

Opening the door to a change of consciousness is different for each person. That said, everyone arrives at a point in life where a success strategy that once worked for them is now an obstacle and will need to evolve in order to more effectively meet the challenges of a more complex life.

Mentoring—Consulting—Coaching

In my experience, most leaders have sought guidance along their trajectory of success in at least one of three ways.

- Mentoring typically involves an individual with much more experience in a specific role helping another person develop their expertise. A mentor will serve as a sounding-board, provide guidance and help the mentee develop or improve particular skills. This is typically an informal and often long-lasting arrangement.
- Consulting involves hiring a person for their specific subject matter expertise in order to improve a situation or context. Simply put, this is the purchase of someone's knowledge.
- Coaching is based on the belief that all the resources a person needs to succeed are internal to that person. The coach, through inquiry and conversation, pulls those resources to the surface and designs a set of actions that builds competency and confidence in a particular area. Coaching is not about supplying answers, it is all about the right question that needs to be asked. "The quality of the question determines the quality of the outcome."

Gordon Bernhardt and I share a mutual enthusiasm for people and discovering their stories. We are both fortunate to work in professional fields that allow us to regularly engage interesting and successful people throughout the Washington D.C. area. In sharing the details and personal perspectives regarding their failures, disappointments, successes and achievements, each of the leaders profiled in this book has a lesson from their life to teach us. No matter where you are on your trajectory of success, this is good reading.

– Peter Schwartz
Master Chair | Best Practice Chair Vistage Worldwide

Peter Schwartz is a Vistage Chair working with chief executives and business owners who want to become better leaders, make better decisions, and produce better results. Vistage D.C. serves more than 500 businessmen and women from companies that generate $15 billion in annual revenues and employ more than 60,000 people. In 2020, Schwartz received Vistage's highest honor, the Don Cope Memorial Award. In 2015 he was named Vistage Chair of the Year. He is a four-time "STAR' award and nine-time Chair Excellence Award winner. As a former Host of Executive Leaders Radio, he has conducted hundreds of elite interviews of prominent CEOs, COOs, CFOs, CIOs and presidents focusing on "what makes people tick."

BERNHARDT

WEALTH MANAGEMENT

Introduction

"Close scrutiny will show that most 'crisis situations' are opportunities to either advance, or stay where you are."
– Maxwell Maltz

Being a C-suite executive or business owner has always entailed managing potential crises of one kind or another. Those who have had years to work out their leadership muscles understand that navigating new and ever-changing priorities with limited time to react is often just part of the job. But in 2020, a once-in-a-century pandemic took the word "crisis" to a whole new level. Leaders in every sector of life, some seasoned and some new to the role, were all thrown into the same situation for which very few of us were prepared to manage.

As usual, I'm setting aside the politics of this pandemic. No matter your personal views regarding the threat or governance associated with this crisis, you could not ignore it. As leaders, we regularly manage the needs and concerns of different constituents, all with varying points of view, whether we are in crisis mode or just a normal day at the office. But the scale of unwavering and divisive positions touched every person, business and leader throughout our country, making it that much more challenging to navigate. It's been said that a crisis can manifest the worst and best of humanity. It can also reveal a lot about the type of leader you are, and that of those around you.

In what felt like an instant, COVID-19 struck and scrambled all of our priorities. Focus switched from innovation, revenue and market share to physical health and safety, digital work transformation, and mental health and wellbeing. In other words, people eclipsed all other concerns. Empathy, flexibility and communication became the winning skillset for successful leaders.

Empathy

"How are you doing, today?" Once a benign question usually followed by an equally placid response has now transformed into a vital tool for leaders to truly understand how others feel and what they need to succeed. Numerous studies show that in a business environment, empathetic leaders perform better and cultivate more loyalty. This becomes especially critical during a crisis when everyone is looking to leadership for an example of how they should be handling the upheaval. Trust is earned when people believe the management team genuinely understands their pain points and is striving to support them. Remember the video clips of cats walking across the computer screen and toddlers bursting in on Zoom calls—combined with the sky-rocketing statistics for depression and anxiety?

Flexibility

COVID-19 dramatically altered the workplace, perhaps permanently. I know I personally prefer to have our entire team back in the office together and seeing our clients in person. But the forced need for everyone to transition to a digital life demonstrated that it is possible to do things differently. Companies, especially retailers, that acted quickly to reimagine ways to continue providing goods and services came out ahead of those that couldn't or wouldn't act with speed. In times of crisis, expediency over perfection is essential.

Communication

Successful leaders swiftly process available information (even when that information is changing by the hour), determine what matters most, and make decisions with conviction. Then communicate, communicate, communicate. By getting a consistent message out quickly to all constituents there is no room for speculation that clients or staff may be receiving different information than the executive team or board members. Don't be afraid to be transparent about current realities—including what you don't know or that what you know now will likely be changing as more information becomes available. By sharing the disheartening realities along with a clear directive for moving forward, leaders can keep everyone focused on a shared purpose.

Many point to New Zealand Prime Minister Jacinda Ardern as an example of effective leadership during a crisis. According to Suze Wilson, a professor at New Zealand's Massey School of Management, the country's COVID-19 messaging campaign "was so well communicated that people just got it." She described Ardern as "calm, focused, practical, and decisive" in her daily briefings and Facebook-live streams to the public.

When asked to describe 2020 in one word, more than half of responses to the Fortune/Deloitte CEO Survey used decidedly negative words. The most common word was "Challenging." In comparison, 27% of CEOs in the latest survey wrote "hope" or "hopeful" to describe 2021. Other common words included "opportunity," "optimism," and "recovery." As the path out of this crisis seems to be clear, I also feel positive.

Our team and business fared well, as did our clients. Now, we are taking time for a retrospective review of our detour during COVID-19 in order to discern what we could have done differently and which changes, originally thrust upon us, will we continue as a regular part of doing business. I have written often about Bernhardt Wealth Management's core values of Character, Chemistry, Caring and Competence. I believe making decisions and maintaining a culture consistent with those values throughout this crisis, kept our attention where it needed to be in order to continue the journey forward.

Buen Camino!

– **Gordon J. Bernhardt, CFP®, AIF®**
Founder, President and CEO
Bernhardt Wealth Management
www.BernhardtWealth.com

Since establishing his firm in 1994, Gordon Bernhardt has been focused on providing high-quality service and independent financial advice in order to help his clients make smart decisions about their money. He specializes in addressing the unique needs of successful professionals, entrepreneurs and retirees, as well as women in transition throughout the Washington, D.C. area. Over the years, Gordon has been sought out by numerous media outlets including MSN Money, CNN Money, Kiplinger and The New York Times for his insight into subjects related to personal finance.

Profiles

BERNHARDT

WEALTH MANAGEMENT

Andrew Bennett

Life is a Precious Gift

When Andrew Bennett was three years old, his mother left him with his grandparents one afternoon. She was taking Andrew's seven-year-old sister, Kelly, to the dentist, and Andrew had a cold. "I'm leaving my boy with you," she told her mother. Later that day, Andrew's mother and older sister were killed in a car accident, the victims of a drunk driver. With their daughters' final words echoing in their ears, his grandparents chose to take him in permanently.

He was too young to remember his mother, but he heard stories of her growing up. So much so, that he feels as if he knew her. "I know when somebody passes, people can put them on a pedestal," Andrew reflects. "But my mom sounds like she was beloved. She was a really bright ray of sunshine in our community. I'm thankful that even though I didn't know her, she's been that positive, real, optimistic, joyful presence with me."

For about a year, his father and older brother, Brad, moved in with his maternal grandparents as well. But eventually, his father moved out and remarried, taking Brad with him. Andrew stayed with his grandparents, and for years struggled to understand why his father had left him behind. In retrospect, he realizes the situation was more complex than he could've understood at the time. "From my dad's perspective, my grandparents wouldn't let me go," he relates. "He came on the Thanksgiving after he'd remarried to collect me, and my grandpa and he had a fist fight. Grandpa cleaned his clock, and basically said, 'you'll never take our boy.' I think in a way, my grandparents needed me. I looked so much like my mom and my sister. They needed something to give them solace from their loss."

It was a dramatic start to life for young Andrew, but his childhood in picturesque Beulah, Michigan wasn't all tragedy. In fact, his youth might best be described as both the best of times, and the worst of times." Once he was settled with his grandparents, the three moved from a little house in downtown Beulah to a 150-acre cherry farm a mile outside of town. Though it was more of a hobby than a money-making endeavor, the cherry orchards were fully functional, with migrant workers coming to pick the cherries every year. "Growing up there was magical," reminisces Andrew. "My buddies came over to play, and it was like we had our own park. We played in the orchard, and the empty farmhouse on the property became our clubhouse. We also had horses that we would ride. Those were the days when you could run out in the morning and come back when it was getting dark. My grandmother would ring a bell when it was time for dinner."

Growing up, Andrew called his grandmother "Nin," a baby's permutation of "Nana" that stuck. He was wonderfully close with both Nin and Grandpa, both of whom exemplified kindness, caring for others, and a wicked sense of humor. "They were characters," Andrew smiles. "They were funny as hell. I am so grateful that I got that sense of humor; it's been a big savior in my life." He remembers spending long hours with his grandfather in what they called the "fly-tying" room. "He was an avid outdoorsman and loved hunting and fishing. He tied his own trout flies," explains Andrew. "He would sit in the fly-tying room with a Tiparillo cigar in his mouth, listen to classical music, and make his own trout flies. I would come in, pull up a chair, and chew the fat. We did that all the time."

At the age of seven, Andrew got his first magic kit. He began doing tricks at school and became notorious as the local magician. By 12, he was doing shows at local venues like the grange hall. He had business cards printed up and would hand them out to anyone he met. Through it all, his grandparents were his biggest fans, and his grandfather helped write his act. The family always ate dinner each night together, and Andy would show off any new tricks he had learned. In the morning, his grandfather would go to work; he was President of a local bank. But on the counter, he'd have left a script to accompany the new trick.

Andy's grandfather had a keen business sense. He had risen from janitor in the bank where he eventually became President, and he helped Andy manage his burgeoning magic career. "When I started to get paid for my magic, my first fee was $25," recalls Andrew. "Grandpa taught me how to write contracts. He got a typewriter from the bank for me, and I converted my toy room into my office. How many 12-year-olds are writing contracts, promoting themselves, and putting ads in newspapers? I was never just an entertainer. I was a businessperson, too."

Andrew's magic business was taking off, and he was thriving in school. He did well in class and was popular with the other students. Everything was going so smoothly; then, tragedy struck once again. Andrew was 13 when his grandfather was hospitalized during a severe mental health crisis. "I saw him in the hospital," remembers Andrew. "I saw him literally fall apart. He went from being my hero to being delusional and hallucinating. I think that's when I realized I'm going to have to take care of myself." From that time, Andrew's grandfather never spent more than two weeks back home with the family before taking his life three years later.

"By that time, he had been in institutions all over Michigan," describes Andrew. "They tried everything including electroshock therapy and valium. When he killed himself, he had been home for two weeks, and he was the best he'd ever been. It was like we had him back. I've since learned that that is oftentimes when people take their own lives. Because they're terrified they might go back to that darkness. After he died, I had this feeling of the world collapsing. Like everything was closing in. My grandma was the rock. She was a tough, incredible woman. I put so much emphasis on my grandfather being my hero in my life, but my grandma was the foundation. She was always there, and, my goodness, she was tough."

Andrew notes that it would be years before he fully grappled with the loss of his grandfather. At the time, his way of dealing with it was to keep his head down and throw himself into work, school, and magic. By then, Andrew had already had a local TV show for two years. The opportunity had come about somewhat fatefully. His grandmother was getting new carpeting installed, and the worker happened to notice his magic props. It turned out that he was a magician, too, and was part of a club. Andrew was invited to join, and though he was the youngest by decades, he loved spending time there. One of the other club members, Jim Matthews, was a producer at the TV station in nearby Traverse City.

"He started saying I should have a kid's show on Saturday morning," says Andrew. "A local, live kid's show. So, *The Andy Bennett Show* was created. There was a live audience, and we would show cartoons. I was on for maybe five minutes during the show. But Traverse City was a big tourist destination in the summer next to Lake Michigan. So all these celebrities would come and appear on *The Andy Bennett Show*. Pat Paulson, Telly Savalas, William Shatner, Vivian Vance, and Christopher Reeve before *Superman* were guests."

Andrew also began working at Jim's tourist shop showing off magic tricks, and even opened at Louie's—a local strip club. The local paper ran a column called 'Andy Bennett Entertains' with a calendar of his live shows. And on top of all his success in the entertainment world, Andy was still thriving in school. His grades were average, but he was Class President every year and won Homecoming King as a senior. He developed a love of public speaking, a skill he continued to hone throughout his career.

Although his grades weren't stellar, he scored high on the ACT and got a full ride to Michigan State. Going into college, Andrew was considering a career as a radio broadcaster. His first job in college was with the campus radio station. He used the audio recordings from his show to get a summer job in his hometown radio station. He realized a career in broadcasting wasn't for him and switched his major from radio and TV to general communications. He knew he wanted to be a manager in the business world, and in 1983 he was recruited into the management training program at Joann Fabrics.

It wasn't a dream job, but it was a good training program and a decent job. During his 18 months with Joann Fabrics, Andrew ran a store in East Lansing and later another one in Northern Detroit. Then he met the mentor who would steward him through the next decade of his career: Ross Perot. A friend was working for a Dallas-based company called EDS, a then medium-sized company with about 4,000 employees. "My friend told me, you have got to meet Ross Perot," relates Andrew. "Back then, no one knew who Ross was. But she told me she'd get me a conversation with him. It wasn't an interview, just a sit-down. So I went to his office in Troy, and we talked for an hour and a half. I just thought he was down-to-earth, relatable, and inspirational. He called the next day to inform me he was selling EDS to General Motors. He needed someone in Detroit to take care of his personal stuff and asked if I would be interested even though I wouldn't be a manager. I said, 'absolutely.' But it just so happens that I was open to a change due to a recent experience at Joann Fabrics. A $700 deposit had gone missing. Even though I was cleared of any wrong doing, they insisted on taking the money from my paycheck. That hurt and left a bad taste in my mouth. Therefore, I was ready for a change."

For six months, Andrew worked directly for Ross as his assistant. Later, at the office Christmas party, Andy got out his old magic set and performed for his colleagues. Ross' reaction was one Andy took to heart. "He challenged me to use magic in business," Andrew recalls. "He told me he'd seen a side of me he hadn't seen before. He could see the authenticity of my love for magic, and he encouraged me to use magic in my business presentations. It's something I have done ever since."

After that, Ross began to rotate Andrew through all the divisions of the company. First, he was sent to HR, where he quickly picked up recruiting. EDS was hiring people hand over fist at the time, as they had been purchased by GM and were filling a large number of new support roles. While there, Andrew made a potentially career-ending mistake. He overlooked the fine print in a buyout clause with a contract programmer that required EDS to pay $15,000 if we hired him. This was a fee we could have avoided because we had an abundance of candidates who wanted to work for us. Andrew knew Ross would be upset. The next morning, Ross called Andrew into his office. He offered Andrew his chair, then sat on the opposite side of his own desk. "You're me. What do you do?" he questioned Andy. Andy had been mulling it over all night and told Ross the business couldn't afford $15,000 mistakes. He should be let go. "Ross slammed his fist on the table and said, 'That's exactly why I'm not going to fire you!'" remembers Andrew. "He told me he'd just invested $15,000 in my education. My jaw must've hit the floor. That was the kind of leader he was."

On his next rotation, Andrew moved from recruiting to business operations management. He struggled to get his sea legs in the new department, but Ross continued encouraging him. EDS was a data processing business at the time, and Andrew's job was to liaise between the data processing centers and GM. Without a technical background, he felt adrift, but slowly learned the ropes. After that, it was on to a tenure in marketing from about 1987 to 1989. From there, Ross decided to send him to manage an account in Australia.

Andrew's time in Australia was another case of growing into his role. Initially, everything was going wrong. The client, a breakfast foods' business called Uncle Toby's, was furious with his management. Andrew's crime was saying yes to everything they requested. "The client would come to me and say we want this and that and I'd say, 'Yes,'" laughs Andrew. "The list kept growing. They kept changing priorities. Every day the wind was blowing in a new direction which meant we got little done."

"At one point, Ross met with them, and I thought I'd be going home on the next flight," continues Andrew. "Instead, he sat me down and said, 'I know you're trying to make them happy. But trying to make them happy is making them very unhappy. When you start telling them 'no' because it's in their best interest, then we stop being a vendor and start being a partner.'"

After their meeting, Andrew apologized to his team. He described the situation, acknowledged what he'd done wrong, and any tension was immediately released. His Australian team was more than happy to help Andrew rectify his mistakes and build a healthy new culture. What began as a failure became an unmitigated success story; the contract grew from $5 million to $65 million in just two years. By the time Andrew left, Uncle Toby's was a $3 billion company.

Andrew was a hero when he returned to the States. He began consulting internally at EDS and helped other account managers restructure their contracts.

Around this time, Ross left the company. Although he'd achieved success by every possible metric, Andrew felt restless. "Up until then it was all about the bottom line; work hard, climb the ladder, get the titles. But I wasn't happy," explains Andrew. "I asked myself, 'Is this all there is?' I've had so many great opportunities. Why am I not happy? So I made a change in my career to pursue other interests. I had learned that leadership and culture make a huge impact on a team's quality of life and on whether they lead a compelling life. So there was this connection to me: how do we make the work part of life more meaningful? My definition of success shifted from money, titles, car, and house, to how do we make a difference?"

Andrew decided he wanted to work in leadership development and organizational culture. He took a job with a consulting firm in Seattle and promised himself he'd only stay for five years before going out on his own. About four and a half years, he got laid off. "It was a blessing, because I don't know that I would actually have gone out on my own," says Andrew. "I was comfortable, making a good living, and doing good work. Then it ended, and I thought, 'This is God's way of saying that I'm moving you on.'"

Thus, 23 years ago, Bennett Performance Group (BPG) was born. From the ashes of tragedy, Andrew became an entertainer. Now, on the foundation of his first career, Andrew built another. As the President of BPG, Andrew spends much of his time in speaking engagements and conducting workshops. He also conducts consulting engagements and coaching to leaders to hone their leadership skills, management teams to create harmonious balance, and companies to provide an enjoyable and productive culture for all employees. He has worked with over 120 organizations including Google, Microsoft, Ford Motor Company, and the U.S. State Department.

Generally, his consultancies last at least a year. He'll work independently, or he'll draw on a small team of trusted fellow coaches to fill out his roster. BPG has done 39 long-term projects over its 23 years in operation, for clients of all sizes. Their largest was Sun Microsystems; their smallest, a family-owned commercial coffee roasting and distribution business in Detroit. They have clients everywhere and have worked on five continents. Largely, Andrew attracts new business through word of mouth.

"I help people thrive," Andrew says of his work today. "I help people lead fulfilling lives. I started out climbing the corporate ladder, but as time went by and I got experience, my influences led me to care more about people and their lives. Life is really, really precious. I want to make the most of this precious gift. And I want that for everyone. I want people to feel fulfilled."

Today, Andrew is living a life of fulfillment. He has a strong faith, and a wonderful marriage. He met his wife Jennifer in a leadership program, and she has been a wellspring of support since their marriage in 2013. Andrew considers his wedding band to be his most treasured object. "She's a superstar in business and she's the Chief Learning Officer for the National Credit Union Administration," Andrew says proudly. "She has her Master's degree in Leadership, so she and I are peers. I admire her tremendously as a colleague and as a person. I just can't believe I'm married to her. My wedding band is my most treasured object, and I never take this ring off. There's nothing more important to me in my life."

Along with Jennifer, Andrew notes that he finally, once more, feels at home with a family. "Jennifer came with a family. I now have a family," he smiles. "Her mother and I in particular developed a bond. I feel like I got a second chance at having a mom. She's an incredible, good woman. I've had so many great things in my life, and I've had a lot of really tough things in my life, and I think those tough things made me grateful. I always say, I'm grateful to be grateful. I'm glad I don't take for granted that I get to experience this amazing gift of family. Most people love and appreciate their family, but I treasure them."

As a leader, Andrew emphasizes lifting others up. "It's continually acknowledging people for their strengths and really calling that out publicly and privately," he affirms. "I want to make people strong in terms of belief in themselves. I want to do what Ross did for me."

To young people today, he advises working for a purpose. "Life is a precious gift," he repeats. "You never know when it could be your last day. Mom never suspected, when she was 33, that that would be it. So make sure that your life matters. There's only one you, and there will only ever be one you. How do you bring all of who you are to bear and make this place a little bit better?"

Lenny Berger

Rebuilding

The story of Lenny Berger's family is quintessentially one of American success. His paternal grandparents were immigrants; both of them, in fact, were Jewish refugees fleeing the Nazi regime. Growing up, he knew that his paternal grandfather had successfully worked as a handyman after running a grocery business for many years. He knew his grandparents fled Eastern Europe with their infant son (Lenny's father) and arrived in Aruba, where his aunt was born, before eventually relocating to the United States. But he knew little of the heartbreaking realities they had left behind when they embarked on their immigrant journey.

"When I was growing up, our family would not speak about that time period," Lenny relates somberly. "It wasn't until my 30s that the stories began to come out more. My grandfather was about 10 years older than my grandmother; I always thought that was unusual. In his

80s he finally told my grandmother that he had been married before. During the war, he was conscripted into the Soviet army and had to leave behind his wife and young child. On his way back home, he was stopped by villagers he knew, who informed him he could not return to his town which was now under Nazi occupation and everyone there had been killed. He never talked about that part of his life. Whenever anybody asked him questions, he'd say, 'We don't look at the past, we only look to the future.' As I've read more stories about the Holocaust and visited Auschwitz, I've learned that "survivor's guilt" is common.

Lenny's grandmother, meanwhile, also went through incredible hardship. She was one of four children—two sisters and one brother. Both of her parents, as well as her younger brother, were killed in a Nazi work camp somewhere in the Ukraine. During the chaos of escapes and evacuations, she also lost touch with her two sisters. By sheer happenstance, she was reunited with her younger sister, Genia, in a bomb shelter in Western Russia. They stayed in contact, but Genia went to the Ukraine and then to Israel. Lenny's grandmother went to Poland. Eventually, Lenny's grandparents met when his grandfather was paid for work with a sack of flour. He asked someone what he should do with it. He was told to visit a house where a young lady could use it to bake him bread. That young lady was Nechoma, my grandmother. They fell in love, and two days after my father was born they received permission to leave Poland and moved to Aruba to live near his grandmother's aunt, where they established a successful grocery business. Genia moved with her family to the United States and Lenny's grandparents followed in the mid-1960s.

Their oldest sister, Leah, was sent to a different Nazi work camp and was presumed dead by the rest of the family for 14 years. Eventually, Leah contacted the aunt in Aruba via a letter and re-established contact. After the war ended Leah was sent to Bucharest, Romania for resettlement and became locked behind the Iron Curtain for 30 years. It wasn't until 1980 that she received permission to emigrate to the United States as a political refugee and the family saved enough money to bring Leah to the U.S. where the three sisters were permanently reunited after decades of separation.

"It's absolutely amazing to me what my family left behind to come here," reflects Lenny. "My grandfather was in his 50s by the time they moved to the U.S. I can't imagine being 50 and having to start over again. They never complained about the hardship; they were always proud and grateful. When you finally hear these stories and learn what they went through to make it possible for my generation to thrive, I can't help but feel fortunate and grateful."

Although his grandparents and Genia have passed away, Great Aunt Leah recently turned 101 and still lives in her own apartment. Lenny sits and talks with her about the past. Lenny's grateful that she's been able to watch her family begin to grow again after seeing so many killed and others separated during the war. "The next generation is getting married and having kids," smiles Lenny. "One of my nephews recently got married and I was talking to Great Aunt Leah. She was so proud that she's lived long enough to be able to see the family grow and thrive. She mentioned that in the old country that there were 400 relatives in the town. I thought it was unbelievable, but she said, 'Yes, our family lived there for hundreds of years.' It was a little town called Lipkoni and still exists today in Moldova."

This heritage of strength and survival has driven Lenny both to appreciate what he has, as well as to reflect on how best to spend his time and talents. He's also developed a much deeper relationship with his Jewish faith and considers his grandparents' Kiddush cup—a cup over which a blessing is said on the Sabbath—to be one of his most prized possession. "My grandmother passed away six years ago and my grandfather six years before that," explains Lenny. "When we sold the house, my sister and I went over and my aunt asked if there was anything we'd like to keep. The Kiddush cup was what I chose. It's an item that brings up so many memories. Now my wife and I have it in a display on top of a little secretary in our dining room. It's not a fancy cup, it doesn't have a high dollar value, but it definitely brings back a lot of great memories."

Perhaps it was his grandparents' willingness to start over along with his grandfather and father's work in repairs and construction that drove Lenny to leave a twenty-year technology career to launch a remodeling business. Today, HandyMensch Home Remodeling is the unlikely success story that followed two IT start-ups and a meaningful sabbatical spent travelling and volunteering.

Lenny was always drawn to computers and enjoyed many of the jobs he'd held in the IT field. Still, after a disappointing end at his second start-up, he was beginning to reflect on what he wanted the rest of his life to look like. Not one to rest on his laurels nor one to forget the importance of living life to the fullest, Lenny embarked on a quest to consider his next move. He travelled in Africa for a month before coming home and volunteering with Habitat for Humanity.

"For a while I just met and talked with people," remembers Lenny. "I knew I liked being entrepreneurial and really wanted to see if I could build my own brand. It was the height of the real estate boom in 2007, and I was finding that there was a lot of demand for handymen who could do small to medium sized projects. So The HandyMensch was born. I started focusing on handyman services. For the first four years we did primarily hourly or fixed price assignments. But then I started noticing something. I was coming in and doing $800 worth of work, but there was another $10,000 or $20,000 worth of work going on in painting, carpeting, and things like that. Over time we evolved toward a more project-based model and took on whole kitchens, bathrooms, basements, etc."

"Today I describe our services as sitting between the neighborhood handyman and the big general contractor that does additions or whole house remodels," Lenny goes on. "We work within the footprint of the existing house, but we're doing things that involve a lot of different trades like electrical and plumbing. We will even bring in a structural engineer to open up a load bearing wall. Typically, our clients have a challenging project that needs good management and a good process but is smaller than what a large general contractor would want."

The business model has paid off in spades. Lenny said his efforts to carve out a specific space for HandyMensch has been particularly successful because competitors in the business—both bigger and small companies—don't' view him as a threat, but as a partner filling a different role in the market. In fact, they will often recommend him or send business his way. Today, HandyMensch typically takes on about four to six projects at a time and has five in-house employees, as well as 15 different subcontractors across many different specialties. This ensures that clients have access to experts from plumbers, to electricians, to engineers, etc. This has been particularly crucial to Lenny's business model and to a project's success.

Although Lenny never planned to get into home repairs professionally, it's a talent he comes by honestly. His father was in construction throughout his career and did remodeling himself for a number of years before eventually going to work at Whiting Turner in their corporate offices in Towson, Maryland. Lenny's mother, meanwhile, presided over the family's Baltimore City home and raised Lenny and his sister. "We were three blocks from the racetrack," Lenny recalls of his childhood home. "I could hear the races being called outside my window. The Preakness was always a bit crazy every year."

Lenny was never much into sports, but he did well academically. His father took note of his interest in computers early on and encouraged him. "If there was something that sparked my interest, my dad was really good about finding a way to help me pursue my interest," says Lenny. "He would sign me up for a class or figure out how to make it happen." First, he enrolled Lenny at a class at a local computer store. The class came with four additional hours of lab time. But by the time Lenny had used twenty, the store had run out of patience and

Lenny had long since run out of hours. So his father found a way for him to continue his studies.

For high school, Lenny had been sent to an Orthodox Jewish academy. Unfortunately, the school, while academically rigorous, didn't yet offer any computer courses. Lenny's father instead signed him up for classes at a nearby community college at the age of only 14 and even bought him a personal computer. "By today's standards, that computer would be a joke," laughs Lenny. "But that was several thousand dollars at the time. I don't think that amount of money really computed for me, but now I realize, 'Wow, that was a huge amount of money for my father to spend to encourage me."

Despite his young age, Lenny thrived while being surrounded by older kids learning about computers. He even took a volunteer position in the computer center at the community college. Although within two weeks, he found the role didn't live up to what he'd been expecting. He was lowest man on the totem pole and would take printouts off the printers, return magnetic tapes to the library and would generally be killing time. Again, his father encouraged him to dream big. "He told me to go talk to the head of the department and tell him I wanted more to do," remembers Lenny. "I was unsure but went to see him anyway. While I was waiting, his secretary told me that the Department Head, Wally Knapp, had already noticed me."

Wally would go on to become a mentor who remains close to Lenny to this day. He had been impressed with Lenny's hustle right away, and was even more impressed that Lenny came to express an interest in programming. He told Lenny that he didn't yet have enough programming experience but that the department needed help on the networking side of things. Lenny continued volunteering with the lab every summer through high school and later transitioned into a paid role while in college.

For two years, Lenny attended Catonsville Community College and continued his work in the computer lab for a basic work study hourly rate. However, by this time his work was much more complex than a typical student's. "I was getting paid the same as someone who was sitting at a reception desk," noted Lenny. "I was actually running the college's entire network with ten remote locations. There were multiple incidents where the network had some issue, and no one could solve it because I was in class! By the time I graduated, I had four years of experience in networking."

After two years, Lenny transferred from Catonsville to University of Maryland, Baltimore County, but he still kept up his work on the Catonsville network. After graduation, Lenny saw an opportunity to gain a real resume boost when IBM came to Catonsville, did a study of their IT department, and recommended that they hire a Manager of Network Services. The school didn't have the money to fund it; Lenny offered to do it for his same work study salary in exchange for the title. He did that for a couple more years before finally deciding it was time to find a position that would pay him what he was worth.

He applied to a Network Engineering job at Johns Hopkins University and was quickly selected. Through this job, he met the owner of a firm called RPM Consulting, and he ultimately jumped over to work for RPM through the dotcom boom.

Over the next five years, Lenny thrived at RPM. He was asked to move to North Carolina and later to Atlanta where he built BB&T's network for them. He then moved to the DC area. "We basically started before most people knew what the internet was," points out Lenny. "This was when having an email address on your business card was a big deal. We were building networks for the likes of Fannie Mae, T. Rowe Price and Discovery Channel, to name a few. Most people just didn't yet know what the internet was or what the potential was."

Also during these years, he became engaged to and then married the love of his life, Lynn. "She's always been supportive of me," affirms Lenny. "We were dating when I was debating leaving Johns Hopkins to join RPM. I thought it might be too risky, but she encouraged me to take it. She told me 'Everything you've told me about these guys is exactly what you're looking for so what's the worst that can happen?' I may not have taken the leap without her support and encouragement. She's also very extroverted while I'm more of an introvert. She can talk to anyone and make you laugh. She's a very independent minded person, and like me, she loves to travel. One of the earliest trips we took was to Thailand and Bali."

Lynn's advice proved correct. About five years after Lenny joined RPM Consulting, they ended up selling to a larger firm, and he was given a piece of the company in the buy-out. Lenny moved on to another start-up—one that was focused on CRM systems for car dealerships. He was hired as the CTO, but over the next several years, he saw the writing on the wall. The company made some bad decisions, and by the time he left, the company was on the rocks. It was then that Lenny decided to take his break to reassess his future. He was burnt out on the unpredictability of the tech world. "When you're in the position that you're not worried about paying the mortgage the next month, you have some runway to really consider your future and what you want to do," explains Lenny. "At that point, I didn't know anybody who'd gotten out of tech. But I knew I wanted a change. I've always had a creative side and knew I wanted to build another business. I just needed time to explore something new. And that became HandyMensch Home Remodeling."

As a leader, Lenny describes himself as "the conductor." "I'm the conductor of the orchestra," elaborates Lenny. "I understand the role of each instrument on our projects; I understand what makes that instrument important and how it works. And at the end of the day, I've got to make everybody play well together. If you're not conducting properly, projects can fall apart. If things start to get out of tune, you have to nip that in the bud and get things back on track."

To young people entering the job market today, Lenny advises hard work and patience as he reflected back to his years working in the

Catonsville computer lab for a tiny salary. "You gotta work hard and you gotta earn it," he points out. "I worked for free or a very low wage to build real experience."

Like his grandparents before him, Lenny wasn't afraid to start over and swing for the fences. "I haven't become Mark Zuckerberg," he reflects, "but that doesn't mean I haven't built success. At the end of the day, I always want to feel that we've done good work and we've built a great team. We have clients that like working with us, and that's what's important."

Gordon J. Bernhardt

From Farm Values to Urban Impact

Despite months of preparation and planning and firm commitment to his end objectives, Gordon Bernhardt wasn't sure he would be able to go forward. Crouched over a toilet in a small town in the French Pyrenees, he was thousands of miles from home and felt sick to his stomach.

Saint-Jean-Pied-de-Port, in France, is the jumping-off point for travelers on the Camino de Santiago, a centuries-old pilgrimage through northern Spain. Since learning about the ancient pilgrimage seven years before, Gordon had set a cherished goal of hiking the 500-mile Camino route from France through northern Spain known as the Camino Francés, or "French Way." But on this misty, cool July morning at the outset of his journey, doubts were beginning to creep into his mind.

"After hugging the ivory throne for a few minutes, I knew I was experiencing anxiety, not a stomach bug," he said later. "I had set a goal and announced it to anyone who would listen, but because of an earlier failure in a similar effort, I was doubting myself. If I couldn't complete a 184.5-mile hike on the C&O Canal three years earlier, my mind was questioning whether I would be able to complete this much longer hike."

Gordon decided to take his first step. Pulling himself together, he walked onto the trail and began his journey, accompanied by other fellow pilgrims—peregrinos. "Before long, I was joined by six other peregrinos from different parts of Europe. We talked, provided encouragement, and bonded. By the end of the day, when we reached our destination in the small town of Roncesvalles, Spain, I knew that I had ascended past my fears and doubts; I was on my way to what would become the best experience of my life."

A similar vein of determination led Gordon to found Bernhardt Wealth Management (BWM) in 1994. "After working as a CPA for seven years, including experience with what is now a Big Four firm, I concluded that I wasn't making the kind of difference in people's lives that I wanted to make. I thought that working in financial services would allow me to create the kind of impact I was hoping for." However, the focus on proprietary products and the sales-and-commissions orientation of the two different brokerage companies Gordon joined soon proved antithetical to his hopes. "I disliked the obvious conflicts of interest. I needed to be able to look myself in the mirror at the end of the day and believe that I had served my clients' needs, not just sold them something that the company wanted me to push. I realized that the company expected me to place its interests above what was best for my clients. That became unacceptable for me."

Realizing that an independent environment would allow him to provide important investment and wealth management guidance without the conflicts of interest that were making him uncomfortable, Gordon launched BWM, building it on the principle of fiduciary care: providing guidance, service, and advice that places clients' needs ahead of everything else. "I had finally found a way to make the kind of difference I hoped for," Gordon says. "By placing my clients' interests first, I knew I could meet my own goals and accomplish something that would be important for others. This was the kind of impact I wanted to make when I left the CPA profession." Today, after more than a quarter-century in business, that same ethic still guides every initiative at BWM.

But it wasn't easy at first; launching a new company never is. Gordon had to build a client base, open accounts and gain sufficient assets under management to make his advising business sustainable. A year after opening the business, he had liquidated his retirement accounts, depleted his savings, and run up $45,000 in credit card debt to finance the company. "It was the lowest point in my life," he remembers. "I didn't feel successful when comparing myself to my peers from college, but I kept focused on my mission of helping people. I was determined to build the business."

Gordon wasn't afraid of hard work or a stranger to the concept of doing whatever it took to succeed. "Failure and giving up wasn't an option for our family when I was growing up, and it wasn't an option when I was starting BWM." There were mistakes, false starts, and one or two mid-course corrections, but the same determination to succeed that impelled Gordon to begin walking the Camino de Santiago helped him push forward, creating one of the most successful and nationally recognized independent financial advisory and wealth management firms in the Washington, DC area.

It turns out that Gordon's upbringing prepared him for this challenge. In fact, he often says growing up on a farm gave him the foundation to be a wealth manager. What he calls "the unglamorous work" of caring for animals and crops was his introduction to the meaning of hard work, as well as the need for patience while waiting for the fruits of his labor to be revealed. He also learned to prepare for the unexpected and to stay focused on what you can control as he watched the devastating costs associated with a sudden hailstorm, blizzard or drought. "Just as the future can't be predicted on the farm, it can't be predicted in the financial markets," Gordon explains. "In many ways these are the same lessons we try to teach our clients. We can't be certain when the next financial crisis will happen or where the next market bubble will occur, which is why it is important to have a strong plan on which to rely in good markets and bad."

The desire to help people and to leave a positive impact on their lives is what Gordon describes as the most rewarding part of his job; another characteristic cultivated during childhood. "I remember the time my father borrowed a shovel from a neighbor when we were building an addition to the house. After Dad was done with the shovel, he washed it thoroughly to remove any dirt, used a steel brush to remove as much rust as he could, then he sharpened it. Dad returned the shovel in better condition than when he first borrowed it." The lesson from this memory has had a profound impact on Gordon, including his decision to start his own firm and how he would conduct business.

"Dad's obligation was to just return the borrowed shovel, no matter the condition. I compare that to an advisor who follows a suitability standard. My dad didn't just meet his obligation, he went above and beyond to do what was in the neighbor's best interest by delivering an improved tool. That is the equivalent of a fiduciary standard by which my business must operate."

The culture at BWM is built upon what Gordon calls the "Four C's: Character, Chemistry, Caring, and Competence." Gordon has assembled a team of professional, fee-only wealth managers who operate with integrity, striving to do what is right for both clients and their colleagues, 100% of the time. And that level of personal caring has fostered an extraordinarily loyal client base. "During the 2008 financial crisis and again in the spring of 2020, as the coronavirus pandemic was devastating the economic landscape, we had clients calling, not to seek reassurance about their investments, but rather to see how we were holding up," Gordon says. As Gordon and his advisors work to help clients remain calm, rational, and focused during volatile markets, client calls and meetings often end with the clients thanking them for providing reliable, logical, and accurate information and advice. "We are vigilant about staying in touch with our clients, in good markets and bad," Gordon says. "After all, our goal is to function as our clients' personal chief financial officer: to take from them the burden of managing the daily details of their investments and financial plans, allowing them to focus their energies on their greatest priorities. As business owners and leaders in the community, our clients' purpose is people, and their business and investments are their legacy. We believe it is important to protect that legacy and to help them make wise decisions around complex financial matters so that they have the freedom to focus on what matters most to them: their businesses, their families, and the causes that are important to them."

Another way that Gordon seeks to help and advance local entrepreneurs and business leaders is through his "Profiles in Success" program. Gordon seeks out and interviews outstanding leaders in the Washington, DC Area, eliciting from them not only their life stories but also the keys to their success in industry, in relationships and in life. He has gathered these profiles into a series of books that carry the collective title, *Profiles in Success: Inspiration from Executive Leaders in the Washington, DC Area.* In 2021, Gordon started the Profiles in Success podcast where he continues to feature business and community leaders. Gordon views the "Profiles in Success" program as another way to give back to the community by highlighting its outstanding leaders and expanding their influence. In addition, the stories in Profiles in Success serve as a source of inspiration for the next generation of leaders.

Gordon is looking to the future of BWM, as well, working to ensure it remains a solid company for years to come. The firm currently consists of multiple generations of advisors who have the opportunity to become equity owners in the company. In this way, the advising team members benefit financially when the firm does well for its clients, further incentivizing them to continue acting in the best interest of all involved. The culture Gordon has fostered at BWM is indicated by the tenets of the 26-point "The Bernhardt Way," which includes fundamentals like "Put clients first, always," "practice transparency," "honor commitments," "invest in relationships," and "keep it fun."

Gordon's family farm was located outside Hay Spring, a small town in northwest Nebraska. They raised cattle, sheep, and pigs, and also grew wheat and hay. "I had learned to drive a tractor by the time I was five years old and was working in the fields with my father," Gordon says. "And no joke, I really did get up before sunrise to do chores." The second of five children, he learned early on, along with his four sisters, that there was almost always something that needed to be done to keep the farm operating smoothly. His first eight years of education took place in a one-room schoolhouse, and he graduated from high school in Hay Spring, where the average class size was just over 30.

One of Gordon's memories is from a time when he was just eight years old and riding in the pickup with his dad. "It was a hot summer evening, and we were on a narrow country road. A Native American waved us down from his pickup as we were meeting on the road. The man told my dad that he needed some money to pay for a new chain saw, which he used to cut cedar posts for sale. He told my dad he'd give him a great deal on fence posts, if he could help him out." Gordon knew his family didn't have a lot of extra money, so he was astounded when his father pulled out his wallet, took out a few bills, and handed them to the other man. "That was a defining moment for me," he says. "With that one action, my dad taught me the importance of giving back to others." That orientation toward service has stayed with Gordon ever since, he says.

Gordon also relates an experience that happened during his first year as a student at Chadron State College, in Nebraska. During that year, he developed an inner conviction that he belonged in

Washington, DC. He decided to apply for an internship in the office of his state representative, Congresswoman Virginia Smith. His family was not wealthy or politically influential, but Gordon believed in following his inner guide, and he mailed his application—which was declined. Not to be defeated, Gordon developed a plan for his next attempt, the following year. He recruited fifty people, including local businesspeople, his high school teachers, student leaders at his college, professors, and the president of the college, to write letters of recommendation for him. After sending his application, he then asked those fifty people to begin mailing their letters. "After a few weeks, I got a call from the congresswoman's office," he says. "They told me to stop sending the letters; I had the internship." His determination to succeed enabled Gordon to set himself apart from the other applicants and paved the way for success, as it would during future years when he was building BWM—and walking the Camino de Santiago.

He arrived in Washington, DC in time for the inauguration of Ronald Reagan in January 1981. "It was an incredible experience," he remembers. Not long after his arrival in Congresswoman Smith's office, a staff member left, and Gordon was offered a paid position. He worked for Congresswoman Smith for two years before landing a staff position with the US Senate Finance Committee, chaired at that time by Bob Dole. Subsequently, he was admitted to the McIntire School of Commerce at the University of Virginia, where he finished his undergraduate studies and received the prestigious McIntire Faculty Award for Leadership.

Upon graduating, he accepted a position at Pricewaterhouse-Coopers, working on the audit staff. Three years later, after a brief stint at a government contracting company, he began working for an environmental consulting company based in Arlington, Virginia. By 1992, he had determined that he needed to be in a line of work that would allow him to make a bigger impact in peoples' lives, sensing the call to giving back that he had learned from his parents on the farm so many years ago. He decided to move into financial services in 1992, which eventually led him to found BWM, two years later.

Gordon's life is a testament to hard work, determination, and the power of giving back, and when he speaks to young people launching their careers, these core values ring through. "You have to put yourself out there and be willing to demonstrate your unique strengths and abilities," he tells them. "Cultivate a willingness to take on new challenges and try not to worry too much about who gets the credit. If you're passionate and focused, your employer will see your value to the organization and reward you with additional opportunities. If you always act with integrity and watch for chances to serve others, your career will ride a rising tide of good reputation and expanding prospects." Mindful of his debt to those who helped him during his youth, Gordon started a scholarship to help young people from his hometown of Hay Springs attend college and another scholarship to help transfer students at the McIntire School of Commerce. In addition, every holiday season, he makes a donation in the name of each of his clients to a charity of their choice. "All these are ways of paying back a small portion of the many good things I've received from the caring people in my life," he says.

Gordon believes the future is bright as long as young leaders keep rising up who understand the value in helping others. "The essence of effective leadership is effective service," he says. "The determination to succeed is important, but unless it is coupled with an ethic of helping others, it can too easily turn to blind ambition. That's why we place such importance on relationships at BWM: relationships with our clients and relationships with each other. We believe that by helping our clients make the best possible decisions for the legacy of their wealth, we are setting them free to create the impact they want to be able to create. It's hard to overstate the value of the leverage created when good people use their resources to make the world a better place. Our goal is to help them do that more effectively, every day."

Returning to his experience along the Camino de Santiago, Gordon explains that peregrinos greet each other in passing with the words, "Buen Camino." The simple phrase literally translates to "have a good journey." However, it also embodies a wish for fulfillment and for true discernment of one's purpose. Today, Gordon and his team extend the spirit of Buen Camino to clients, colleagues, and everyone they encounter professionally. It reflects their purpose to be dependable traveling companions for the financial journey—providing encouragement, guidance, and expertise while trying to lighten clients' loads and helping them stay on the path to their most important life goals.

"Buen Camino!"

BERNHARDT

WEALTH MANAGEMENT

Dani Canubas

Something Out of Nothing

When Dani Canubas was growing up in a small village in the Philippines, coming to America was the furthest thing from his mind. In fact, he'd never even heard of it. His parents were high school educated, and his father spent years at a time travelling to Saudi Arabia and Singapore to work as a laborer. Meanwhile, his mother stayed home to raise Dani and his brother and tend to the family farm. At the local elementary school—a tiny, one-room building that taught about 10-15 kids—Dani learned alongside the other village children, but resources were limited. The students were taught languages and math through fourth grade; then they had to travel a bit further afield, to a bigger town.

In the bigger town, Dani began to struggle with his studies. The other students had had better training, and he was already behind. "It was a culture shock, because the other students knew more than I did," he remembers. "These kids were more advanced, and that made it quite challenging for me. That is when I started hating school because I couldn't keep up."

During high school, the divide between the richer and poorer students only worsened. He was again sent to a larger town, and for the first time, he began to encounter kids who were wealthy. "There is no middle class in the Philippines," explains Dani. "You're either rich or poor. I could see from the get-go that there were places I wouldn't be invited. Classmates of mine got dropped off by their drivers, while I took public transportation. I started to notice the difference between the wealthy kids and the rest of us. That is when I started dreaming because I noticed that the parents of those wealthy kids were entrepreneurs."

Today, Dani is the Founder and CEO of American Esports, a rapidly growing business in a rapidly growing field. "Esports is competitive video gaming," explains Dani. "It used to be for leisure, but now it's become a profession. It used to be part of the gaming industry, but in the last ten years it has become an industry in and of itself. Today it's considered the fastest growing technology industry in the world."

Dani launched the company in May of 2018 after eight months of exhaustive research. He hadn't known anything about esports or video gaming previously. In fact, he'd never even played a video game before. But the more he read on the industry, the more he saw the opportunity. "A total of $4.4 billion dollars was invested in esports in 2018," he notes. "Before I started my research, I didn't know how much the total investment would be. I saw investments of $10 million here and $20 million there being made. And they were focused on three things—publishing, leagues, and professional teams. Publishing is video game makers putting out new games. Leagues are then built upon the publishers' games. And professional teams are the teams in the leagues. You have to have deep pockets to get involved in those three things."

Dani was hesitant about plunging into any of these three major investment areas given that each was tied to a particular game, and particular games run their course in terms of public engagement and popularity. "I didn't see how you could sustain it in the long term," Danni points outs. "What if that 'it' game is no longer the 'it' game in five years. Then the league is gone, the game is gone, and there's a new one. So I knew we had to do something different and realized we could build the infrastructure around it. We don't participate in those three, but we support them."

Instead, American Esports builds venues, large egaming centers which are often located on college campuses or military bases, as well as hardware like gaming chairs, tables, monitors and more, all under one brand. They provide all the products and services of the esports industry, and with their venues, are providing spaces for large groups to gather and form teams and leagues around whatever game they may be interested in.

"We want to bring back the community, so our foundation is building these centers in big cities. We're building one or two in DC now that are 5,000 square feet," Dani describes. American esports is also interested in institutional development; they're the leading company providing esports development programs to colleges and even high schools. Colleges are interested in building their own esports centers and programs because those programs help to attract and retain students. "We provide a turnkey solution to help colleges build an esports program within 90 days," says Dani. "Now we're talking with major schools like Cornell and American University." Not only that, but American Esports is also working on its own college and putting together a curriculum to certify people who want to become trainers, coaches, and tutors.

Additionally, American Esports is creating an app that will launch within the next year, as well as a media platform including an ESPN-like television show for esports. They've even brought in a former ESPN executive to head up the project. And finally, they hope to construct their own leagues, but these will be public rather than built around a publisher's game. Another idea is building a collegiate league that is similar to the NCAA. "There are a lot of leagues in colleges right now, but they're regionalized," explains Dani. "We're creating an umbrella so all of them will be playing under us."

Currently, the team has raised about $1 million and employs about 35 people. Dani was careful to hire a mix of experienced business leaders and energetic young egaming experts. "I built two teams—a team of seasoned people and a team of millennials," describes Dani. "We then mixed them up so they can leverage each other and feed off each other. All the members of my team are equity holders of the company."

Dani chose the name "American Esports" as both an homage to his chosen home and with an eye to its branding power. "If you go anywhere and ask them to give you 10 global brands, what do they say?" asked Dani. "Ninety-five percent of the time, they mention companies like Coca-Cola, McDonald's, Nike, Adidas, and Starbucks. They say American companies. I came to the conclusion that the number one brand in the world is America. If it succeeds here, it succeeds globally. All we have to do is succeed in America, then we go international. So this is a global play."

If Dani's ambitions are grand, perhaps it's because he's already come so far. Casile in Cabuyao, Laguna was the name of the tiny village he grew up and is about an hour outside Manila. Laguna didn't have electricity or running water when Dani was a kid. "When I go back today, I don't recognize it," says Dani wistfully, "There are big houses and mansions today. It's actually tough to go back because I don't recognize where I came from."

His father was a carpenter, and, like many Filipinos, he travelled abroad to make money for the family. In fact, Dani notes that the Philippines is one of the leading countries that provides workers around the world, from construction workers, to nannies, and to nurses. Dani has seven nurses in his family and his wife's nursing career is ultimately what brought him to the U.S. So Dani's father was one of many who would leave home for long periods of time. Generally, he'd leave for two to three years before coming home for several months, after which he would go back to Saudi Arabia or Singapore. Dani was in high school before the family was doing well enough that his father could stop travelling.

His mother, meanwhile, cared for the children and ran the family farm where they raised pigs, cows, and chickens and grew bananas and coconuts. From the age of 10, Dani was selling bananas in the market to make extra money. He and his younger brother were expected to help care for all the farm animals as soon as they could carry a pail of water. In his free time, Dani loved to play basketball, which is wildly popular in the Philippines, and spend time with his grandfather who was a respected leader in the village.

"I enjoyed hanging out with him and enjoyed listening to the older people's conversations," reflects Dani. "All the leaders from different villages would come, and I would sit there and just listen and enjoy it. I continued that until I came here. The majority of my business partners and associates are older than me, and that's how I learn, by listening. I learned about things like philosophy, leadership, solving conflicts, and other things from my grandfather. Eventually, I was tapped as a leader in my village, too. If I had stayed, I probably would have gone into politics."

Although neither of Dani's parents had a college degree, they stressed the importance of education and were adamant that Dani should get one. He never loved school, he worked his way through it to honor their wish. "As parents, they wanted us to have a better life than they had," Dani explains. "They thought that if we finished college, we'd have a better opportunity. That was their goal for us at the time."

Dani attended a religious university close to the village for two years where he decided to study psychology and marketing. While there, he began selling magazines door-to-door, and continued to cultivate his natural gift for sales. After two years, he left for the big city of Manila. It was there that he completed his education and got his first post-college job doing sales at a staffing company, acquiring clients, and sending workers for jobs in Taiwan and Hong Kong.

People began to notice Dani's potential almost immediately. After a year at the staffing company, he was recruited by a toothbrush company after the owner promised to double his salary. Instead of selling door-to-door, Dani was selling to companies. "I was building relationships with purchasers and with the people who own the store," says Dani. "One of the things I learned in sales and psychology is the first thing you have to sell is yourself. Once you're able to do that, then you have a very good chance at selling whatever products or services you have. Because if you're not able to sell yourself, no matter how great your products are or if people don't like you, they aren't going to make a deal with you."

Dani's career was going well, but around this time his girlfriend and future wife, Ruth, was recruited to come to America. "She was my college classmate, and I fell in love with her because she was kind, simple, pretty, and charming, and she was the smartest person in the class," smiles Dani. "When she took the board exams, she was in the top ten in the entire country. She had always dreamed of coming to America and had relatives here. Those relatives would send her things from America when she was a kid. So when she got the opportunity to go, she knew she wanted to go."

Dani followed Ruth to America where he knew no one except his wife and her family. He accepted a job for two weeks at a local Taco Bell and would drive to work every day with his mother-in-law. He next tried out a job at a bookstore but found the work to be boring. "All I was doing was checking the inventory. Around 2:00 PM I would go in the bathroom and fall asleep," laughs Dani. "I was so bored. I can't be in one place doing the same thing for eight hours. So after about a month I left that, too.

Then he decided to become a distributer for packaged nuts. Each morning he'd fill the trunk of his car with packaged nuts and drive from gas station to gas station selling them. Dani enjoyed this far more than being cooped up in one place. He began to learn how to communicate, to make connections, and to hone his selling skills. A few months later, he was introduced to Cutco Knives and decided to try his hand at selling knives for Cutco. "They doubted my capability and access being a new immigrant, but I asked them to give me a chance," remembers Dani. "I asked them to give me 30 days to prove myself. I ended up becoming the No. 1 salesperson in that office, and ended up the No. 3 producer in the entire company that same year.

While selling knives, he happened to meet and befriend a former VP for Equitable Insurance who offered Dani a place at the company. "I was uncertain why he asked me to join him, and he said that he knew I could do it," says Dani. "I accepted it and asked him to show me the ropes. He taught me about residual income, and I became more interested." Dani became a financial planner for several years.

Once Equitable was bought out in 1996, Dani decided to leave and became an Independent Distributor for Market America now SHOP.COM to build a substantial residual income. After building the global distribution business, Dani decided to retire in 2003. By this time, Ruth and Dani had four children—they now have five—and they decided to take the children back to the Philippines for several years so they could meet their family and better understand their heritage. While there Dani started another international staffing business that placed nurses and other workers in the U.S. After 9/11, though, this became increasingly difficult, and ultimately, Dani and the family returned to the U.S.

After several years living only on residual income, Dani took a consultancy job as VP of Sales and Training for Market Philippines and led Market America's expansion there. "With Market America/SHOP.COM, I learned many aspects of leadership there," he recalls. "I spoke in public, ran conferences, and led trainings in front of as many as 25,000 people around the world. My horizon was expanding as I travelled globally and I was becoming more entrepreneurial."

After a couple of years back in the U.S., Dani joined the Tower Club and became an advisory board member. He met and became friends with more entrepreneurs and leaders from various industries.

In 2017, Dani's father died suddenly in a tragic accident, and Dani accompanied his mother to the Philippines to bury his father and mourn. "My dad was one of those people who never made an enemy," smiles Dani. "No one was ever mad at him. He was a quiet man but was always helping others. In fact, even though we had very little, both of my parents were always helping others as I was growing up. They always found some way to give back to others."

It was during this trip home that Dani had time to take a step back and begin to research new business opportunities. It was during this research that he discovered esports. "I stopped everything I was doing and disappeared for a while," recalls Dani. "I fell in love with reading again which is how I learned about the industry. I feel like my father paved the way for me to achieve my goals. It was almost like he helped me find this platform that can empower young people."

Ruth has been another major influence in Dani's life. "She's been very supportive, but she's also my number one critic," laughs Dani. "She's smarter than I am and better than me in many ways. She's disciplined and very organized. Her thoughts and ideas help me since I know she doesn't always tell me what I thought I wanted to hear. She supports me and holds me accountable."

As a leader, Dani sees the importance of teamwork and making sure your team gets the credit they deserve. "Leadership, to me, is doing what you want other people to do. I see the difference between leadership and management. Many people confuse the two," observes Dani. "I let people know that I don't want to walk in front of them and don't want to walk behind them. I want to walk with them. I love teamwork. The essence of teamwork, for me, is about giving the credit instead of taking the credit. What I've experienced in life is that the more you give, you more you receive."

To young people getting ready to face the world, he advises them to focus on personal development, to never quit, and to make adjustments to get better. He also said it is important to have balance and to remember to give back. Dani also shared that he loves the philosophy of ants—they never quit, are always moving forward, and are working as a team.

"One of our missions in American Esports is funding the American Esports Kids Foundation," says Dani. "It's focused on social responsibility, education and wellness. I think that's what's missing right now. There are a lot of Gen Zers and millennials who are into wellness and education. But what's missing is social responsibility. I would encourage them not to overlook that."

He also looks to his own past as he encourages college graduates to dream big, because everyone can exceed their dreams. Dreams do come true. "Had I not believed that I would succeed because I was not rich, or because my parents were not rich, then I would have just given up on my dreams," he reflects. "I shouldn't have been dreaming the way I was, but I did. I wanted to create something out of nothing. To me, that's the true definition of entrepreneurship."

Karl Colder

A Man with a Mission

Karl Colder had already applied to the DEA once when a college classmate offered to connect him with her uncle who was a Special Agent in Charge in Philadelphia. The classmate, Theresa Hill, saw potential in Karl, and encouraged him to call her uncle anyway. Karl was double majoring in political science and criminal justice, and Theresa knew he was committed to his coursework and to social change.

The next day, Karl called the uncle, John Wilder (Norton Jonathan Wilder, Sr.), who would turn out to be a lifelong career mentor and friend. He asked Karl two questions: Whether he had a suit, and whether he could make it to Philadelphia that week to meet. Karl replied affirmatively to both and drove into the city that week for an introduction that would change the course of his life.

Karl explained that he'd already applied to the DEA once, but John assured him that there was a new recruitment coordinator, Walter

"Wally" Gambrell, working in Philadelphia and made the introduction. The application process was rigorous, but a month later Karl was back at the office preparing for a panel interview. "Mr. Wilder told me, 'Here's what I want you to do,'" recalls Karl. "'Go down to the cafeteria, have some lunch, come back, and then take your job.' I went down, ate a turkey sandwich, and took my job when I came back. Mr. Wilder loved to tell that story and would say, 'I don't know what Karl ate downstairs, but it worked!'"

Mr. Wilder passed away in 2012, and Karl shared the story during the memorial service. "It's a remarkable coincidence that during his career, Mr. Wilder also served as the Special Agent in Charge of the DEA Washington Division where I ended my career with DEA as the Special Agent in Charge."

It took almost a year to get through the background check process, but in February of 1986, Karl headed to basic agent training for an intensive five-month program that launched a decades-long career. During that time, Karl was reassigned eight times and continually promoted. He ultimately ended his tenure with the government as the Special Agent in Charge of the Washington Division.

In the DEA operates, mandatory retirement is enforced at the age of 57 or after 25 years of service, whichever comes first. In Karl's case, having started with the DEA at the early age of 22, he hit 25 years of service before the age of 50, and he knew he still had a lot more work to do. Working with the DEA, he had had a front-row seat to the ravages of the opioid crisis, especially given his work in the region. Maryland, DC, Virginia, and West Virginia were hit incredibly hard by the influx of opioids. Over time, Karl and his fellow agents began to see that "arresting our way out of the problem wasn't working."

Now, as the President and Founder of Colder Allied Consulting, Karl is able to continue his work confronting opioid addiction in myriad ways—often through approaches that weren't available to him when working through the government.

As a consultant, he brings three decades of law enforcement experience to businesses and contractors who need them. As a volunteer, he brings his expertise in drug addiction to help prevent dependence before it begins. Colder Allied Consulting works with businesses small and large to help them navigate the world of State and Federal contracting, introducing them to the right people, connecting them into the proper channels, and ensuring that tax dollars are spent efficiently and productively on projects making real impact. Specifically, some of this work is done through his subcontracts with the MITRE Corporation and the Thompson Reuters Corporation.

They also work with non-government clients like EagleForce Associates, a Veteran owned company in the healthcare space that provides real-time analytics for prescription drug monitoring. When it comes to the opioid crisis, keeping tabs on manufacturers, distributors, pharmacies and doctors is crucial for understanding supply.

Karl also works with a company called TagIt Technology, a business that is working to prevent counterfeiting of products or in this case, the newly popular CBD, a therapeutic oil derived from hemp. He has also partnered with AGX, a veteran-owned company that provides holistic healthcare services through the VA. "In the VA system, you have insurance codes for things like tai chi, yoga and chiropractic care, but in the private system those don't exist," explains Karl. "So, when you see that, you realize there's no real alternative to pain medication. There aren't many options for people other than these prescription drugs to help people who are in severe pain."

By working on alternatives to opioid use, Karl hopes that he's doing more to confront the epidemic than ever before. He also works heavily on the treatment and prevention side, as a volunteer for various groups including Mentor Foundation, an organization dedicated to educating teenagers about drugs. At Mentor, young people are trained to be ambassadors to their own communities and utilize their social media skills to spread information about the consequences of drug use.

Additionally, Karl has maintained a program he spearheaded at DEA, the training of first responders in faith-based organizations. While working at the DEA, he noticed that while faith-based organizations often volunteered heavily to help with the drug crisis, they never received any training to administer Narcan and to provide substance use disorder referral services, which has saved countless lives by reversing the symptoms of opioid overdose. Karl had always been active in the Episcopal Church, but, aware of the potential difficulties of combining Federal business with religion, he proceeded with caution.

First, he met with the bishops from his region to ask what they were currently doing about the crisis. The Episcopal Church is broken down into provinces, and eventually, Karl was contacted by Province III of the Church—an area comprising Delaware, Maryland, Pennsylvania, Virginia, West Virginia, and Washington DC. They asked Karl to hold a workshop to educate the Bishops about the opioid crisis, teach them about the DEA, and educate them on what can be done in terms of prevention, treatment, and emergency response.

After a successful workshop, a task force was established, and Karl was asked to serve as Co-Chair of the Province III Opioid Response Task Force. He still serves there, promoting education, and training volunteers to administer Narcan. He's been as far afield as Mississippi, Michigan, and Georgia putting on workshops and organizing what he refers to as the "faith-based response." It empowers churches and clergy to play a direct role in healing and lifesaving.

"When you look at it overall, my company takes a deep dive into the future of drug prevention," Karl affirms. "In terms of healthcare, in terms of substance use disorder, and in terms of how you deal with it. It's about technology, analytics, and learning about all these different spaces. Now that I'm independent, I can do more of this out-of-the-box type stuff; I am able to do things I couldn't do before."

Although Karl hadn't grown up planning to work for the federal government or in health, his father spent his career working for the

Postal Service while his mother was a lab technician at a New York hospital. In some ways, his career reflects the influences of both parents. Karl was born in Spanish Harlem on 106th Street between 1st and 2nd Avenue in Manhattan. He had two older sisters and was often living with an aunt, or two, or several cousins. The family home in New York attracted visitors and migrants from their extended clan down in Jacksonville, Florida and Chester, Pennsylvania. Very often, the Colder house was a way station as relatives established themselves in the city. Karl's extended family in Jacksonville is enormous; his mother was one of 14 siblings.

Both of Karl's parents knew how to stretch a dollar. His mother was a seamstress and often made clothes for the family. Both parents were great cooks. Karl's dad was heavily involved in the community, and both parents were involved with the Episcopal Church.

In New York, Karl developed his independence at a young age. His father worked the graveyard shift, and his mother left early for her job. Karl, therefore, became a latchkey kid and would be responsible for himself during some parts of the day. He learned how to navigate public transit and would hop on a train or bus to meet his parents downtown, attend basketball games at Madison Square Garden, or see dollar movies on Lexington Avenue. "Sometimes my friends and I would say we were going to the movies but catch the train to Shea Stadium in Flushing and watch New York Mets games from the platform, or the Bronx to see Yankee Stadium," Karl laughs. "We'd get back on the train before the 8th inning and beat the rush home."

The neighborhood was diverse, and Karl loved having friends from all backgrounds, cultures, and ethnicities. He'd walk to school—a magnate school (East Harlem Block School) on 110th Street and Madison Avenue—and liked learning. He was responsible about doing his homework and was never attracted to joining a gang as some of his classmates began to do in middle school. His older sister and aunt looked out for him, keeping him out of trouble.

When he turned 12, the family made a big move from New York City to Jacksonville. The change was an adjustment for Karl. He noted that Florida was less diverse and more segregated. "We left a melting pot," he reflects. "In Florida at the time, it was more just black and white. That's where I really learned about our nation's racial divide." Karl continued to play his favorite sport of basketball, but found it wasn't as popular in Florida. He began playing football, a sport most of his classmates began playing at six years old. He played football for several years before deciding to focus on basketball throughout high school.

Karl's parents emphasized education and enrolled him in classes like Greek, Latin, and Chemistry in order to get him into a more challenging high school. His grades were average; He remembers earning C's but points out that C's at his school may have been A's at less challenging schools. While in high school, he had the defining moment of being doubted when a guidance counselor told him to forget about 4-year-college. "I didn't like somebody telling me I couldn't do something," he remembers. "So that was a moment in my life when I chose to prove somebody wrong."

Karl decided to attend Cheyney University, a historically black college in Pennsylvania. At the time, he wanted to be a lawyer and got heavily involved in student government and eventually served as Vice President of the Student Government. However, Karl decided to change tracks when both of his parents fell ill with cancer. His father was diagnosed with Hodgkin's Disease and his mother with multiple Myeloma. He decided he needed to make money more quickly rather than taking on the financial burden of more loans. Thus, classmate Theresa's fateful offer was particularly well timed.

After acing his interview, Karl had to find a job while waiting for his clearance to begin training. He got a gig as an intake counselor at an alcohol and drug program in Philadelphia where he began to grapple with drug addiction close up. After working there for a year, he went to basic agent training which he completed in June of 1986.

He was one of the youngest in his class and became a senior agent quite young as a result. He was leading enforcement groups and task forces and doing undercover work. During his time at the Philadelphia DEA, he met his wife, Sherry. Coincidentally, Sherry was from a small town called Chester, where Karl's father also grew up. As it turned out, Karl and Sherry's father had been friends growing up. During the ten years Karl spent in Philly, his mother also passed away from her cancer at the young age of 55.

In 1995, Karl decided he was ready for a change and requested and received a lateral transfer to the Virgin Islands where he learned the trans-shipment side of drug enforcement. A few years later, he received a promotion to become a Group Supervisor in Dallas. By then, he and Sherry had three children—Karl Jr., Cory, and Ashley. Karl Jr. was turning seven and sending kids to private school in St. Croix was quite expensive. The family relocated to Texas where Karl became the Supervisor for the Dallas-Ft. Worth Airport Task Force. A year after that he became Resident Agent-in-Charge in Ft. Worth.

In 2002, he received another lateral transfer to DEA headquarters in Arlington. While there, he was made Inspector in the Office of Professional Responsibility (OPR); in other words, he was working in internal affairs, conducting investigations concerning allegations of misconduct lodged against DEA employees. "Nobody wants to see you!" he laughs. In 2004, he moved to Newark, NJ to continue working in internal affairs as the senior inspector with a team of four inspectors under him.

The following year, Karl was transferred back to Philadelphia where he became the Assistant Special Agent in Charge with responsibility for all the DEA task force groups in the city. While he was there, Karl's father fell and hit his head, causing some traumatic effects including memory loss. Immediately, it was decided that his father would move in with them. "The family banded together and committed to taking care of grandpop," Karl remembers. "My kids had done some community service in elder care facilities, and they, too, didn't want their grandparents in that type of environment. It was automatic that he'd come live with us."

His father's fall happened in 2007, and he later passed away in 2013. Karl is proud of the legacy he left, reading from his obituary the seemingly dozens of organizations with which he volunteered and was involved in. Organizations like Disadvantaged Youth, The Cultural Heritage Center, Community Center, Prison Ministry in the Episcopal Diocese, NAACP, Urban League, American Legion, and the co-founder of Tri-Forrest Athletic Association (Athletic Program for inner city youth). "My parents really instilled community service in me," Karl nods. "They were huge influences in my life. Helping others was always important to them."

In 2008, Karl became the Acting Special Agent in Charge for Philadelphia and returned the following year (2009) to headquarters as the Deputy Chief Inspector (Senior Executive Service) of OPR where he oversaw internal investigations for the agency, and served as the principal advisor on integrity matters to the DEA Chief Inspector and the DEA Administrator. And finally, in 2013, he finished his career as the Special Agent in Charge of the Washington division. "I ran out of time at the DEA," he reflects, "but I was ready for something bigger."

Through it all, Karl has had the stalwart support of his wife, Sherry and their three children. "Sherry is a great mother and a great wife," smiles Karl. "Look at all these moves she had to put up with in my career. She's been beside me through it all." All three children, meanwhile, are thriving, with the two boys out of college and embarking on their careers, and Ashley set to graduate soon as well. All three of them thrived in athletics in high school, and all three were State Champions—the two boys in football and Ashley in cheerleading. Karl's face lights up with pride when talking about their achievements and he considers their championship rings to be his most prized possessions. "I live vicariously through all of them," he laughs. "They've given me all the rings to keep. I have all of the team plaques, the championship photos, and the framed jerseys. I've got it all!"

As a leader, Karl considers himself a people person and stresses the importance of empowering others. "Being able to identify talent is crucial," he points out. "If you're in a leadership program and you're trying to manage and oversee programs, you want to be able to have the best people—people that may even be smarter than you. You have to put friendships aside. You have to select the right people because they're qualified, and they bring value to what you're trying to accomplish."

To young people entering the working world today, he encourages patience and advises them to find mentors. "Everyone needs a mentor," he says. "Don't pick one based on whether they're male or female; be open to whoever it may be. Find someone you can rely on and not someone who just tells you what you want to hear. A good mentor will tell you what you don't want to hear as well." Karl admits he was fortunate to have several mentors he could depend on throughout his career.

Karl also attributes his belief in God for his success, spiritual strength, and perseverance. He also attributes his affiliations to Kappa Alpha Psi Fraternity, Prince Hall Free and Accepted Masons, and the Brotherhood of St Andrew for also being a support base in achieving his goals. "I had no older or younger brothers, so involvement in fraternities filled the void. I now have millions of brothers."

In addition, Karl served as the National President of the National Association of Black Narcotic Agents and served as the organization's President for eight consecutive years (2004-2011). "To lead an organization consisting of colleagues and counterparts was extremely critical in my development as a leader and professional.

Karl feels blessed to be able to continue to pursue his passion of dealing with the drug crisis and to do so with more flexibility than ever. "When you're in a government law enforcement system, it can be a rigid system," he explains. "Outside of that system, you can begin to discover new things. Discover things that are related to what you've been doing but, were things you couldn't necessarily do in the government. I knew we couldn't arrest our way out of this crisis, and I began working on ways to help victims. I wanted to be able to look at all options and see how they would work. It's about taking chances. And this was my chance to learn and to make an impact."

Karen Doner

The Butter Knife

Karen Doner was only a fifth-year attorney when she won the case she remembers best. She was practicing employment law as a midlevel associate for the large firm Williams Mullen and was representing Oncore Construction in a suit against a large local construction company. There were other partners on the case with more experience, but Karen was handling the bulk of it and developed the client relationship; ultimately they saw her as their attorney. The case was a classic David and Goliath scenario, with the smaller Oncore expected to lose.

Instead, Karen and Oncore won the suit, and the President of the company was more than grateful. As a thank you, he gave her a gift which, today, she still considers to be one of her prize possessions. "At the conclusion of the case, he gave me a butter knife," she smiles. "He told me, 'Karen, you cut their heart out with a butter knife.' That was a turning point in my career. When you're a mid-level senior associate, and a client compliments you in that way, you start to realize that I might actually know what I'm doing. You start thinking more like a strategic lawyer."

"That statement—'I cut their heart out with a butter knife'—actually is my style to this day," Karen continues. "I'm reasonable and happy to get along with opposing counsel. I want to be reasonable since it is so much more pleasant to get along with the other attorneys. But I'm there to do a job. My job is to zealously represent my client and, of course, win. The President of Oncore is a friend of mine to this day. He recognized that skillset in me early in my career. It felt good, and it gave me a lot of confidence going forward."

Karen continued rising in the ranks at Williams Mullen. She stayed for ten years and ultimately became a partner at the firm and was the first female elected to the Board of Directors. After a decade learning what she could there, she and two other attorneys decided to launch a small firm of their own. That business, Roth Doner Jackson, did very well, and again, Karen gained valuable experience that she would carry with her into her own practice. She stayed for about seven years before taking the leap and founding her own firm, Doner Law, PLC, in January 2017.

Today, Karen is running a successful practice and employs two other female attorneys—one full-time and one part-time. Karen made a particular effort to ensure there would be roles for part-time attorneys at her firm since many law firms do not have meaningful positions for part-time attorneys. "There's a whole body of mostly female litigators with families who ultimately have to drop out of the practice of law because of the difficulty in balancing family and law," she explains. "Even when bigger firms say they have work/life balance and part-time opportunities, those opportunities are not truly part-time or they are financially punitive. I discovered at my last firm that hiring these women is really a win/win situation for both the firm and the employee. The firm can really benefit from someone providing however many hours they are able to provide, whether that's 5 hours a week or 20 hours a week. A firm benefits from that because these are top-notch attorneys who didn't have the opportunity to keep working in their field. And obviously it benefits them because it's a job that's flexible and understanding." In fact, Roth Doner Jackson won the DC Bar Quality of Life Award for its commitment to offering a positive work environment by embracing this same model.

Although Doner Law is a small firm, Karen tries to offer all the benefits and resources of a much larger firm. She believes it's crucial to invest in amenities like a nice office space in a well-located area with access to shared conference rooms, as well as employee benefits like paid maternity leave and a monthly childcare stipend. She has an administrative assistant and bookkeeper to ensure that she isn't bogged down with administrative work and can focus on the clients. One thing that sets her apart from other law firms, she believes, is her responsiveness and her decisiveness.

"It's surprising, but a lot of attorneys are not responsive," Karen notes. "That doesn't make sense to me. If you're successful based on your clients, why wouldn't you return a call in a timely manner? Even if I'm in trial, I let them know I'm in trial and will get back to them in two days. In the meantime, I let them know who they could contact in the firm. So I cultivate those relationships, and I do try to get to know the client on a personal level as well." She is also results-driven and gives decisive results. Lawyers from larger firms tend to identify the pros and cons of each situation and then shy away from making a specific recommendation. Karen, on the other hand, assesses the risks involved and then offers direction. There is no waffling back and forth when you are talking to her about a legal issue.

As she has since law school, Karen practices employment law, generally representing employers when they face litigation over discrimination or harassment suits. She also provides counseling to employers on day-to-day matters like terminations, instituting fair policies, and avoiding litigation in the first place. That makes up 60 to 70% of the practice; the other 30-40% of her time is devoted to commercial litigation—business-to-business disputes and contract disputes.

"I believe in doing two things well for our clients in her employment practice: First, helping a business in any way I can to prevent them from being sued by an employee. Avoiding being sued means treating people fairly, not discriminating, and not engaging in anything unlawful. I know we provide excellent guidance on these matters. The second thing we do well is defend them in litigation when it is appropriate. In my experience, there are a very small percentage of valid claims that employees bring against companies. That doesn't mean there aren't any because there are. But they are of a much smaller percentage than the frivolous claims that I see. So I feel very good about defending against those claims."

Karen's clients run the gamut from tiny companies with five employees to giant firms with more than 10,000 workers. Although she's had great success getting her name out to prospective clients, her secret isn't networking. In fact, she doesn't do much networking at all. Instead, she just does a great job for the client, and relies on her reputation to push her practice forward. "I always try to find a way to do what the client wants to do," Karen affirms. "When someone asks me, 'Can I do this?' typically my first response is, 'Well, is that what you want to do?' And then I try very hard to do what they want to do. Every client is so different; I try to get to know my clients so I can mold to their personality and what they're looking for."

Karen grew up middle class in the DC area and is proud that her success has allowed her children more privileges than she had growing up. But she's quick to thank her father for the work ethic that got her here; it was he who gave her a solidly middle-class upbringing after his own childhood of poverty. He and his brother were given up to a foster family when he was only three, and the foster family was too poor to ever adopt them. For years, Karen's father and uncle shared a couch as their bed in the living room of their small apartment in the Bronx. He was the first in his family to go to college. And he went on to become an aerospace electrical engineer for the Naval Research Lab. "I think about how he grew up, and then about how I grew up which was so much better," Karen reflects. "And then I think about how my children are growing up, which is even better. That is amazing to me. My father is definitely my number one fan; he has always been extremely supportive of me and my career."

Karen's mother, meanwhile, was Canadian, and Karen was actually born in Montreal before she, her parents, and her older sister relocated to the DC area before she turned one. In Maryland, her mother worked as an administrator for the Montgomery County government. "My mom and I have similar personalities," smiles Karen. "She always volunteered for various things. I don't think she tried to get me to do it, but she led by example. My mother is very service-driven. That's important to her, and she does it regularly." Although she didn't go to college, and although Karen's father was the first in his family to go, she remembers that college was expected for her and her sister.

However, Karen was a late bloomer when it came to academics. She was more focused on spending time with her friends than studying. Until high school, her report cards suffered. Then she got involved with the local B'nai B'rith Youth Organization (BBYO), an international youth group for Jewish teenagers. There, she began to come into her own. "I had been getting into a little bit of trouble," she laughs. "And my parents forced me to go to this group. But it really changed the course of my life. There I was part of a strong group, and I'm still friends with a lot of those people today. I ended up becoming the Regional President of the Washington area."

Still, getting into college was tricky. She'd improved her grades since being involved with BBYO, but her transcript still left something to be desired. With her heart set on University of Delaware, she followed the advice of a counselor and applied to their Agricultural Education Department. Then, after starting at the school, she transferred out of the Ag department, began to pursue her passion, and majored in two fields—criminal justice and political science.

Everything was going swimmingly. She joined a sorority, and after years spent working at various waitressing and retail jobs, she landed a competitive internship at then-Senator Joe Biden's district office. She was enjoying her classes and loving the social life. Unfortunately, at the beginning of her junior year, she was badly injured in a freak accident at a sorority hayride.

Karen was run over by a wagon with 20 people on it a week before Halloween. The tractor driver had headphones on and was unable to hear the screams for him to stop. Karen had fallen off and was pinned to the ground underneath the wagon. She had broken her back. "It was a very serious accident, and I was helicoptered out," says Karen. They didn't know whether I was going to walk again. The spinal cord injury was tremendously painful."

She was in the hospital for several weeks, then in the National Rehab Hospital for several more weeks before being able to return home to Gaithersburg. She took the rest of the semester off and was lovingly cared for by her parents. It was a depressing and painful time for Karen since she was basically bedridden and had to relearn how to walk and perform other daily life activities.

Finally, she returned to school for her second semester, but everything felt different. She needed a back brace and a cane to get around. She no longer enjoyed going to parties or participating in the college social scene. Instead, she buckled down, focused on her studies, and went to physical therapy regularly. During her recovery, Senator Biden reached out to offer his condolences, and when Karen decided she would attend law school, he gladly wrote her a letter of recommendation. "I applied to Syracuse, his alma mater," she laughs. "And I was accepted there within 24 hours of them receiving his letter."

Ultimately, Karen felt the need for a change of pace and decided to go to law school at Loyola University in Chicago. Now free of her cane and back brace, Karen loved law school and immediately developed an interest in employment law. She even started an Employment Law Society on campus, and to this day, she stays in touch with her employment law professor, who has been the strongest female mentor in her career and who Karen describes as a lifelong friend.

In the summers, Karen would return to DC, as she knew she wanted to practice in the area after graduation. Back home, she worked as a cocktail waitress, but in Chicago she landed a gig at a boutique employment law practice through her mentor. By the time she graduated, each of the seven attorneys in the practice were happy to reach out to connections in DC to help her get set up in the area. She landed her first job out of law school at a firm called Hazel & Thomas, before moving on two years later to Whiteford Taylor and Preston. "My first few years I was just trying to figure out what felt best and where I wanted to be," says Karen. "But I always practiced both employment law and commercial litigation. I've done that at every firm because I do love the trial work."

Two years after that, she landed at Williams Mullen. There, she met many mentors, although all of them happened to be male. In fact, the only sexism she encountered in her career came from fellow female attorneys. Because of these experiences, Karen prioritizes being a mentor to other young female attorneys who may have faced similar prejudices. The difficulties of juggling the responsibilities of both law and motherhood are the reason she's so committed to offering excellent benefits, maternity leave, childcare stipends, and part-time schedules.

Karen has been fortunate to have a supportive partner as they raised her son and daughter. Her husband, Andy, actually attended the University of Delaware with her, but the two didn't begin dating until they reconnected at a school homecoming four years after graduation. Their children are 17 and 14, and now because they're more independent, Karen has begun to make giving back more of a priority. She's volunteered for a variety of causes, but the project closest to her heart is the work she's done toward getting housing for a homeless man, Marvin, in her neighborhood.

Her friendship with Marvin began around four years ago. Karen and her neighbors in Vienna had organized a monthly community service event, and it was her turn to host. She had seen Marvin from time to time and offered him food or a cold drink on a hot day. But she felt she wanted to do more to help. "I met with him, and we put together a list of stuff he would need to get through the fall and the winter," explains Karen. "Since that time, our relationship has really grown. We are close and lifelong friends."

Marvin is 75 years old and had been homeless for almost 50 years. One day he asked Karen for help finding a job so he could afford a place to live. Karen dove into the project knowing nothing about homelessness or the resources available. She connected him with The Lamb Center, which provides services to homeless people, as well as FACETS, an organization that paired him with a case worker to try to find him housing. With his permission, she even reached out to his relatives and located two sisters and several first cousins, some of whom are in the area. Last November, Karen found Marvin a place to live. It took some time to get him settled into a new place and routine, but Karen reports that he is doing well and is very happy. She continues to take him to doctor's appointments, the grocery store, and checks in with him regularly.

Karen thinks back to her time at BBYO as she reflects on what it takes to lead. "I learned in youth group that a good leader is someone who really listens and collaborates with others," she says. "It's got to be a team effort. I try to do that in my practice now and get input from others. People need to feel included and valued."

To young people entering the working world today, she gives the simplest, but often best advice—work hard. "It seems so obvious, but

I don't always see that," nods Karen. "That is how I was able to build a practice and be successful. I worked hard from the very beginning, proved myself, and never stopped. My work ethic is what got me to where I am today."

Jonathan A. Evans

Building a Championship Team

Athletics were a major part of Jonathan Evans' childhood. Both of his parents were in physical education; his mother was a local health and PE teacher, and his father was a respected teacher and coach-turned athletic director. The two imbued him with a love of sports at an early age.

In fact, Jonathan's father had won a state championship in his role as basketball coach at a high school in nearby New Haven, but when Jonathan was born, he gave up his successful coaching career for fatherhood. Additionally, as soon as Jonathan was able to swing a bat, his father, a hometown hero for the championship under his belt, was out on the field showing him the ropes of Little League. "Now the big city coach was coaching suburban t-ball and coaching kids playing basketball on little 8-foot hoops," laughs Jonathan. "I think with my father coaching me, he was definitely pushing me harder than any kid on the team. I wanted to be the best, and as the coach's son, I had to take on a leadership role. I couldn't pick a fight. I couldn't disobey because that night my dad would tell me, 'you've got to set the example, you're my son.' We were the first ones there. We were the last ones to leave. So my father coaching me really helped shape me. It set an example of hard work and leadership, and it pushed me toward that role."

All through high school, Jonathan pursued and thrived in athletics. But as he grew into adulthood, he took those leadership skills learned on the basketball and tennis courts, in the pool, and on the baseball and football fields, and turned them into professional assets. "In business, especially consulting where you're working on projects, it's never just an individual contributor kind of scenario. Government contracting is about teaming, putting teams on the ground and building the most effective teams. So the ability to work with others, incorporate a strong work ethic, and integrating the strengths of others on your team is huge."

Today, it's clear that Jonathan took his parents' lessons to heart. He is the President and CEO of B&A, a government contractor providing IT integration and application development services. Along the way, he reorganized a rapidly growing business to achieve a new level of success for the entire company by building new teams and creating previously unseen efficiencies between departments.

Founded in 1988 under the name Bart & Associates (B&A), B&A celebrated its 32nd Anniversary last year. For its 30th Anniversary the company underwent a rebranding to reflect its changing leadership and structure. However, the new name, B&A, pays homage to the founders and where the company came from.

Over the last several years, annual revenue for the company has averaged about $45 million, and it employs approximately 250 resources. Although B&A received 8(a) status in 2002, entitling it to pursue small-business set-aside contracts, it outgrew this designation by 2011 around the same time Jonathan joined the business full-time. His mission as Vice President of Service Delivery was to both solidify the delivery organization and improve communication between departments, all the while ensuring that B&A didn't fall back into small business status. "A lot of small businesses take this really dramatic hit when they outgrow 8(a), where they lose half their revenue," explains Jonathan. "You can't compete with the big companies, so all of a sudden you're back in the small business game. We solidified our organization, put the proper processes in place, made the appropriate investments in people, and leveled out where we are, but we are definitely poised for growth. We've structured the company with the ability to scale, because we've made those investments in people and process. Plus, we have zero debt on the books and a healthy balance sheet. We're able to look at acquisitions, pursue highly competitive contracts, and be aggressive in how we bid. Before, we were at $80 million in revenue with about 20% full and open contracts, we're at $45 million now with about 70% of that from prime contracts in the full and open space. We've had to compete against companies like IBM, Accenture, Deloitte, and Northrup Grumman. We're going to be very strategic and stay focused in our areas and double our full and open revenue again."

B&A's work focuses along four service lines: human capital management, operations and enablement, integration and analytics, and modernization. They contract for several federal agencies, most significantly the Department of Homeland Security as well as the Department of Commerce, and also work for the U.S. Senate and the Judiciary branch, ensuring federal employees are paid and the government continues to operate. "We make a real impact on society," nods Jonathan. "Whether it's the mission critical system we implement on the borders that protect our nation, or the people processing systems we've implemented within airports, or a payroll system that we've implemented to pay every Senator so our government is operational. The impact that we have at this company continues to drive me. I get up every morning, I enjoy going to work, and I want to continue to make that impact."

And make an impact he certainly has. When B&A hired Jonathan in 2011 as VP of Service Delivery, only one—or possibly one and a half, Jonathan winks—of the four partners thought he might be suited for the CEO role and eventually taking the reins. Jonathan, despite having no personal connections within the company, won them all over with his tireless work ethic and talent for creating efficiencies.

Jonathan had worked with B&A for years as a customer of theirs at IBM, and then as a supplier and vendor of theirs at his own small business. He first came onboard part-time to provide assistance growing their projects and their business. By the time he switched to full-time, he was ready with all sorts of ideas to streamline the company. "I helped restructure the organization for the future," explains Jonathan, "At that time the departments and the partners were operating in silos with no oversight at the top. If one partner handled an HR situation one way, someone might go to another partner to get a different answer. So I took over operations and solidified the organization by standardizing how we deliver value to our customers, establishing consistent operating processes and procedures, and instituting annual strategic growth plans. I found myself the glue between three executives—me as the VP of Service Delivery, the COO who controlled Operations, and the VP of Business Development and Sales. Each of these areas really needed me to drive."

Over the next several years, Jonathan began to bring in his own management team. In 2015, he was named President of the company, and in 2018, he was officially named CEO. At that time, three of the four partners agreed to step back from the day-to-day running of the business to form a Board of Directors, with the fourth already retired. "From 2015 to 2018 I began to restructure the business. I brought in a new VP of Service Delivery, a new VP of Sales, and promoted someone I had previously brought in to take over Operations," says Jonathan. "Once the company was restructured, we needed to solidify the role of the partners going forward and that's why we created the Board. Our 30th Anniversary celebration in 2018 was not only a celebration of 30 years of business but was also an opportunity to thank the four partners for their service and influence. It was also the formal changing of the guard so to speak as the leadership team was formally announced. It was a great celebration. Everyone in the company appreciated it, and we honored the partners with mementoes from all of us to mark the milestone."

It's impressive that Jonathan has risen so high at such a young age, but especially so given his background. He had no connections in DC, nor any contact with the world of federal contracting. He grew up in the small town of Hamden, Connecticut, just outside New Haven, in a house his parents still live in today. Both his mother and father, as mentioned, were in physical education, and pushed Jonathan and his younger sister to do their best in both academics and athletics.

Sports were particularly important to Jonathan, not only because of the life and leadership skills he learned, but because of the diversity it exposed him to from a young age. New Haven was close enough that the suburban kids from Hamden got to know the inner-city kids who played on their teams, and Jonathan learned never to judge his peers by their skin color or background. Somewhat unusually, he also celebrated both Christian and Jewish holidays throughout childhood, as his father is Jewish, and his mother is Catholic which meant the family was in synagogue just as often as they were in church. At the age of 11, Jonathan's parents asked him to choose a religion, and, excited to have a Bar Mitzvah like those he'd attended for his older cousins, he chose Judaism. He ended up having a B'nai Mitzvah, or a group Bar Mitzvah with some other inter-faith kids, complete with a big party, gifts, and one meaningful one in particular.

At the B'nai Mitzvah, his father gave him a ring—a Chinese initial ring—that Jonathan today considers one of his most prized possession. The rings are a family tradition for the Evans', and for years Jonathan had worn the ring of his paternal grandfather, Albert. He felt a special connection with his father's father, although the two never met, because Jonathan was given the middle name "Albert" after his grandfather. He grew up hearing stories about how beloved his grandfather was in the community. "The ring has my initials on it. It represents the past and the history of my father's family," explains Jonathan. "But it also represents the memory of a grandfather who I never met. It's not something I wear every day. But when I do wear it on special occasions, it reminds me of my family and the importance of family."

At school, Jonathan thrived. His parents' demands for excellence didn't end on the court. His mother could be strict and once even encouraged his school to suspend him for skipping school. Jonathan laughingly admitted that their nickname for her was "Inspector Gadget," because if you did anything wrong, she was sure to sniff it out. He spoke at his sixth-grade graduation, went on to take Honors classes as he got older, and finished high school in the top 10% of his class. He was later recognized as a Distinguished Alumni inducted into the Hamden High School Education Fund Hall of Fame in 2019.

Meanwhile, outside of his schoolwork and commitment to athletics, he also took on summer jobs and worked on weekends. From mowing lawns in the summer, to shoveling snow in the winter, to working at sports camps, to cleaning apartment buildings owned by his father and uncle, Jonathan kept busy and earned his own spending money. Once he was able to drive, he became an assistant tennis pro. "My parents really instilled that work ethic in me," reflects Jonathan. "I got exposed to a lot of different jobs. It was never an option not to work. My parents were okay financially so it was not out of necessity that I worked. They encouraged me to work knowing it would enhance my work ethic. There was no slacking off in the Evans' household.

By the time he got to high school, Jonathan had to make some decisions about his sports teams. He was getting older, and could no longer play several sports during the same season; he had to commit. He chose to take a chance with football in the fall, basketball in the winter, and tennis in the spring, giving up swimming and baseball. Although he loved athletics, when it came time to think about colleges, Jonathan knew athletics wasn't going to be a career for him, and wisely chose to focus on academics. "I was good enough that I could have played at a Division III school," Jonathan points out. "But I accepted the fact that I wasn't going to be a professional athlete. And attending a small liberal arts Division III school the same size as my high school didn't appeal to me."

Jonathan was more drawn to universities in the Big Ten conference. He was impressed by their size and the energy he felt on their campuses. His father, a Syracuse graduate, tried to lobby for Syracuse, but once Jonathan set foot on the Penn State campus, he'd already decided. He applied to Penn State and left for State College, PA the next fall. The decision turned out to have been a strong one; not only did he love his time there, joining a fraternity and making time for tailgates, he was able to study abroad in Spain, and double major in both Business Logistics and International Business.

In the summers, Jonathan took on internships hoping to get a foothold in the professional world. Following his freshman year, he went to work at a family friend's business but found it wasn't quite what he'd signed up for. "My father's friend had a business where they broke down IT equipment for metals," Jonathan recalls. "He told me I could intern there and be exposed to business," recalls Jonathan. "But they didn't have enough work for me and threw me in the warehouse to separate metals from computer parts. What I wanted to truly get exposed to was the operations side of the business and unfortunately that didn't come to fruition."

The next summer, he had more success, living with relatives in Nantucket for the summer, ordering supplies and learning the logistics side of business. Finally, he had enough credits to be placed with large corporations via a program at Penn State, and he was able to work with Photronics on the technology side and then later with Staples on supply chain and logistics.

Because his double major required additional credits, Jonathan stayed at Penn State for four and a half years. Upon his graduation at the end of the fall semester, he wasted no time launching his career. "I graduated just before Christmas, got home on December 20th, 2003, and on January 10th, 2004, my parents dropped me off in DC and wished me luck," laughs Jonathan.

Thanks to his work ethic and the impressive internships under his belt, Jonathan had been offered a position with IBM, where he quickly displayed a talent for the business world. Only a handful of years later he was growing his own business into a multi-million-dollar business. By 2011, he was offered VP of Service Delivery at B&A—a mere seven years after his parents had dropped him off in DC and wished him luck.

To young people looking to replicate his success, Jonathan's advice is simple and straightforward: work hard. "Working hard is first and foremost and is crucial to your success," he affirms. "Put in those extra hours. Be committed to things. You have to set yourself apart, and the only way to set yourself apart when it comes to business and success is doing the work that is required. When you look at stories of people who achieved success, nothing is given to them. When I came to DC, I didn't know a person in the business world, I had no family connections. If I had gone into education, my dad probably could've made a call and gotten me a teaching job, but I took that risk because I knew I could work hard, and I could put those extra hours in, and this was something I was passionate about doing."

When it comes to leadership, Jonathan is all about using the teamwork skills he learned so long ago from his parents and on the court. "I'm a hands-on guy," smiles Jonathan. "If we have a proposal due at eight in the morning, and we're working late to get it buttoned up, or get the printing done, or get it boxed, I'm there with the team. I'll even run and grab dinner if needed. I think all of these things—how I lead and how I engage with my team—it all came from that early exposure to sports. Of course, my father's coaching helped shape me as a leader. I wanted to be the best on the field and on the court when I was a kid, and I want to be the best in business."

Patricia A. Ferrick

A Home-grown Leader

Trish Ferrick considers her prize possession to be an old college sweatshirt, but it's not from her alma mater. When her father Ed passed away, it was an item she took from his closet. The two had a close relationship, and the sweatshirt reminds her not only of her beloved late father, but of the many lessons he handed down to her including an unshakable belief in herself.

The sweatshirt reads "Atlantic Christian College", a school her father attended but never graduated from. In those days, he wasn't focused on school, and his transcripts were full of incompletes before he ultimately dropped out in his second year. When he went to interview for his first professional job at Univac, the transcripts were a problem. Ed sent them over, and the man who had interviewed him quickly called him back in disbelief. The interview had gone so well, but the transcripts were a hard sell up the ladder.

Still, Trish's father persevered. He convinced Univac to give him a shot on the strength of his honesty, charm, and commitment to buckle down. "I'm not surprised they gave him a chance," smiles Trish. "He was so genuine and humble that I'm sure he laughed with embarrassment but didn't make excuses for his shortcomings. He never took himself too seriously, but he worked hard and always encouraged us to do the same. He wound up working there for 35 years—against all odds!" Today, Trish says the sweatshirt reminds her of her father's determination and humility every day. His experience with schooling left him a committed advocate of education. Though he regretted his own inattentiveness in college, he always emphasized that his own kids would attend and graduate.

"He told us we could be anything we wanted to be," relates Trish. "I wanted to be around him whenever I could. If he was going to the store, I wanted to go with him. It was a chance to spend time together and talk about everything. He would always let me know he was proud of me and he was always encouraging in whatever I was trying to accomplish. One of the benefits of his encouragement was that I was motivated to be successful and do more, to push myself. He instilled in me the value of providing that same encouragement to others."

Her mother, the introvert to Ed's extrovert, was supportive in her own ways. She was a stay at home mom throughout Trish's childhood, and could always be found attentively cooking and cleaning for her five kids. However, she also had attended Stanford and was conspicuously book smart and accomplished. Her parents' marriage was a happy one, and she remembers her childhood in Annandale, VA, nostalgically.

"Mom was such a good cook," Trish beams. "She was always in the kitchen making dinner when I came home from school. I remember loving how the house smelled. Every night she went through the trouble of making a big dinner for all of us, and it was such a comfort walking in and knowing she was there." All seven family members gathered every night around the dinner table to discuss everything from work and school to sports and friends. And Trish could be more than a little competitive with her sister and three brothers.

Trish is the fourth of her five siblings, with a sister and brother seven and eight years older, as well as two closer brothers, two years older and two years younger respectively. She looked up to her older siblings while spending most of her time running around the neighborhood with her other brothers and playing games with the other kids who lived nearby.

"If I had homework, I'd do it fast and then run out to join the action," remembers Trish. "Everyone met in our yard, about a dozen neighborhood kids—some of them are still my friends today—and we'd play until dark." Trish loved playing with both sports and dolls, playing with boys and other girls alike.

In school she thrived, heeding her father's advice to take her education seriously and always earned good marks academically. She attended a private Catholic school through eighth grade, then attended Annandale public schools during high school. In both settings, she did her best to succeed and relied on the support of her family at home. For extracurricular activities, she played piano and was the only kid in the family who took piano lessons. Three nights a week she had to come in from the outdoor fun and practice, a situation which she remembers being none too pleased about. "I wanted to be out there throwing the football with my brothers or playing with my friends," she laughs. "Even when I was young, I got excited about my brothers' football games. I wanted to be right there in the middle of it."

Although girls couldn't sign up for football, she found an outlet for her athleticism on the high school cheerleading squad, where she quickly established herself as a leader. She had been nervous to try out as a freshman, but quickly became team captain on the strength of the other girls' trust in her. And the cheerleading squad wasn't the only place her burgeoning leadership skills were recognized; she also held class officer positions every year of her high school career. She also ran track, and often joined the family for her brothers' athletic events as well.

"My father was always excited about what we were doing," Trish recalls. "I remember when I was running track my freshman year and was competing in several events at the first meet. I was really looking forward to the competition, but I broke my ankle at practice two days before the meet. When my dad came home that night I was in a lot of pain, and he knew how disappointed I was that I would miss most of the season. I could tell that he could sense my pain and disappointment. He tried so hard to make me feel better. He was always supportive, and he always let me know how much he cared."

Trish decided to follow in her brother's footsteps and apply to Virginia Tech early decision. She knew it was a good school not far from home, and that many of her friends from Annandale were planning to attend. She was accepted on the strength of her grades and began thinking about what she'd like to study.

Throughout high school, Trish and her father had always gotten along swimmingly. But their relationship was briefly strained when she announced as a college freshman that she and her high school sweetheart Rich were engaged. "I knew Rich had already asked for my parents' blessing, and my dad liked Rich, but he was afraid that the engagement would distract me and that I might not finish college," explains Trish. "He thought I was too young to make such an important decision. He didn't like it when I showed him my engagement ring; he wouldn't even acknowledge it. It really killed me that he was upset with me. I felt like I let him down. When we finally really talked about it, I promised him I'd finish college before getting married, and he reluctantly accepted the idea. As time went on, he realized that we were both committed to finishing our degrees and he became more and more accepting of our intentions."

The young couple did wait, tying the knot only after they'd finished college. Trish's mom, ever the accomplished homemaker, actually sewed her wedding dress. "She could do anything," exclaims Trish. "In fact, she's 87 now, and she can still do anything. She had a quiet strength about her that complimented my dad's outgoing personality." Her mother still lives in the family home where Trish was raised and has such fond memories of. Today, Trish and Rich have three grown children and four grandchildren of their own.

At Virginia Tech, Trish decided to major in accounting. She was attracted to discipline and liked the rational way specific rules produced predictable results. After college, she went to work for KPMG and passed her CPA, but she never really fell in love with public accounting and began to get restless. After four years she took a job as director of internal audit at a local bank. About a year after that, she was asked to take on the role as the controller, and she's been in banking ever since.

It's no wonder, with her strong upbringing and the encouragement of her family that Trish thrived in her chosen career and quickly rose through the ranks. Through it all, her parents were supportive, and her dad remained a trusted confidante. "Whenever I had problems at work, I would call him," she affirms. "He was my sounding board. He was always worrying about me, always wanted to make sure I was ok, always wanted the family to get together. And he had a really good mind for things and always gave me good advice."

After serving as a controller at several different institutions, she was offered a CFO job. In spite of her strong self-confidence, when she was first presented with the opportunity, she balked. A fellow female banking executive named Georgia reached out to Trish maybe ten times before Trish decided to go ahead and meet with her. She found Georgia exciting, but a bit intimidating. Initially Trish was offered a consultant role and was shocked when the offer changed. Georgia wanted her to come onboard as CFO.

"I started telling her all the reasons I shouldn't do it,"Trish remembers. "I didn't have the experience. I didn't feel sure I was ready. And she's like, 'Trish, this is an opportunity here. This is not a bad thing. This is a good thing. You'll be fine. Don't worry.' So I accepted the job, and it was a great experience."Trish served as CFO there for four years before moving on to become CFO at several other banks.

In 2006, Trish suffered the loss of her father to lung cancer. She remembers how hard it was being unable to discuss her work and life as he grew sicker. "The bank I was working at was in the process of being sold. Those types of things were exactly the kind of things I would usually sit and talk to him about," she reflects. "I had this big new opportunity I knew he would love to hear about. But he was too sick by then. So he wasn't with me to go through that next big step, the first step I really made on my own without his mentorship. But I did it. And the rest is history."

Thanks to wonderful mentors like her father and her bank leaders, it's no surprise that today, she's one of the few female bank Presidents in the country. In 2007, she became one of the four founding executive officers of FVCbank, after present-day CEO David Pijor invited her onboard. The two had met through mutual acquaintances, and David invited her to lunch. There, she learned about his vision of a community bank with investors who would actually help build and grow the bank. He had a team of directors and shareholders ready to go, and Trish jumped at the chance to play a role. She began doing some part-time work for the team before joining full time that September.

"We're a commercially focused community bank, relationship-focused, with small to mid-sized customers. As we grow, that customer base is expanding," describes Trish. "In this sophisticated market, it was important to be able to offer our customers all the products and services that a big bank could. So we invested in the infrastructure of a bigger bank, thinking, 'Let's build a billion-dollar bank from the outset as opposed to developing it along the way.' We invested in a good team at the beginning and were committed to superior customer service, a suite of products to support our efforts, and a team of exceptional bankers. We had a good platform with a hundred or so local investors who were committed to make referrals and bank with us. David knew a lot of people. I would say this bank is David's vision, and I embraced it completely. It just got me excited—he didn't have the typical job description or work structure, he really thought way outside the box.

He looked to his team to advise him how we could do what he wanted to do within the confines of banking policy and regulation, so I felt like I was part of strategic direction from day one."

David and Trish worked to build their bank on a firm foundation. Rather than stress over each little expenditure, they invested in their future. Their strategy paid off. With a 25% compound annual growth rate over a four-year period, the bank grew to $1 billion in assets by year ten, with over 90 employees. "All the metrics look so good," Trish says. "Our trajectory is great. We've tried to keep it disciplined. We're in a great market and a lot of things are in our favor. We tried not to be too many things to too many people, but just to focus on things we do well." FVCbank acquired Colombo Bank in October 2018 and now has eleven branches throughout Metropolitan Washington, with 130 total employees. The company is also listed on NASDAQ and completed a public offering during the same time period.

"We deliver," Trish asserts. "We've got a smart group of people who have significant experience and understand community banking. We've worked hard on building a reputation for doing the right things. If we say we're going to do something, we're determined to do it. That is meaningful when you hear that customers feel they have been misled by bigger organizations. We work at having the best products and technology available for our customers to make their work easier, but, at the end of the day, it's the people. Everybody wants a relationship. It sounds so cliché, I know it does, but I really think it's the incredible people that we have who embrace the bank's culture and are personally motivated to go above and beyond each and every day. That resonates with customers."

Trish also promotes a strong sense of service to the bank's customers, community, and employees. Many of them volunteer and support local charities. Trish herself served as a director of Ronald McDonald House of Greater Washington, D.C. for six years, which she calls a "moving experience."

Trish credits her husband, Rich, with being a pillar of support through it all. "Rich comes from an even larger family and we had similar experiences growing up," Trish notes. "In addition to being supportive of our children, he has always been very supportive of me and my career." He's a retired teacher and coach, and an extraordinarily dedicated father. Trish feels fortunate, however, that over time she was able to adjust her schedule and spend more time with her children as they grew up. "I needed more balance and asked for that from my boss at the time," Trish recalls. "Someone I trusted once said to me, 'you have to ask for it.' So I did. And since then I haven't worked anywhere where I wasn't fully supported. I've been fortunate to work with leaders who believed in me throughout my career. And I was fortunate that Rich did whatever needed to be done to help balance things."

Trish describes her leadership style as collaborative. "I want to know what other people think," she says. "We work together collaboratively so we can determine the best course of action. Banking involves many specialized activities and we rely on our team of experts to provide input to get to the optimal result. I always try to actively listen and then it's my job to make sure we are working towards accomplishing our goals. We work hard at being deliberate and nimble, so we don't hear somebody say, we talked about that six months ago and we still haven't done anything. In my role as president, in addition to having more time with our customers and prospective customers, I work more closely with our talented team of bankers to champion our strategic objectives and help move our priorities forward."

Her advice to young people would be: "Work very hard, be open minded, and take advantage of opportunities. Don't take opportunities for granted. Be grateful when someone gives you a chance. Go out and make a difference."

Mitch Gorochow

The Search for the Secret Sauce

Mitch Gorochow grew up around entrepreneurialism. His father owned his own small business in which he manufactured and installed blinds and shades. Mitch's father got great satisfaction from running the business; so much so that as he got older, he lived in fear of being forced to retire and move to Florida by Mitch's mother. "My mom says it was the happiest day of his life when she told him she wouldn't make him give up the business and move to Florida," laughs Mitch. "You could tell he was personally fulfilled with his work. He chose to work right up until he passed away."

Mitch's father never complained about the business. He loved what he did and seemed to always be at work. Despite his tireless efforts, however, the little family struggled to make ends meet. From an early age, Mitch wondered about this. His father was working so hard, and Mitch wondered why that wasn't translating to more financial success?

"The business paid the bills but not much more than that," recalls Mitch. "Seeing how our family struggled to get by motivated me to make sure that I ultimately was able to combine having that sense of fulfillment with having financial success. That's what motivated me to become a student of business, a student of what separates a successful business from an unsuccessful one."

Throughout his career, Mitch did just that. He not only started his own business soon after graduating college, he built it from the ground up from a staff of two to a staff of 200. Ultimately, he sold his accounting firm to the prominent accounting and consulting firm McGladrey and became the Partner-in-charge of the Mid-Atlantic Region until his retirement in 2011. Like his father before him, though, Mitch isn't quite ready to hang it up. Instead, he still takes on consulting clients for McGladrey from time to time in order to share the business expertise he's learned throughout his career.

As a consultant and an accountant, Mitch always saw himself as a counselor to businesses. He wasn't just someone who came in with spreadsheets and numbers, but someone who could take a bird's eye view of the business and provide real, time-tested advice to improve efficiency and increase revenues. "I've had the good fortune of being able to study business because of my career," nods Mitch. "In my role I basically become a counselor to various businesses and continue to get a better understanding of business. I'm fascinated by how a business operates and what the secret sauce is. I've read a lot, and I've examined a lot of experiences with a lot of companies. What motivates me is taking that knowledge that I've been able to ascertain over many years as a student of business and help others move their agenda forward. At the same time, I'm continuously learning by examining different businesses and observing what attributes contribute to a successful enterprise versus one that is ordinary. I'm motivated to continue to learn, to understand, and to provide counsel to organizations to help them reach their potential. I get to figure out the various factors that will be the key to unlock their success and help them succeed."

Mitch's efforts throughout his career have not only been professionally rewarding, he's also been able to inspire those around him. When he retired, his colleagues at McGladrey created a special gift for him. It was a beautifully framed plaque honoring his time there and was covered in quotes from 15-20 partners at the firm. The quotes all speak to his talent and mentorship, and Mitch considers the gift to be his prize possession today.

"As you move on to the next chapter of your life, I hope you do so knowing the profound and lasting effect you've had on so many people and their careers, including myself," reads one particularly poignant message. Other messages read, "I'm grateful for the many opportunities you provided me and the trust you placed in me. You taught me and many others the business of our profession and showed us the skills required to be successful. You lived what you preached and asked of others, and in the process were our leader, mentor, teacher, taskmaster, partner and friend, all at the same time. I've come across few individuals in this world that possess the unique talent of being able to fill all those roles simultaneously, and you do an outstanding job at each of them. You're truly one of a few. A million thanks."

As a kid growing up in Yonkers, New York, young Mitch certainly never imagined the heights he'd reach in his profession. The family remained lower middle class throughout his childhood, something Mitch didn't always admit as he climbed the corporate ladder. "It's funny, but depending who was asking, I'd say I was born and raised in Westchester County," he laughs. "It has much more of an upscale tone to it! But truth be told, I was born and raised in Yonkers, just outside of the Bronx."

Though the family sometimes struggled, Mitch remembers his time in Yonkers positively. He reminisces about playing baseball in an old sandlot with the neighborhood kids, putting on plays, and shooting hoops whenever he could. He grew up close to Yankee Stadium, and he loved to jump on a bus to the subway and pay 75 cents to go see a double header. However, he would *not* be rooting for the Yankees. "I hated the Yankees because they always won!" exclaims Mitch. "They had Mantle and won every year. It just took the fun out of it. Who wants to root for someone who always wins? I rooted against the Yankees. Eventually the Mets came in, and I became a Mets fan because they were horrible! I liked that; rooting for the underdog is just more fun."

In school, Mitch got by with decent grades, but he recalls that he was never very motivated with his studies until college. In his free time, he'd often help out at his father's store. He swept the floor as a little kid and later would string the blinds by the time he was 11 or 12. At first, he loved getting to spend more time with his father and learning how to do the repetitive manual tasks. But as a teenager he became bored of the work. However, the experience came full circle when, as an 18 and 19-year-old home from college, he again appreciated the opportunity to help out his father and help out the family.

Mitch's mother stayed home with the kids while they were young but returned to part-time work only after Mitch and his older sister were in school. She and Mitch's father were both very involved in the local synagogue and presided over several community organizations. They took their commitment to community seriously. Mitch remembers that they were constantly entertaining friends and getting together with folks from the neighborhood. One fun annual tradition was their insistence on dressing to the nines for the synagogue's yearly Halloween party. Then, when it was time to trick or treat, Mitch's father would change into a huge gorilla suit and accompany the kids from door to door. "He would scare the hell out of the other parents until they knew it was him," laughs Mitch. "Then they would give him a roll of toilet paper or something instead of candy. The funny thing is that I continued the tradition when my kids were little. I went around dressed up in the gorilla costume, and I got a real kick out of it!"

Another family tradition was a strict adherence to their 5:45 PM dinner time. Mitch remembers that his father, while never mean, was stern about this. Both his parents also taught him to respect his elders. And even as an adult, he never swore in front of his father.

It's clear that during his decades of success, Mitch never lost sight of his parents' legacy of honesty, hard work, and humility. "They taught me not to focus on my ego and not to be driven by that," observes Mitch. "Your ego shouldn't be what motivates your existence. They were humble people. They also taught me that it's important to acknowledge the contributions of others. Those are two attributes I'm really thankful for; they showed me, demonstrated to me that that was the right thing to do."

Still, that lesson took time to learn. Mitch recalls that he was motivated more by his ego while pursuing leadership opportunities at his high school. He was first elected Vice President of his class, then President, and initially, he was only interested in the recognition the titles brought. "I was a kid, so in that first leadership role, I'd say I wanted people to see me, I wanted to have influence," Mitch reflects. "But it exposed me to the fact that being a leader is not as easy as it seems. I learned that there's more to it than just barking out orders and telling people what to do. People don't follow that type of leader for long. It was the beginning of an awakening. It took a lot of trial-and-error, a lot of reading, a lot of self-reflection on my part to develop leadership."

He also learned about leadership on the basketball court, where he spent most of his free time. In high school, he was still playing informal ball in the neighborhood while also playing on the school's team. He was never the star, but he learned how to lead. "I had limits in terms of my skills and my height," explains Mitch. "But I wasn't a bad ball player. I was the guy who tried to keep people motivated, who called for teamwork, and who tried to make the other players feel good."

After high school, Mitch attended the University of Maryland where he chose a math major because the logic came easily to him. While he had a major, he still didn't know what he wanted to do. He figured law school was a possibility but concluded his undergraduate years were a waste of time. And if he was going to waste his time, he might as well get a degree in accounting since it was logical like math and would give him a skill.

And eventually, he began to get serious about his undergraduate studies. The motivation? His girlfriend and future wife, Monica. "I wasn't a bad student before meeting her," muses Mitch. "I received mostly A minuses and B pluses. But she motivated me through her actions in terms of really taking on learning and dedicating myself to studying. My wife has incredibly high standards; she continues to show me the standard I should try to attain in whatever I do, because whatever she does, she always puts forth a supreme effort and always produces the best results regardless of whatever it may be." Monica went on to receive her Ph.D. in Psychology and even did post-doctorate work in the field.

As Mitch buckled down, he found mentors at Maryland, professors who pushed and challenged him and with whom he built close relationships. One business professor in particular became a confidante and sounding board for Mitch as he entered the working world. "A lot of times he'd just pontificate about his experiences, good and bad, in the business world, and that was really influential," remembers Mitch. "He really opened my eyes to the impact leaders can have on an organization."

After graduation, Mitch quickly landed an interview with the accounting firm then called Ernst & Ernst, now Ernst & Young. Mitch still wasn't sure what he wanted to do. He considered going to law school, but the opportunity at Ernst & Ernst was better than he anticipated. He found another mentor who guided his business development during his two years there.

After two years, Mitch was due to begin law school, and he knew he couldn't balance both the rigorous schedule of Ernst & Ernst and the coursework of law school. He left his job to work at a small accounting firm. After one year he discovered that law school wasn't for him. He found his work at the small accounting firm to be transformational. "It was tremendously rewarding," beams Mitch. "I got to work directly with business owners and impact them. When I was able to deal directly with small and medium-sized business owners, that's when I started to think, 'I want to understand what those attributes are that contribute to success.' I loved it, and I was good at it. I was really good at helping clients, being an advisor, being a counselor, and being part of their team. I found my calling."

A year after that, at the young age of 26, Mitch and a partner founded their own accounting firm with a staff of two. Quickly, they were able to bring on two more hires, and over time the little business grew from 4, to 10, to 20, to 50 and beyond. At first, Mitch focused heavily on sales and developing the company's growth culture. He also offered high salaries and attracted the best people by overpaying them while the business ramped up. Lastly, Mitch was quick to see that the business would do better by focusing its services into certain industries and becoming industry experts rather than generalists. They soon acquired a reputation, particularly in the field of government contracting.

By the time the firm hit 80 people a decade later, Mitch had his sights set even higher. He decided to merge with another small firm to bring their staff up to 120 people. "It's interesting because your brand is somewhat defined—maybe not always rightfully so—by the critical mass you have," explains Mitch. "We recognized that if we wanted to be more impactful, if we wanted to play against the larger players and compete for larger, more profitable clients, we needed to have more of a presence. So the motivation for the merger was to jump-start that."

Another decade passed, and by the end of the 1990s, Mitch was looking to sell the business to a larger firm. And in 2000, he finalized the deal with McGladrey. "I truly did it for strategic purposes, not financial purposes," stresses Mitch. "Our motivation here, again, was to continue to move upmarket and to have access to more national resources. It was very successful, it worked exactly as we expected. It took a while; we had to build the brand recognition in this region. McGladrey didn't have recognition on the East Coast yet, they were more of a Midwestern firm at the time. But we were able to do that, and once the brand was defined, we really took off."

As Partner-in-Charge of the Mid-Atlantic Region, where McGladrey had previously only had one office in the Carolinas, Mitch was able to continue running his old office and expand his leadership role. He also became a board member as well as an executive committee member of McGladrey. He took on a number of other national responsibilities and strengthened his influence at the firm over the next 11 years. Through it all, he maintained his emphasis on serving as a counselor.

"My hope is to have an impact on business leaders, that can then have an impact on their business," explains Mitch. "The only way I can do that is to develop a real relationship with the business owner and that they in turn develop a trust in me knowing that my advice is valuable and can in fact be used to help them move the organization forward."

It's no surprise then, that Mitch considers his leadership style to be "servant leadership," emphasizing the importance of valuing your team. "I think it's really paramount in terms of the attitude you have as a leader," elaborates Mitch. "Helping others to be lifted on your shoulders, taking pride in the accomplishments of your team, and being there to help them fulfill their potential. Those are the ways you effectively move an organization forward."

And what about that secret sauce Mitch dedicated his career to discovering? Turns out, there's no one size fits all answer, but there are a lot of things that help. "There are components that I see as critical if that business is going to separate itself from the pack," points out Mitch. "Things such as relentless focus on execution and making a plan and sticking with it. Too many companies go with the flavor of the month and don't have the fortitude to focus as strongly as they should on execution. It's also about building a collaborative environment where people are contributing, where the thoughts of others are valued, and where they are part of the team. Have a real strategy, figure out what you do best, and really focus on that. So these are a few key things, but there is no one secret sauce."

To young people embarking on their professional career today, Mitch again speaks of leadership. "I want to make sure they know that leadership isn't about the position you hold," he asserts. "You can be a leader regardless of that, it's nothing to do with the title. It's how you act. How you collaborate with others. How you help others and how you put forth supreme effort. What I've found in my career is that people that do that, that act as leaders as they go about their day-to-day lives, eventually get the title and the rewards of being a leader come along with it."

Jacqui Higgins

Be Curious

At the age of 15, Jacqui Higgins received some startling news from her parents: they were moving to India. Her father worked in civil engineering and was offered a position overseas. The little family packed up their Illinois home for an eighteen-month sojourn in a very foreign place.

The Higgins were hardly strangers to travel; Jacqui had been born in Nigeria before moving to England, where her parents were from. Since their move to the United States, they'd frequently relocated. At first, these relocations occurred across the Boston area, but recently they'd moved to Illinois. Through it all, Jacqui learned adaptability and began to shed some of her innate shyness.

It wasn't until the trip to India, however, that she fully came into her own. For the first six months of the trip, life was almost like a fairy tale. The whole family resided in a luxury hotel—The Taj Mahal Palace in Mumbai. Jacqui, young, curious and precocious, spent her days befriending the staff. There was Gerard, the handsome French maître d', the general manager, and Rudy, who worked on oil rigs. Often the group would sit around the pool, telling Jacqui fabulous stories about their travels. "They viewed me to be their little sister," smiles Jacqui. "They took me under their wing, made sure I was invited to the right parties and met the right people. I was meeting dignitaries, politicians, and other important people. I went to more black-tie events in those six months than probably the rest of my life combined!"

Eventually though, she had to come back to reality. With the monsoon season over, she needed to get back to school. Her parents sent her to a missionary boarding school in the Southern tip of India, a second culture shock. This one was a lot less pleasant. Jacqui missed the black-tie events, the opulent food, and the dignitaries. Suddenly she was crowded into a dorm room with two roommates. Glitz and glamour had been replaced by the drudgery of schoolwork. She had so much trouble adjusting, in fact, that she decided to run away.

"I wanted to go back to Bombay, so that's what I did," she laughs. "To get from Kodaikanal, in the mountains, you have to take a bus to a tiny village. Then a train, crowded with livestock, to Madras, then a flight to Bombay. I traversed all of that, and my parents didn't know I was coming home. I probably covered a quarter of India by myself as a 16-year-old with no one knowing where I was. I was fearless. I had no thoughts that anything bad could happen with this plan!" Her parents were relieved she'd made it home safely, but she still had to return to school. This time, she began to make friends and enjoy herself.

"The school was only about 30 kids, grades 1-12, mostly dignitaries' children," recalls Jacqui. "The education I got there was at a collegiate level. Our instructors were amazing; we were always studying and cramming for exams. I joined the running team and field hockey team. And once I adjusted, I liked it. Boys and girls weren't allowed to spend time together unless there was an official reason so my roommate

Sheila and I started a social committee for the school. We had a big record collection so we began holding dances. We would decorate to the hilt, and everyone had a great time."

Jacqui began to thrive academically, athletically, and socially. She came fully out of her shell; the once-shy preteen became a worldly and confident teenager. And after growing up in relatively privileged, homogenous Wellesley, MA, she learned much about the world beyond her doorstep. "All of a sudden I'm seeing poverty and destitution," she reflects. "There's a beauty to India and a beauty to the people. I learned not to judge through one lens. It taught me so many things about myself and how I looked at the world; it helped me see things more broadly. Hearing from the other students about their lives and their homes, made me more tolerant and accepting of differences. If I had stayed in Wellesley, I think I might have been much more myopic. It gave me a completely new view of the entire world, which I'm so grateful for."

Jacqui's experience in India had been a deeply transformative one. But coming home was a second rude awakening, one that in some ways was even harder to navigate. While she had been travelling the world and expanding her horizons, her classmates had been continuing their typical suburban high school experience. Jacqui had grown; the people around her had not. Now it was difficult to relate to anyone around her. She was drawn to older people and was wary of her peers. She took a retail job at a local department store, Winkelman's, and began socializing more with her adult coworkers rather than other students.

From then on, Jacqui leaned into her independent streak. She became not only confident and curious, but creative and ambitious. Her time in India reframed the horizon of the possible for her; she'd navigated an enormous country, built a new home for herself, and encountered all kinds of people. Looking back on her career, it's clear that she took each of these experiences to heart. Through it all, she's maintained her curiosity and love of adventure and is always looking to the next horizon.

In 2019, Jacqui launched her second business, J Designs Consulting. Currently, she's working with two large clients, and bringing a broad portfolio of skills and talents with her. With a mixed background in both marketing and sales, Jacqui works to find a business's niche and then effectively communicate that messaging to the sales team. She doesn't believe in trying to outdo competitors by meeting them on their turf; instead, she advises businesses to find their own "sandbox to play in." In other words: find what sets your business apart and communicate that unique value to customers. Be proactive, not reactive to others' messaging.

Jacqui worked with an esports start-up dedicated to building out the infrastructure and community of the competitive gaming industry. "It's an amazing industry," she exclaims. "I'm not in the company's demographic so I conducted a lot of research when they asked for my help. We think of video gaming as nerdy kids sitting in a basement, and there's certainly that element. But there is also the reality that this is the fastest growing tech industry in the world. And nowadays, you can turn your passion into purpose. You can become part of a team or a league, and you're no longer sitting in your basement. You may not be playing soccer on a field, but you're still learning those same basic tenets of interpersonal skills, development, and leadership."

The organization owns centers where people can play communally and sells gear and merchandise. But with Jacqui's help, they've moved beyond that, too. Now, they're focused on building leagues around schools, businesses, and regions. They're teaching people as well, offering a curriculum in esports and working with schools to offer scholarships. "These kids can go on to study coding, design, event management to name a few," she lists. "There are so many facets of this that they can pursue, and at the end of it, they can get a meaningful job out of college. Tying that all together makes this a neat little tapestry."

Jacqui knows that the key to good sales isn't your product or your size; it's your story. And as she discusses the esports start-up, she tells the story of this business from an emotional perspective. "When I went to school, you had the jocks and nerds," she points out. "But now, these kids who were previously nerds have a voice and can get recognized, too. You don't have to be a traditional athlete to be viewed as an athlete or make money. It levels the playing field and opens it up to people with disabilities; it's changed the whole paradigm of how athletics is viewed. It's good for autism, good for PTSD. I love that inclusivity component of it."

J Designs Consulting offers strategic sales and marketing positioning, branding, and strategy. Step one is empowering the organization to define themselves in the market. What is the purpose of the company? What is the story of the business, the reason customers will emotionally identify with it? After she works with companies on defining themselves in a compelling way, she moves into sales enablement. This means going to the sales team and working on how that story can be effectively presented. "Often marketing people create marketing content in a vacuum," she explains. "Then they go to the salespeople, and the salespeople don't know what to do with it. I'm able to look through both lenses and translate between those departments." This talent has been evident in another engagement where she's helping a healthcare start-up refine their messaging and marketing approach. The company, SmithRx, is visionary, purpose-driven organization that offers a disruptive approach to pharmacy benefits management. Crafting the message through the lens of the client: what's most important to them.

Translation and communication have been key throughout Jacqui's career so it's no surprise she developed those skills throughout her life. Although India was the first major trip she remembers, she was actually born in Nigeria. At the age of two, her parents moved her home to England. Her father worked as a civil engineer, while her mother occasionally took hairdressing clients at home. Jacqui had a brother who was five years older and was already attending college during her time in India.

The family stayed in England until Jacqui was eight. Though she once had an accent, she lost it over the years, partly due to her desire to fit in. From that early childhood, she remembers happy times with a couple of best friends, and visits to her nearby extended family. Her aunt and uncle owned a bakery, and she fondly recalls them picking out the prettiest Easter egg for her each year. Another uncle owned a restaurant and club, complete with a swimming area and bowling alley. She loved Uncle Bernard, who was "like Superman" and an owner of several beloved rabbits.

But she was closest of all to her maternal grandmother. Jacqui would often spend hours in her home playing in the greenhouse and learning to pot plants. Her grandmother, a talented artist, also taught her to draw. Quickly, Jacqui began drawing imaginative comics. At Christmas, the family had a big traditional English celebration, complete with Christmas pudding, custard, and English Christmas cake covered in marzipan.

It was a charmed childhood, but at age eight, Jacqui experienced her first big move. The family relocated to Wellesley, Massachusetts, a nice suburb of Boston. And the family continued to move every few years. In retrospect, Jacqui realizes her parents were flipping houses. "It was a joke in my family that they would fix it up to the point they liked it, then sell it," she recalls. "My mother, to her credit, was a very astute businesswoman. She should've been a realtor; she would've made a boatload of money. She was always very communicative and social. She would learn things just by talking to people. She knew where to buy and when to sell from talking with people."

Both of Jacqui's parents are still alive and in their 90s. Her father, unfortunately, suffers from dementia, but her mother is as sharp and feisty as ever. Both of them were tremendous parents. "My father was always very kind, charming, and even-keeled," Jacqui reflects. "He's a gracious warm person who is easy to connect with and to talk to. He had a lovely strength of character I admire. He's also a very humble man. I've learned from him that humility is one of the greatest traits you can possess."

"My mother has been my mentor," she goes on. "I saw her manage so many things, seemingly with ease. Moving a family around all the time to different countries or neighborhoods. She always flowed with everything; when they moved, she was the one who made sure they got involved in the community. I love her strength and her resilience. She instilled in me a belief that there wasn't anything I couldn't accomplish if I put my mind to it. I never felt there was a limit on what I could achieve."

One anecdote in particular illustrates their supportiveness. Jacqui was something of a tomboy growing up. She loved the outdoors and became fascinated by a movie called "The Other Side of the Mountain" about a little boy who ran away. She was packing to run away when her father stumbled on her trying to crawl out the window; he sat Jacqui down and asked about her feelings. Then, her parents bought her her very own pup tent, where, except in severe storms, she chose to sleep outside for over a year. Sometimes, her parents would come out and join her for a bonfire or smores.

In school, Jacqui got along with the other kids and did well both academically and in gymnastics, but as mentioned, she had trouble transitioning to normal after returning from India. She decided to take a gap year before attending college at Northeastern University. She took some courses in interior design and loved it, but ultimately decided to go into the IT space.

Her first adult job didn't end well. She'd scored a marketing associate position at a telecommunications company, but quickly became a victim of the CFO's unwanted advances. When she commented on the harassment, she was let go. "I walked out and started sobbing in my car," remembers Jacqui. "I really did think my entire life and career were over."

Soon after, she noticed an ad in the newspaper for a job at Wang Laboratories. "The role was International Public Relations Specialist," she smiles. "I definitely was not qualified for that job. I knew nothing about the role, but I was determined and was able to talk my way into it. I think it was the determination I showed." At Wang, she met her first mentors, Cheryl Garelik and Jane Carpenter. They taught her the marketing and international business ropes.

From there, Jacqui moved onto the operations side with a job at MASSCOMP. She wanted to learn more about software and management; she did both, but ultimately decided the role wasn't for her. She was back in marketing at AAA when she was diagnosed with a severe illness. She was just about 30, and she'd come down with a thyroid disorder called Graves' disease. For five years she struggled with her illness; at the same time, she struggled to learn to rely on others more.

"My whole life went into a tailspin," she relates. "I couldn't make it through a whole day. My heart rate was off the charts. I was exhausted and would have to take naps in conference rooms. My friends would watch out for me and wake me up. I was fortunate because I had three very dear friends who would always help me. I always knew I could turn to people if I needed to but was always reluctant to do so. It was a progression for me to accept being more dependent on other people. Part of that goes back to moving all the time. I had become very self-sufficient and independent."

After five years, Jacqui fully recovered and knew immediately that she wanted a change. At first, she considered a move to Tampa but ultimately settled for Washington, DC. Here, she developed her skills in international sales and marketing while working for Learning Tree International. Five years later, she decided to go out on her own and launch her first business.

That first business was called Accents by Design. It focused on commercial interior design, with a heavy emphasis on the value add of design. It wasn't just about creating nice spaces; it was about working with businesses to understand their needs, and fill those needs with smart design. She started with nothing but her presentation and public speaking skill. She launched a series of "lunch and learns" at the Tower Club and found clients that way. The business thrived for several years before the economy made it difficult to compete. Ultimately, she tried her hand at working for a larger design firm before deciding it wasn't for her. Ever the independent one, she refocused on a new business with a fresh strategy: J Designs Consulting.

Jacqui emphasizes the importance of leading by example. She also reflects that leaders should inspire their subordinates to be better versions of themselves. "Your role in leading them is to help them elevate their strengths," elaborates Jacqui. "I'm curious about people and want to hear their stories and learn what makes them tick."

To young people entering the working world today, Jacqui advises a willingness to learn from others. "I want to instill in them the value of knowledge, and that knowledge comes from experience many times," she nods. "Take what you can learn from other people; that will make your journey easier. Be astute enough and curious enough to ask people about their journey and learn from them."

BERNHARDT

WEALTH MANAGEMENT

George W. Hinckley III

Providing Solutions

George Hinckley III was smart, but growing up he didn't take academics very seriously. Neither of his parents had gone to college, and only his mother had finished high school. Among George and his three brothers—one older and two younger—he was the only one of the four who pursued higher education. But that might never have come to pass if he hadn't first joined the United States Marine Corps.

Throughout high school, George maintained a "C" average. He was careful never to dip into the failing range, but he hardly tried to do his best. As his years in high school ended, he wasn't sure what he wanted to do next. But he knew he wasn't ready for college. So instead, he met with a Marine recruiter. While there, he noticed a picture on the recruiter's wall of several Marines in full dress uniform. Something about the picture spoke to George. "I didn't just like the uniform; I also liked the demeanor, the bearing, and everything about them," he reflects. The Marine recruiter was also impressive. "There tends to be something more there, with Marines, and that's what I thought I was seeing. And after 20 years, I believe that that something really was there, that I saw something special."

Before he knew it, he enlisted in the Marine Corps with a guarantee that they would send him through avionics training. He'd once hoped to attend the Air Force Academy, but his eyesight disqualified him. So the avionics career that the Marines offered seemed like the next best thing. At first, things went very well. At boot camp George stood out for his impressive marksmanship skills at the range, and for his overall physical fitness.

After a day spent outside shooting in the cold, however, George began to come down with something. A couple of days later during mess duty the head cook at the Mess Hall sent him back to the barracks because George was coughing all over the food. Over the next few days, George spit up mucus all night and struggled to keep up with his duties. In the military, there's a stigma associated with illness and injury and so, like many of his fellow recruits, George tried to push through.

Finally, he went to the drill instructor to explain that he was wasn't well but instead, passed out in the middle of his explanation. When he awoke, he learned his diagnosis: severe pneumonia. The doctors told him that without medical treatment he may have died in another day or two. George spent the next three weeks in the Beaufort Naval Hospital. By the time he was released from the hospital, he couldn't rejoin his original platoon because it had moved on in the training cycle while he was hospitalized. "The one thing you never want to do in boot camp, is to drop from one platoon and join another because joining a new platoon is hell," explains George. The drill instructors harassed the hell out of him, joked about his pneumonia while blowing smoke in his face, and had him running wind sprints to regain some of his compromised lung capacity.

Still, despite the rough treatment, George soon distinguished himself again. In fact, the Senior Drill instructor called him into his office one afternoon to tell George that if he had been an original member of their platoon, then he'd have been designated both the Honor Man and the High Shooter—two distinguished honors awarded at the end of boot camp. Unfortunately, because he wasn't an original member of the platoon, he wasn't eligible.

Fortunately, his shooting skills weren't the only thing the military saw in George. When he expressed an interest in becoming an officer, his Marine Corps career counselor encouraged him. "They had something called the BOOST program where if you weren't in a good enough place academically, then they'd work with you to get you ready for officer training. But when I went to ask about that program, the counselor looked at my transcript and told me that I was actually overqualified. So the counselor then said, 'Let's go ahead and put your officer training package together.' As it happens, twenty-two were selected for officer training that year, and I was among them." After considering several schools, George applied to and was accepted by the University of Missouri, where he later received a Bachelor of Science degree in Mechanical Engineering.

Generations of the Hinckley family served in the armed forces, to include his father and all three of his brothers. Not one, however, had risen to officer rank since his great grandfather. George knew that his parents, particularly his father, were proud of him. And it was his father who kept him on track after a particularly challenging summer spent at the Officer Candidate School (OCS) at Marine Corps Base Quantico. While there, George began to have doubts about continuing in the program after watching a good friend—someone who he considered quite smart and competent—fail to meet the academic expectations of the program, and then leave it. "That was one of several occasions when my dad drove all the way from Massachusetts to Missouri to encourage me." George's dad said to him, "What are you doing? You need to get your head back in the game and finish this. You have opportunities that I didn't have." For George, that encouragement was a major turning point.

Perhaps it was because of the instrumental role the U.S. Marine Corps played in getting George a higher education that he ended up doing the work he does today. Today, George is the CEO of Crossroads Innovation Group (Crossroads), a business he founded along with two partners last year. Crossroads is so named to invoke the spirit of Marine Corps Base Quantico, which has long been considered the "crossroads" of the Marine Corps. Decisions made at Quantico impact Marines around the globe, hence the name. With the establishment of Crossroads, George created a platform upon which he might pursue and fulfill opportunities he felt were being missed in the military training process, ideas which he had been exploring over many years working with the armed forces both as an active duty Marine and as a private sector member of the defense establishment.

Crossroads' mission is simple: to work with military and educational institutions to make it possible for servicemen to receive educational credit for the military training they undertake. In many cases, the training they've received for their role within the military tracks closely with courses offered by colleges and universities. In those cases, Crossroads works to bring the military training establishment and select colleges together to examine the intersections between their curricula, as well as assessing how much credit a service member would be able to receive at each select school for the training he or she has already completed.

The first seeds for the idea were planted when George was introduced to Northern Virginia Community College (NOVA) during the course of his independent consulting in 2011. NOVA, as it is commonly known, is a Designated Center of Academic Excellence for Cyber Education, a subject which is critical for all branches of the military. George decided to put two and two together and approached the Marine Corps with the following proposal: what if the Marines and

NOVA worked together to map the Marines' training courses already offered to NOVA's curricula, and then put in place a process by which Marines could receive academic credit for their training?

"When we evaluated the learning objectives and content that the Marines were teaching, it mapped to two three-credit courses that NOVA was teaching," explained George. "That's when we decided to take a deeper dive. The Marines looked through the NOVA course catalog and identified courses that they thought might map to their program of instruction."

This was the first step toward creating the program called "MOS to degree"—MOS stands for Military Occupational Specialty which is essentially the job role and responsibilities of an individual Marine. For instance, George's MOS at one time was "Avionics Technician". A MOS provides an entire career path for a Marine. Next, Paula Worthington at NOVA spent five months identifying which MOSs received training that could map to courses offered at NOVA. Ultimately, she came up with eight MOSs that can qualify for anywhere from six to twenty-six academic credits in the Information Systems Technology department.

"Roughly three thousand Marines annually complete MOS related programs of instruction, and now, any of them can apply to NOVA and be eligible to receive credit for their prior learning," says George proudly. "Recently, fifteen Marines at Quantico attended NOVA for thirty-one more credits to add to the twenty-six they already have. So by the middle of spring semester in 2020, those young Marines will come out of NOVA with fifty-seven credits toward a sixty-seven-credit data engineering degree. All the general education stuff is on them to actually finish the degree up. But getting them to fifty-seven is absolutely transformational. That's why I'm so passionate about this."

The feedback so far has been fantastic. George recently received an email from a Marine General who affirmed that credentialing the Marines' training has begun a sea change for the Department of Defense. "She also reached out to thank me because they're accustomed to vendors knocking on their door and selling them things," notes George. "They're not used to people providing solutions. So they really appreciated that. That's what we do."

Despite the great work Crossroads is already doing, the business is technically in its infancy, and George has his sites set much higher. The partnership between NOVA and the Marines is going very well, but what about the other branches of the military? What about other colleges and universities across the country? This successful model could easily be applied to thousands of courses of study, and George has already begun working with George Mason University to put together a project focused on cyber security.

"The Marines asked NOVA if they could scale and they said they could by accommodating another twenty-five students," notes George. "But we're thinking in terms of thousands and thousands of people. So that's one of the things we're focusing on now. How do we scale content to a broader enterprise? We're developing a platform to make that possible."

George has certainly come a long way from his blue-collar childhood in the Boston, Massachusetts area. He was born in the rough part of town in Brockton. It was there as a young boy that he began to get into trouble doing things like playing on the railroad tracks and accepting dares to steal cigarettes from the local convenience store. Eventually, his parents decided that Brockton wasn't the right place to raise their four sons; so they moved the Hinckley family to the quieter, smaller town of Whitman when George was six.

George's mother stayed home to do the tough work of raising four boys while George's father worked as a mason and bricklayer. He was a man who worked with his hands and relished seeing the final product of his labor. He'd learned his craft from an Italian immigrant who knew the business well, and his work was widely admired. As George grew older, he often helped his Dad build chimneys and lay bricks with the other workers.

In Whitman, George began to get involved in more wholesome activities. He developed a passion for football, basketball, and baseball. He even became the Captain of his pee-wee football team in eighth grade. However, by the time he hit high school, he had begun to enjoy the sport less and less. "I was a running back but our team was undefeated because our defensive line was just monstrous," George remembers. Every practice was brutal. I'd come home with both my forearms bleeding. So I eventually convinced myself that I didn't want to do that anymore."

Instead, George got involved in motorcycle racing. He notes that his father was a "gearhead" and encouraged him in the sport. "My dad was a hardass, but he was a real soft boiled egg kind of guy. You know, the one who is tough on the outside but has a huge heart," smiles George. "If you had an interest and you were committed to that interest, he would do his best to help you be successful." To this day, George still considers his first motorcycle racing trophy—a second place finish—to be a prize possession. "My father told me, 'When you win on that motorcycle, we'll get you more competitive equipment'" recalls George. "And shortly after that, I won my first race, he bought me a new high-performance motorcycle, and I won six straight races!"

Eventually, his father sold the motorcycles when George tired of racing and took more of an interest in girls. "Dad wasn't going to leave expensive equipment lying around when no one was using it," laughs George. "He taught me that if you're going to do something, commit to it and do it well." If I was really trying, he was supportive. When I wasn't, he wasn't nearly as supportive!"

Chasing girls did have one positive side effect for George. He ended up taking typing classes for the purpose of meeting girls. But those lessons ended up being instrumental in pushing him into Signals Intelligence as his military career progressed. George was first stationed in Hawaii, "a tough assignment,“ he says with a smile. He would later be sent to Taiwan, Okinawa, and the Mediterranean during the fighting in Beirut.

After that, George attended the U.S. Naval Postgraduate School for graduate work.

Coincidentally, one of his fellow classmates in that program was a Marine Captain by the name of Gordon Steele, who had been in Lebanon at the same time as George. Not only that, but George's ship had provided naval gunfire support to Gordon's men when they were under attack in 1984. Their reunion in 1988 at Quantico led to an amazing friendship that continues to this day. Gordon was even the best man at George's wedding to his wife, Julie, with whom he has been married for twenty-five years.

Julie has been a constant source of support since they met working on a project together. "I've learned a lot about myself since I met Julie," admits George. "She's a superb coach and a superb teacher, and she's become my sounding board. Now I bounce things off of her because she gives great, pragmatic advice. She's been a great balance for me over the years. She's been amazing. I wouldn't be the same person without her."

After leaving the Marines in 1992 with over two decades of service behind him, George headed to a company that produced and sold satellite communications systems. Within a year, he was the supervisor of his group. From there, he moved over to a smaller company in 1996 and rose to the level of Vice President before departing in 2005.

Finally, George took a position with a business called MTCSC, where he developed advanced capabilities for tactical systems. The business, founded in 2000, grew from a tiny fifteen employee organization to over three-hundred-fifty by the time it was sold ten years later. After the sale, George toughed it out for about seven months but found that working for a $3 billion business didn't really fit his independent style.

It was then, in 2011, that George began consulting, and it was through this work that he fatefully came into contact with the Northern Virginia Community College. The rest, as they say, is history.

It's no surprise that, when it comes to leadership, George emphasizes being a mentor. "A big part of leadership is developing future leaders," he affirms. "Helping them identify what they're good at and supporting their development is crucial for a leader. It's important for young people to find their way. That's why I'm passionate about the work I do with the Marine Corps; none of them know me, but they're going to benefit from what we did."

To young people themselves, George advises hard work and integrity. "I believe you will be successful if you put your heart and soul into what you believe in and into where your strengths can take you," he instructs. "In many instances, you may not end up where you thought you'd be; and that's okay as long as you have the courage to keep moving forward. There are only a couple things you take with you—your credibility and your integrity. You can lose those quickly. If you want people to talk about you in a good way and to have respect for you, work hard to keep your credibility and integrity. That's important."

Tina Hyland

Improvise, Adapt, Overcome

Tina attributes her military efficiency to growing up on naval bases and moving around the country following her father's successful military career. She was born in Patuxent River, Maryland and shortly thereafter, moved to Sunnyvale, California, outside San Francisco. "Well, now you call it Silicon Valley," Tina laughs. "If only we had known that then!"

In Sunnyvale, the family lived on a base in Navy housing in a tight-knit community. Her father specialized in anti-submarine warfare and was often gone for up to six months out of the year. Tina remembers that whoever's dad was in the neighborhood would dress up as Santa Claus or the Easter bunny during the holidays, which were always a special time. "If you needed something, there was always someone right there to help you," she recalls gratefully. "If somebody moved in, you went over to welcome them. It was just that kind of environment."

Both parents were positive influences. Her father modeled hard work; she remembers he never once missed a day of work during his 27 years in the Navy. Her mother had a strong work ethic in her own right, working three jobs before meeting Tina's father. As a housewife, she brought a similar commitment to running the household efficiently. "She's old school and taught me to take pride in your appearance and always look presentable," smiles Tina. "Every day she would get up, do her hair and make-up, and put on a nice outfit whether she was going someplace or not."

Tina was the youngest of three, with a brother and sister 11 and 12 years older, respectively. Although there was a large age gap, Tina was particularly close with her older brother, Gary, who she lovingly called "Bud". He often brought her along to his baseball games and other sporting events. Her mom was a stay at home mom, and her memories of childhood are happy ones. The family had an organ, and Tina remembers she and her father playing *Silent Night* before bed or him reading her a Dr. Seuss book.

When Tina was eight years old, her world changed drastically. The family was moved to Hawaii at the same time her brother and sister graduated high school and moved out of the house. Her brother married right out of high school and joined the Army; her sister, too, married shortly thereafter. Tina and her parents headed to unfamiliar Oahu, and she spent the rest of her childhood growing up as an only child. She and her parents began calling themselves, "the three musketeers."

The move was the first of several that occurred every three years from then on. But Hawaii was an easy place to fall in love with. Despite having to make new friends and attend a new school, all while her father was travelling in Japan and the Philippines, Tina quickly adjusted to her new home. The family was still in military housing, making it easy for them to fit in with other oft-relocated families. At school, Tina loved learning about Hawaiian culture and music in the DoD school. She rode her bike to school and befriended all her teachers, enjoying clapping erasers for them and helping them before class. "It was probably one of my favorite times in school," Tina reminisces. "I never wanted to miss a day!"

The next move was a bit tougher. At the age of 11, Tina had to adjust to life in a new place—Virginia Beach—once more. She had more difficulty blending in, as the other kids had existing friendships, and she often felt marked out by her presence in the advanced sections of classes. However, as time went by, she began to find her footing. "In 7th grade, I went on to the junior high and all the schools were merging," she recalls. "My friends and I tried out for debate team and student government. I immersed myself in school and started taking a foreign language—Spanish. It was one of the best times of my life."

In Virginia, Tina joined the student government and the pep club. She was planning to try out for cheerleading in her ninth-grade year. That year was particularly exciting for Tina; the junior high was a 7th through 9th grade school, and 9th grade was like being the "seniors of middle school."

But fate intervened; her father was again reassigned, this time to Pensacola, Florida. Now 14 and heading into high school, Tina was once again starting over. This time, she was missing out on experiences she had been sorely anticipating. Already a teenager with interests and activities, this move was by far the most difficult.

"People there had a different view of school," Tina remembers. "It was the opposite of what I had just left. If you were in a non-athletic extra-curricular activity, you were considered a geek. There wasn't the same school spirit and activities were looked down upon. In addition to that, all the advanced courses I'd been in weren't even offered until 10th grade, even though I'd already taken them. I had to once again make new friends; I started to get discouraged and lost my love for school."

Although Tina continued to study hard, she never became invested in her school in Florida the way she had in Virginia. She did well, but she'd lost her passion. After high school, she enrolled in a college in Florida, but that summer, her father had a heart attack. Needing to help take care of her father, Tina returned home to be with her family. He ended up having to retire early and as he recovered, Tina enrolled in a local community college. Over the next several years, she balanced coursework and a full-time job. At a young age, she moved up the ranks in retail, first working in the cosmetics department and later being promoted to counter manager of the fragrance department. She was making good money, and proudly purchased her first car on her own with cash she had saved.

Needing more flexibility with her school schedule, she went on to work at McGuires Irish Pub. Tina had already spent some time in Italy before she met her first husband, an Italian Navy pilot then living in the States for three years. The pub was the favored haunt of the local military pilots, and it was only a matter of time before the two met.

About a year and half later the couple was engaged and Tina decided to join her fiance' in his move back to Italy. She had recently begun working as a flight attendant for Continental, a job she loved but had been swept off her feet by the dashing young pilot. "Your first time in love, you think it's going to be your Cinderalla story," Tina laughs. "He had a ten year commitment with the Navy, so we knew we'd be in Italy for at least ten years. The plan was, I'd move over there, learn the language, get settled, and fly for a major airline, either British Airlines or Alitalia."

But over their first few years of marriage, things changed. Her husband was no longer interested in her plans to go back to work with an airline and instead insisted she should be thinking about staying at home and having children. A short time later as Tina continued to express a wish to return to work, he became verbally abusive.

"That entire experience was filled with defining moments for me," she reflects. "I had willingly made so many sacrifices, had left my family, my friends, and my country, and had to learn a new language and culture at such an early age. We made an agreement and now he was changing the rules. I felt so betrayed."

Finally, in July of 1996, after five years in Italy, Tina took back control and decided she was ready to live her life on her terms again. She flew home to the States with little but her beloved six month old puppy Maxine and what she could fit in two suitcases. She headed straight to her brother's home in Boston, dropped off Maxine in his care, and then went directly on to training with United Airlines in Chicago.

Tina launched herself in her new career, where she quickly tapped her potential for leadership and became an admired flight attendant. Within two years, she was selected for Purser training, a lead flight attendant program. "I was the youngest flight attendant to complete the training." recalls Tina. "In addition to special wings and a certificate, it elevated your seniority and what trips you can hold. The majority of the people in my training class had been flying for 20+ years. I'd been flying for just two. It was a big deal and one of my proudest moments."

Soon, she was managing teams of other flight attendants, assigning work positions, and conducting appraisals. From there, she caught the eye of higher ups before being recruited by the White House Press Charter. Often, she would join the Administration on multi-week trips abroad conducting state business overseas. She calls her time with the charters the "best four years of her professional career." She loved flying for myriad reasons: the opportunity to travel, the excitement, the service mentality and honoring her father who also flew during his career.

A few years after Tina returned from Italy, she dealt with personal tragedy when her beloved brother passed away. He was diagnosed with lung cancer at only 45, and it quickly progressed to brain cancer. During the last two weeks of his life, she and her parents moved and lived with him in Boston, holding his hand as he passed away. "I was the only one he would take morphine from," Tina recalls. It was a life changing moment and she promised him she would take care of their parents.

But her nine-year career with the airlines came to an end shortly after 9/11. Unfortunately, the tragedy meant industry wide cutbacks, furloughs, and substantial pay decreases. Within five years, Tina had to resign. She returned to the corporate world and once again proved she had the ability to climb the corporate ladder and successfully assume managerial positions in each industry she tried her hand at.

Tragedy struck again in 2009, her father was diagnosed with pancreatic cancer and passed away within weeks of the diagnosis. Once again, Tina was by his side holding his hand and promising to care for her mother, who had recently been diagnosed with Alzheimer's.

Tina's next move in the corporate world found her as part of the leadership team for a national chain of day spas where she further honed her skills in staff training, corporate development, organizational expansion, and strategic guidance.

She also found herself now happily remarried to a loving, caring partner, Robert, whom she met in 2012 via eHarmony. "Online dating was out of my comfort zone, but it was great how their algorithms worked. Before we could even email each other, we had to go through several layers and list our non-negotiables, our interests, and our values," Tina explains. "By the time we got to our first date, we connected on a much higher level. It took a long time to find the right person and to know exactly what I wanted, but I'm glad I waited. It was worth every minute. He gives me a whole new dimension to my life. He's my best friend and my biggest supporter. When you're a little girl, you picture your Prince Charming. I can say, he encompasses all that, and things I never even thought to ask for."

Her personal life now settled and secured and having had a proven track record for turning around organizations and leading teams, she now wanted to see how far she could go on her own. "I was in management consulting at this point, and, as with a lot of people working in the corporate world, you hit a ceiling," says Tina. "Either you can't grow as an individual, or the work you're trying to accomplish can't flourish because of how they do business, or they're not wanting to implement anything new. I began feeling frustrated, not feeling valued, and not being able to make the impact I knew I was capable of making. It was also exceedingly difficult working a corporate schedule while needing flexibility to care for my mother."

Thus, True Clarity Coaching was born. Initially founded as a life coaching organization in 2014, Tina missed the business side of things and became a certified business coach. She began to reach out to people in her network whom she knew might be interested in her skill set. By 2017 she was solely focused on business clients, particularly small business owners. Generally, she says her clients have up to 30 employees, although that can vary widely. "They are generally generating low to mid six-figures trying to grow and scale their business. What got them to where they are, isn't getting them to the next level. They were in growth mode, now they need to shift to CEO mode, which is a completely different skillset, and they struggle with that transition."

About 75% of those clients are women. "I coach men as well," she explains, "but because I focus on self-worth and mindset, I attract a lot more women entrepreneurs. My experience has been that many women in business struggle with what to charge. They're often afraid of charging too much, apologize for their fees, or are uncomfortable talking about money and hesitate to ask for the sale. This is often why they can't sustain or grow their business, so we do a lot of work around pricing, selling with confidence, and authenticity."

True Clarity's results speak for themselves; the majority of Tina's clients double or even triple their price point during their 16 weeks in her business accelerator program, and in a relatively short amount of time, clients across the board see the promised growth and revenue increases.

As a leader, it's no surprise that Tina considers herself supportive and encouraging, but she adds a caveat that she's also no-nonsense. "I have a couple of mantras—One is: mediocrity is not an option. I'm not okay with you doing the bare minimum," she elaborates. "I see their potential, and I challenge them to give their best. And then a Marine Corps motto always served me: improvise, adapt, and overcome. There's always something that we can do. We're never totally hopeless. And if things don't go our way, there's always something that we can tweak, or course correct to get a different result. I'll lovingly kick your butt into action!"

"My coaching is not about creating a dependency," she affirms. "I'm all about giving you the roadmap, helping you along the way, but then letting you ride the bike on your own, without the training wheels. As a coach, I believe you know the answers, and it's my job to help you pull them out. That way you'll take more ownership of your choices, your actions, your successes and you'll uncover important lessons that will impact your future results. It's the whole idea of teaching you to fish."

Her methodology isn't a drawn out, multi-year process; it's a system that gets you into action and generates results quickly. Her three- and six-month programs are intensive one-on-one experiences for established business owners, while the 16-week accelerator is a more affordable option for startups or those looking for a "business in a box" structure. It's usually the go-to option for businesses that aren't consistently generating multi six figures or may not have the capitol to invest in one-on-one coaching.

In the initial phases, clients fill out an extensive questionnaire, then jump on a strategy call to determine whether the partnership is an appropriate fit. Once details are hammered out, coaching consists of bi-weekly calls, weekly assignments, and a weekly tracker to review performance and provide accountability. True Clarity looks at a business's products or services, their business model, and takes a deep dive into operations, financials, company culture and values. Tina makes sure that the business owners are spending their time effectively and strategically. She's quick to emphasize that her work isn't about telling people what to do, but rather, helping them do what they need to do in order to achieve their goals.

To college kids entering the workforce today, Tina advises getting clarity around what you want and why, without paralyzing yourself with options. "I would say hire a coach, get a mentor, and model after someone else who has been successful. Don't try to figure it all out yourself, because you're going to waste valuable time, energy, and money. Instead, pay for speed."

Together with Robert and two stepdaughters, 31 and 36, she has achieved a happy and full family life balanced with a dedication to her craft. Her eldest stepdaughter is expecting a baby this summer. "We're going to be grandparents," she beams. "Business is good, and life is good. I'm proof it's possible to work your business while being present and enjoying family without guilt or sacrificing either's success. It's something I share with my clients who feel they have to choose between the two. At the end of the day, your business may not always be what you have, but family is always going to be what you need."

Tim Koehl

Father Changes Career, Son Finds Calling

At 17 years old, Tim Koehl realized he had a second chance at mastering change.

His father didn't have a college degree, and when he'd come home each day from his job at a cast iron foundry, his clothes were so dirty that they had to be removed outside before he could come into the house. Despite his father's lack of formal education, his hard work and natural leadership skills eventually advanced him to a management role, but he always wanted to take his impact to a new level. After Tim's mother began working for a financial advisor, his father was exposed to financial services, coming to understand the crucial role financial planners can play in the lives of their clients. He knew he wanted to serve the community in that manner.

With that, Tim's father pursued his training and new career, which meant big changes for the Koehl family. They moved Tim and his two younger brothers from their comfortable, beloved house to a two-bedroom apartment in a new town. As a sophomore in high school, Tim had to change schools and adjust to sleeping in a basement room shared with the washer and dryer. "My father was responsible for his own branch, and we had to make a lot of sacrifices as he went from a steady paycheck to the instability that comes from building a business," Tim remembers. "My mother worked tirelessly to support his office, taking care of me and my two brothers while also managing the household in a new community. She was the glue that kept everything together."

The change was hard on Tim, and he initially withdrew from sports and social life. Now, a year after the move and just as he was settling into his new life, his father called the family together to unveil the news that he had been offered a better job in a more established office that would require the family to move yet again. "My immediate thought was despair, but there was something about that moment I'll never forget," Tim recalls now. "I knew my Dad wouldn't ask us to change again unless it was a good opportunity and something in me clicked. I wasn't going to fight against change anymore; I was going to embrace it."

Today, Tim is a Principal and co-owner of Bernhardt Wealth Management (BWM), where he helps clients harness the power of change to garner success on a daily basis. Now he is applying his skills and acumen to help others navigate the unexpected twists of one's financial life. His success dates back to that moment in high school when he first developed the adaptability that would open doors to success and happiness. "Change is a constant part of life," he affirms. "I do what I do to make an impact in my clients' lives and help them successfully navigate change at all levels, whether it's an investment portfolio question or some other important wealth management decision they need to make."

When Tim started with BWM in 2010, he was drawn to its commitment to eliminate conflicts of interest, as well as its investment strategy and dedication to holistic wealth management. "Since coming to the firm, it's been interesting to watch our industry pivot to adopt the best practices our firm has had in place for decades," Tim says. "Clients are better informed now, and they're demanding from their advisors what BWM has always offered: honest, world-class, comprehensive financial advisors that always have their best interest at heart."

Tim has helped the firm almost triple in size to 10 employees, all working together as a team to manage over $500 million in client assets. Today, BWM serves affluent and high-net-worth individuals with a comprehensive process that treats each client holistically. "It's about being able to take some of the weight off a client's shoulders by making sure everything they need gets done, and done right," Tim affirms. "That extends past investments to include tax, retirement, insurance, and estate planning. You cannot look at any one of these aspects in a silo or you will miss opportunities or risks. People are busy and there is just not a lot of time to pay attention to some of these things that are critically important, but that is what we are here for. Staying on top of the client's personal situation takes a lot of time and effort, and many firms do not want to take on this responsibility. It's something that really matters to us and defines who we are as a firm."

Tim has never shied away from hard work—a character trait built early in life that he credits to his parents. Tim spent his earliest years in a rural agricultural setting in Ohio. By the age of ten, he was mowing the lawn at the foundry where his father worked that made cast iron replicas of the Liberty Bell. "We always had a bell at our house, and my mother would ring it when it was time to come home," Tim remembers.

Tim saw his father promoted from the dirty, dangerous work in the foundry to a supervisory job in an office, trading in his soot-covered overalls for button-up shirts and khaki pants. Tim remembers the close friendship their family shared with the foundry's owner, and the enjoyment of taking a break from lawn mowing to enjoy a cold drink in the shade with the foundry workers.

Tim was always looking for ways to make money, like substituting on paper routes, picking up a summer job at the swimming pool, and washing golf clubs at the nearby country club. "My father always had an entrepreneurial spirit and encouraged us in our endeavors," he says.

When his father's entrepreneurial spirit landed him his first financial services job in a new community, that is when Tim's life changed forever. Torn away from the life he loved, Tim was disappointed and depressed. He did not assimilate well with the cliques at his new school.

Looking for something to connect with, he got a job at a small family business that made custom wood pallets. Along with a team of other high school kids, he worked second shift and decided to throw everything he had into it. "My father always told me that whatever job you found yourself doing, you should do the best job possible," Tim recounts. "So that's what I did!"

Tim's work stood out in its excellence, and before long, he was promoted to second shift supervisor—his first foray into leadership. Tim would always strive to meet the quotas set for his crew, and often exceeded them. "I took it very seriously because it was the main thing in my life at the time," he reflects. "I put my whole heart and soul into that job."

Tim will never forget the moment when just a year after their first move, his father sat the family down to announce they were moving again. "I was tired of not thriving in school and in my peer relationships," Tim says. "I decided I was going to embrace change this time and make it a fresh start."

Around that time, Tim's father gave him a copy of the classic book, *How to Win Friends and Influence People*, and he decided to apply its lessons to the life transition at hand. "Starting a new life at my third high school gave me the opportunity to redefine myself as I met new people," he remembers. "The experience was life changing. I learned how to adapt and saw how maintaining a positive attitude made all the difference when faced with the many changes that occur in life."

Through that time, Tim also had the invaluable opportunity to see the importance of his father's work in the community. In a small town where everyone knew each other, a person's reputation was often the difference between success and failure. "Most teenagers are not keenly aware of what their parents do at work, but because of the changes my father's career had meant for me and my family, I became very interested in understanding why he was willing to take such a risk," Tim explains. "I wanted to know just exactly what he was doing to help others and make a better life for us."

Tim saw that people were placing their trust in his father to invest their hard-earned life savings. "Just like one's physical or mental health, one's financial health is complex and multifaceted," Tim says. "Financial decisions can entail strong emotions as clients consider the risks and rewards of investing".

Thanks to a strong letter of recommendation from his time at the wood pallet plant, he was able to land a coveted summer job at a cardboard box factory in town, and he again applied his remarkable work ethic to being the best around. "The work was often difficult, but I always tried to put my best effort into it," he says. "It meant a lot to me to wow my supervisor and show him I could do a better job than some of my adult peers."

Tim attended Miami University in Oxford, Ohio, where he stumbled upon geography courses that soon became a lens for studying regional, cultural, and economic trends. His interest in the human cost of offshore manufacturing led him to study abroad in Mexico. Back at Miami, his interests led him to participate in research that landed him recognition as an author on a published research paper.

As Tim began to think about his post-graduate choices, he considered getting a master's degree in geography and continuing his research into global manufacturing trends. By this time, his father had advanced through leadership positions to become an executive in the firm's Canadian headquarters. Before his parents moved to Canada, Tim attended the going away party at his father's branch office where he was struck by the energy in the room. "I was incredibly moved by his clients who told me how much they were going to miss him," Tim remembers. "They told me they wouldn't be where they were without his dedication, care, and sincere interest he took in making sure his clients met their financial goals. It was a big defining moment for me to see the profound effect he had on the lives of others through his work and I realized I wanted to do more than write research papers people might never read. I wanted to actively make a difference for people."

Upon graduating, Tim followed his father's example and started a career in financial services. He moved to St. Louis to work in the home office of the same firm that had given his father their life changing opportunity. He gained experience in operations and client service by working on a team responsible for serving the firm's extensive branch network.

Throughout his life, Tim had also developed a love for the outdoors. After a few years in St. Louis, he decided to pursue his dream of moving to Colorado to pursue his passion for camping and climbing mountains. He took a job in a financial services call center where he got his first taste of working directly with clients on a daily basis. "The company was very focused on client service, and they had a Quality Assurance team that would listen to your calls at random and give you a score based on how well you took care of the client. I made a point to use their best practices on every single call I took. It became my mantra: every call was going to be perfect." Before long, Tim had the best scores in the entire call center.

Tim eventually transitioned into a training manager position, helping the company adjust to its phenomenal growth while preserving the culture that made it an excellent place to work. Through the highs and lows of the internet bubble, he also witnessed firsthand the challenges that individual investors face when they do not have a sound plan and lack understanding about the risks associated with investing.

Over time, Tim also saw the less desirable side of financial services as he became more and more exposed to the practices of other firms.

"You see a lot of people and companies who are in this business for the wrong reasons, thinking it's about squeezing as much profit as possible from the client," he reflects. "To me, the idea of profit is secondary to just taking care of people and making sure we're always doing the right thing. It is important to me that I am never doing something because of how we might be compensated. That's a unique approach in our industry, and it's a value that my father instilled in me from the day he started teaching me about being an advisor."

In 2003, Tim decided he wanted to pivot from training back to serving clients, and had the opportunity to manage a branch office in Colorado. He grew the practice from $15 million to $50 million in just four years, loving the work of serving clients and the freedom to run his branch office like an entrepreneurial small business. He was living his dream, but the town's isolation limited the opportunities available to his wife and two small children. When his wife landed a compelling job offer in Northern Virginia, a diverse community with better educational and cultural opportunities for the kids, they decided to make the move.

Tim had never been to Virginia before and found himself in a community without any established contacts, friends, or family. Faced with the prospect of building a new life once again, he used the change to create opportunity and success, just as he had done since he was 17. "I believed in what I was doing and that would always be there for me no matter where I was living." he explains. "I knew there would always be a need for trustworthy, honest, professional, ethical financial service professionals." When Tim found BWM, he knew it was the perfect fit for him. "My prior fifteen years in the industry laid a strong foundation that allowed me to step into the firm and immediately start making an impact," he says.

That foundation has become particularly important as BWM has grown, with Tim playing a key role in hiring the right people, charting out roles and responsibilities, and tackling tough business management questions. As a leader, he focuses on effective communication, ensuring everyone on the team is thinking critically about what's working, what is not working, and how to improve. With enthusiasm and a positive attitude, he is firmly committed to always doing the very best possible job. "I will always look at the client sitting across the table from me as if they were my own sibling, parent, or grandparent," he affirms. "With every client, I use the same respect and ethical code I would use for my own family. That means putting my own interests aside to look at what is best for them, earning their trust by doing the right thing, listening, and being a good communicator. I want to be that 'go to' person our clients can always rely on. Ensuring clients make the best decisions for the legacy of their wealth is what we do, setting them free to create the impact they want to be able to create through their business/career and for their family and the causes they care about is who we are. We are passionate about helping our clients create the legacy they want through their profession and for their family and the causes that are important to them."

Today, Tim and his wife, Kathryn, love to show their children the joys of outdoor activities like hiking, camping and boating. "Kathryn and I are very similar in that we grew up with hard-working fathers who preferred spending their weekends doing labor-intensive home improvement projects," Tim reflects. "She has had a very successful career spanning Perot Systems, Microsoft, and Arthur Andersen, so we also have a shared interest in business. More importantly, we have shared values in how we want to raise our children by teaching them the importance of grit and perseverance."

In advising young people entering the working world today, Tim underscores the importance of presenting yourself well at all times. "People around you really do notice how you show up in the world," he says. "It's important to arrive prepared and on time, ready to participate and put your best foot forward. It may seem basic, but it makes a big difference. Always try to wow others, whether it's your supervisor or your customers. Remember that you put your name and your stamp on everything you touch. Be prepared, don't cut corners, and don't make excuses. People who take that seriously will go very far in life."

Beyond that, Tim's story demonstrates how harnessing the power of change can truly transform life for the better. In his office, he keeps a 3-ring binder from a 1980s Forbes stock market course passed on to his father from his maternal grandfather, who immigrated to America from Hungary as a young child and achieved success through a lifetime of learning. The binder was passed to Tim's father amidst the twists and turns of his own career path in his brave pursuit of opportunity, even when it meant stepping far outside his comfort zone. "Successfully embracing change got me to where I am today, and it's my job now to help others do the same," says Tim proudly.

Keith Kruse

Culture First

Keith Kruse's father was a Naval Engineer, and from a young age, Keith had an interest in the military. In particular, he dreamed of aviation, although his poor vision meant he wouldn't be a pilot. But Keith knew that in the Navy, there were many coveted backseat aviation roles. After high school, he headed to the highly regarded ROTC program at Rensselaer Polytechnic Institute (RPI) in Troy, NY. RPI is one of the top engineering schools in the country, and their ROTC program is one of the largest.

Keith did well in his military training courses and scored positive evaluations from his midshipman supervisors. During his senior year, he wound up in one of the top leadership positions in the Midshipman Battalion, the second in command, Battalion Executive Officer. During the summers, his military education continued. After freshman year, he was sent to experience life as an enlisted man onboard the aircraft carrier, USS America. Between sophomore and junior years, he tried out different military communities within the Navy. He spent a time with the Marines, time learning about submarines, time learning about surface warfare, and finally time with the aviation group. "I loved aviation," recalls Keith. "But I tell everyone that the Marine Corps week was the most fun. We would storm a beach and sleep outside. I loved it but would never want to do that as a career." Before his senior year, Keith became a Junior Officer aboard the USS Chandler. The ship was a destroyer out in San Diego, and the experience was a fascinating one for him.

In 1988, Keith finished school with a Mechanical Engineering degree. After graduation, it was time to select which branch of the Navy he wanted to enter. For Keith it was a no-brainer: aviation. "*Top Gun* happened to come out right around that time," laughs Keith. "I had always wanted to fly, but suddenly the top ten midshipmen graduating my senior year were going into aviation. All of us were called into the Captain's office to explain why we had chosen flight school over the nuclear Navy, but he couldn't have done anything to change my mind. RPI was one of the top sources of officers for the Navy nuclear program and the Captain would have to explain to his superiors why they wouldn't be getting the top talent in the nuclear engineering program that year!"

Keith headed to Pensacola, Florida for flight training. "After the initial phase of flight school, you select your aircraft," he explains. "I wanted to go P-3s because they have the best career opportunities for Naval Officers who don't have good eyesight. I didn't want to choose F-14s and ride in the back seat since people always joked that pilots would rather have the extra 200 pounds of gas. On the P-3 you could be mission commander, and I was fortunate enough to get that."

The P-3 is a land-based anti-submarine warfare aircraft. From Pensacola, Keith went to an Air Force Base in Sacramento before going to Jacksonville for more specialized training. Finally, he joined Patrol

Squadron Twenty-Three (VP-23) which was a life-changing experience. "That squadron was unique," Keith reminisces. "We all meshed, and I consider myself lucky to get that assignment. I had some great commanding officers who are good friends to this day. Being in that environment was enjoyable because of the missions we were doing and because of the camaraderie of my squadron. We were travelling all over the world together and were doing deployments and detachments in support of many of the contingency response and combat operations going on at the end of the Cold War. It was exciting to be a part of such an important time in history. We became a very unified group, and they became my best friends. I really enjoyed that culture."

At the end of a three-year tour, Keith returned to the DC area to complete a Master's Program at George Washington University. While completing his degree in Science, Technology and Public Policy, he was still in the Navy. Now a young Lieutenant, he took a position managing a division within the Bureau of Naval Personnel. The job was a major adjustment. "Even though it was a military organization, there wasn't the same tight-knit military culture I experienced in the squadron," Keith reflects. "It was an office environment with military and civilians coming in, working their hours, and rushing home to beat traffic. I realized how much I had preferred the camaraderie in the squadron, and I started to wonder whether it was possible to create that type of culture in the private sector?"

Today, Keith is the President and COO of Federal Conference, and he prides himself on putting culture first. "Wherever I go, I like to put that mark on an organization. It goes back to the first small company I worked for after I left the Navy when I had the opportunity to become Vice President of Operations. I viewed that as my chance to build the company I'd always wanted to work for," Keith explains. "I've tried to build that company everywhere I've gone. While you may not always be able to achieve it, you can still transform an organization's culture by focusing on bringing the best people in the door, helping them thrive in what they're doing, and retaining top talent for the long-term. Building a performance driven culture means creating an environment that attracts capable people and inspires them to do their best. Make them feel like they are part of something larger than themselves, give them clear guidance on what success looks like, and then stand back and let them show you their talents."

Federal Conference was launched as National Conferencing, Inc. in 2006 by partners Paul Trapp and Steve Davis. At the time, the business focused on event management planning for the government. Over time, they began to expand their offerings and moved into the commercial sector as well by starting a sister company, DavisTrapp. Federal Conference focused on government customers, and DavisTrapp focused exclusively on corporate and association businesses. By 2017, the partners wanted to focus more on launching a new business, a franchise-model event planning company called EventPrep and needed someone highly competent to take over Federal Conference.

Enter Keith. The men had met a number of years back, and both Paul and Steve were impressed by Keith's commitment and philosophy. They hired him to take over operations for their government business, Federal Conference since Keith had years of experience as an executive with other government contracting companies. Keith was committed to making change in a disciplined and responsible manner. That meant learning everything there was to know about the business. "That first year I focused on learning about the business, the events, and in particular, the Army Strong Bonds project since it was the biggest program we run. It's a relatively complicated project, but we have a comprehensive training program for all new planners to get up-to-speed. I basically became a Strong Bonds intern to learn the business and learn about our biggest program. It was helpful for me to see all the details and to take notes on what everyone's doing. If I took the time to fully understand what the team was doing and the challenges they faced, I would be able to make the maximum impact."

While Keith was running Federal Conference, Paul and Steve began to focus on their new start-up, EventPrep. Once they knew that Federal Conference was in good hands they moved to Florida and decided to merge their commercial business, DavisTrapp, under Federal Conference and create a new commercial division under Keith's leadership. The merger meant more responsibility and a brand new industry for Keith who had always focused on government customers throughout his business career. "I was learning all of the nuances of how the hospitality industry worked," smiles Keith. "It was all new to me, and I found that exciting. Even though it was a new market for me, the basic aspects of managing company operations and delivering quality service were still the same whether for a commercial or government customer. By this time in my career, I knew operations like the back of my hand so it was easy to focus on learning the differences between the two and how to adjust my decision-making to take best advantage of both sides of the business."

During Keith's tenure, Federal Conference grew from about 50 employees to 67 and revenues more than doubled within his first two years at the company. The new positions are mostly on the commercial and association side which Keith has enjoyed expanding. Government contracts, while more familiar to Keith, are far more onerous to pursue. "There aren't a lot of opportunities for event planning in the government space because often they have their own planners," Keith explains. "Then if there is an opportunity, you go through 18 months of the contracting process. On the commercial side, if we meet a customer and impress them with our expertise and experience, that can translate directly into a business opportunity. It's nice to know that if they like you, and you do good work at a good price, they're going to go with you. No recompetes and dealing with byzantine government contracting rules that often result in unpredictable and perplexing procurement decisions. I love that we can be in control of our own success by focusing on delivering high-quality service and retaining our customers. I have really enjoyed learning the commercial side of the business."

One important aspect of that growth was reimagining the company's marketing pitch and website. Previously, the business had mostly brought in new clients via referral, but Keith realized they were leaving a lot on the table with that approach. While a government customer may look at a business's website during the contracting process, that ultimately wasn't the deciding factor when it came to awarding contracts. On the commercial side, conversely, a well-designed website could well be a motivating factor in the client's decision. Additionally, true to his desire to create a culture of commitment and camaraderie, Keith emphasized the importance of teamwork. "I wanted to be less top-down in terms of defining what our mission was and what services we provided," he states. "I wanted to make sure I had buy-in from my leadership team. We did an off site and reviewed what our service offerings were, where we had gaps, what we were seeing from competitors, and then created a new elevator pitch. Essentially, we offer full-service event management planning for commercial, government, and association customers. What we really try to focus on are customized, tailored solutions which allow our customers to forget the logistical headaches and focus on what's important to them, the content, the speakers, and the experience of their event. We help them bring that vision to life."

Keith has done a fantastic job implementing the Navy values he encountered during his nine years of active duty. But he encountered those values during his childhood long before joining the Navy. He was born in Newport, Rhode Island, where his father was stationed. Like many military families, the Kruses moved frequently in Keith's early years. His father started out as a surface warfare officer in the Navy, then decided he would attend MIT to pursue a Master's in Mechanical and Ocean Engineering. The little family moved to the Boston area when Keith was four and settled in Brockton. After MIT, his father went into the Engineering Duty Officer Program which focused on designing and building Navy ships. For this role, he did have to travel quite frequently to attend to problems onboard aircraft carriers, ships, and submarines he supported, but he wasn't usually gone for extended periods of time.

In Boston, Keith became a lifetime fan of baseball and fondly remembers attending Red Sox games with his father. The team was terrible at the time, but he hung a Red Sox pennant on the wall and watched every game. He was never much of an athlete; his Little League career was short-lived. But he reveled in fandom. Keith's love of baseball continues to this day as a season ticket holder for the Washington Nationals. He also enjoyed hockey, and while living in New England he'd often play with the neighborhood kids on the frozen ponds. He never became a Patriots fan; his father preferred the Dallas Cowboys and Keith became a loyal fan of them, too.

From Boston, the family moved to the Philadelphia area and later to Norfolk, Virginia, before finally settling in the Washington, DC area when Keith was about 12. His father was still taking tours in other parts of the country, but his parents had decided that Keith needed some stability during his middle and high-school years. From seventh grade on, the family home was DC.

That opportunity to stay in one location allowed him to finally build some close and long-lasting friendships. He is still close with his best friend from middle school, Chris, as well as his friend Brian, who lived next door. "Chris and I are like brothers. We've traveled overseas together. We were both each other's best man at our weddings. Our families frequently vacation together during our annual outing to Bethany Beach. Until I met Chris, I never really was in any one place long enough to form a close friendship," Keith says.

As Keith got older, he became more active in school. He was in the gifted and talented program and had a knack for literature. He took AP English and ended up winning the High School English Award from the department. He was in the Junior Achievement program where he learned about business and eventually became the club's President.

Although he didn't yet know he wanted to go into business, he had a strong practical side, and knew that while his English classes were his favorite at school, he ought to focus on a more technical career path. He also loved science and math and knew engineering could be an interesting and lucrative field. Keith also loved aviation and for a time, he even considered becoming an astronaut with NASA. Unfortunately, his poor eyesight nipped that idea in the bud.

Family was important to Keith. His maternal grandparents lived nearby in Silver Spring, and he saw them a couple times a month. They had boxwoods in front of their house, a smell Keith still loves to this day. And somewhat more sentimentally, Keith has a particular affection for a cranberry glass *Gone with the Wind* lamp his grandmother always kept in the window. He liked it so much, he searched far and wide to find one just like it that he could have of his own. Finally, after exhaustive searches on e-Bay, he found one. "That lamp is important to me because it reminds me so much of my grandparents and how much I loved visiting them as a kid, even though it's not really hers," smiles Keith. "It makes me feel at home."

His parents, too, were strong influences. From dad, he got his analytical mind. "He's the person I go to for advice when I'm in a tough situation, even professionally," Keith admits. "He's run large organizations and had a full career in the Navy. He then led the American Society of Naval Engineers for 20 years which was essentially another career. He's been a good role model for me when it comes to leading organizations and getting the most out of people." His mother, meanwhile, keeps things lighter. "We laugh a lot with each other," nods Keith. "I think I get more of my sense of humor from her. And my Catholic faith also comes from my mom's influence as well. When dad was traveling so much for the Navy, my mom and I had plenty of time to bond."

Keith was an only child for most of his childhood, but when he was 17, his parents had a major surprise for him: a baby sister. As a high schooler, he was taking care of the baby, changing diapers, and generally learning parenting skills he'd use later in life with his own kids. "My best friend, Chris, who was also an only child unceremoniously kicked me out of the Only Child Club," Keith laughs. "My sister and I always talk about how we basically knew two different sets of parents. When I was a kid my dad was a young officer, wasn't making much money, but over the intervening decades things changed. When she arrived he was already a Commander, and had been a commanding officer, so it was a very different life experience."

After ROTC and the Navy, Keith got his first civilian job with a then-small company called DFI International Government Services (DFI). He joined as employee number 15 in 1997, doing military policy work for government contracts. He'd been doing well in his role, and in 2001, was offered the life-changing opportunity to move to the operations side. It was certainly a trial by fire. A few months after accepting the role, the entire country dealt with the fallout of September 11th. DFI dealt with the crisis a little differently than most. "There were no new contracts coming out, and it hit our bottom line significantly," he says. "We had to figure out how to conserve resources while trying to keep the team we had. We decided that all the senior leaders would take a voluntary salary deferral." When most companies went directly to layoffs, DFI valued its team. Their bet paid off; the work came back within a year, and the business was stronger than ever. It was a valuable lesson to Keith. "If you have the right culture, people will do what it takes to help the team succeed," he remarks.

He stayed with DFI for 11 years, through their sale to a large British company called Detica. Then, Keith decided to take some time off and reassess. After 18 months, he returned to the workforce, serving as COO at several other organizations before hanging out a shingle as a consultant. It was while he was consulting that Paul and Steve sought him out. The rest is history.

Through it all, Keith has had the crucial support of his wife, Leslie, whom he met in DC just before he left the Navy. Leslie has a music degree and sings professionally, in addition to working in accounting. "She helps me look out for myself," he praises her. "She keeps me from becoming a workaholic which would be very easy for me to do if left to my own devices. She's part of the reason I decided to try consulting and take a step back to find the right fit for myself. She's the core that keeps the family together." The couple have two children.

When asked about leadership, Keith invokes a quote from General Patton. "Don't tell people how to do things; tell them what to do and they'll surprise you with their ingenuity," he relates. "That's what I try to do. I try to set goals and expectations and let them come to me with solutions. I try to be hands-off, where I can."

To young people, Keith advises taking chances. "Otherwise, you're never going to know how far you can push yourself," he points out. "Failure is not a bad thing as long as you learn from it. If I'm going to give people the latitude to try things, I've got to be tolerant of a little bit of failure. They can't be afraid to try. It's the same for young people. You have to experience life and take chances in order to grow and succeed."

Pete Lamont

The Importance of Kindness

Like a lot of recent college graduates, Pete Lamont thought he knew it all in his early 20s. He was working as an assistant administrator at a law firm, and in spite of his low position on the totem pole, he was confident and even bossy. "I was being a little bit of an asshole," he confesses. Finally, a senior partner at the firm pulled him aside for a heart-to-heart. "He told me, Pete, the owners of the firm do not like to be ordered around by their employees," he recalls. "It was a defining moment for me. I was mad because I didn't like to be told I was wrong, and I was disappointed because I knew I screwed up. I was embarrassed. That lesson was 31 years ago and I remember it very clearly. It was one of those moments where you get your head kicked in. You really have to pay attention to what's going on around you. It's part of growing up, and I grew up quite a bit that day."

From then on, Pete always remembered the importance of good manners, sensitivity, and kindness, and strove to leave a positive impression on anyone he worked with. "Using please and thank you goes a long way," he observes. "I say 'please' or 'thank you' in most everything I write now. At the time, I was being very task-oriented and was getting stuff done, but there's a right way and a wrong way to do that especially when the person is your boss!"

His attitude adjustment has taken him a long way from that administrative role at the law firm. Today, Pete is a Partner at INTEGRITYOne Partners, a government contractor that works in IT and Project Management. The five partners employ 36 billable consultants for a total staff of over 40 people. They contract mainly with the Department of Homeland Security (DHS) and have contracts with HHS, ICE, USCIS, and FBI. The main focus of their work is immigration and law enforcement with some additional focus on the healthcare sector.

Coming to the firm from the giant KPMG was a big change of pace for Pete. INTEGRITYOne was founded in 2001, Pete joined in 2005, and he helped build up the firm's project management business. "In a big firm, you stay in your lane since there's so much structure and so much support behind you," he reflects. "When you come to a small firm, you can do everything. Believe me, it's exciting. All of a sudden there's so much to learn and so many opportunities. But you also have to be careful because you can chase butterflies all day long if you don't have clarity about what must be done. So you have to hunker down and bring some rigor and structure to what you're pursuing."

Coming from the hyper-structured world of KPMG, Pete brought that rigor and structure with him. So much so that his coworkers nicknamed him 'Box Boy,' a teasing reference to his need to fill out org charts and carefully demarcate responsibilities. Additionally, he's worked to imbue INTEGRITYOne with the same culture of kindness he learned early on in his professional career.

"On World Kindness Day, I sent a note to everybody," he says. "One of the things I love about the firm is that everyone is so kind and caring. I want to create an atmosphere where my employees are comfortable coming to me with critique. An environment where people are too scared to share ideas or criticism is not productive." Another of Pete's values is his commitment to what he calls "relentless learning." "If you stand still for ten minutes, someone's by you already," he notes. "In the tech space, everything is moving hyper-fast."

There's another reason kindness and commitment to others, and especially family, is so important to Pete. Raised by an alcoholic father, Pete had to deal with unpredictable violence and anger from an early age. He, his mother, and his five siblings became especially close in the face of these outbursts and sometimes even fled the house at night to stay with neighbors. "When he was sober, he was fantastic," Pete remembers. "He was charming, he was funny, and he was one of the smartest people I've ever met. It's really sad that he was an alcoholic. No one sets out to be an alcoholic. But to a great degree, that made me who I am. I wanted to be the dad my dad should've been, the dad he could've been. I think that's why I'm a great dad, and a wonderful husband."

Pete's father was a pilot in the Air Force, and his four older siblings—one brother and three sisters—were born all around the country—Virginia, Alabama, Massachusetts, and Florida. By the time Pete was born, the family had settled in Camp Springs, Maryland. His father retired four years later, a couple of years after his youngest sister was born. Their neighborhood was mostly military, and the kids had plenty of other children to play with. After retirement from the Air Force, Pete's father went to work as an aircraft accident investigator for the National Transportation Safety Board.

Pete's mother stayed at home where she ran a tight ship and demanded attention to manners. "She was the biggest influence on me," he nods. "She was big on table manners and would tell us, 'You never know when you'll be dining at the White House.' She was tough as nails, but she loved her kids. The love never stopped. She made sure I was a gentleman, and she raised us to be good people with good morals."

Because of the chaos in the house, she went out of her way to make Holidays a big deal for the children and would decorate and cook for days before Thanksgiving and Christmas. She was always trying to provide a sense of normalcy and would leave dozens of presents under the Christmas tree.

One of Pete's positive memories of his dad are their trips to a communal farm that one of their neighbors owned. Pete and his dad farmed five acres there. Every Saturday morning from early spring to late fall, they would go there and plant vegetables, pick peaches, or fish in the little pond. Until Pete was about 13, the two went there each weekend, and Pete loved spending time with his dad learning about farming and driving a tractor.

After years of turmoil dealing with his father's alcoholism—years that even included physical fights between his father and older brother—the family reeled when Pete's dad was diagnosed with colon cancer. The disease was brutal and the treatment options were limited in the late 1970s. He quickly declined, and before long he was completely dependent on his wife and younger children to take care of him.

The change in circumstance, though sad, helped to develop Pete's compassion. He remembers lovingly taking care of his father and being able to help him when he was in pain. "I think it gave me a chance to help him ease his pain. I loved being there for him," Pete reflects. "He could ask for anything, and I would bring it to him. Bringing him food and changing his bedding was rewarding. I had a desire to help, and I think it helped me as he was dying to help him pass on in a beautiful way. I took a class in college on death and dying and that's when I realized that we really did give my dad a beautiful death. There was no stress in the house. He wasn't in pain. And while it was very sad, it was the best we could do under those circumstances."

A few months after his father passed, his sister Genise brought home a black Irish Setter puppy they named Clancy. He was a wonderful dog and Pete says Clancy helped the family heal from the tough years they'd been through.

With their primary breadwinner gone, money was now tight. Pete's mother had returned to the work force a couple of years earlier as a secretary at a local high school, but they were still pinching pennies to get by. "We ate a lot of hamburger helper," he remembers. "Anything to stretch that food dollar. My mom even tried to bring powdered milk into the house but that didn't go over well. As I got older, my mom and I had a tradition of going to the commissary together on the weekends. Part of the reason I did it when I was younger was to try and get pop-tarts and the food I wanted into the grocery cart. We continued that tradition until a few weeks before she died when I was in my 40s."

At school, Pete always did well, but was never an extraordinary student. He could earn As when he tried, but often found himself disinterested in his classes and would, settle for more average Bs and Cs. A great teacher though, can be a great motivator. "In 3rd grade, Mrs. Yates was one of my favorite teachers," Pete recalls. "We were learning our times tables and had a competition. I worked my butt off thanks to her encouragement, and I won the competition. That was the first time I really saw how hard work can pay off. When I put my mind to it, I can always do great things. I had that realization that hard work can produce outstanding results."

In his free time, Pete loved to play soccer, and continued to play all the way through high school. As he got older, he also began to work as a paperboy delivering the *Washington Star* and then the coveted *Washington Post.* The gig took up hours of his mornings and afternoons, but he loved the feeling of earning and saving money. Eventually, he got a job at a local gas station, and continued saving until he was able to buy his first car at 19.

In the meantime, he'd started at Prince George's Community College before transferring to the University of Maryland College Park after his first year. "Community college was the right decision," Pete explains. "I wasn't ready to go to college yet. I needed to get my grades up. I didn't love to study and was still focused on making money. My mom encouraged me to get my grades up to prove I was ready to go to college. I took a program called the College Success Seminar, and it changed my attitude on school and studying. It was a fantastic program and gave me the confidence that I was capable. It gave me the tools to be successful. I became a more disciplined and consistent studier and began to see the results."

At Maryland, Pete's first year was tough, but he powered through it. After a semester of low grades, he knew he needed to buckle down and commit. He introduced more structure to his study time and was able to right the ship. Initially, he'd planned to major in computer science, but ended up switching to economics. Throughout college, he worked at the gas station and UPS. Before his senior year, Pete decided he wanted to try an experiment—what would happen if he quit his job and focused on getting straight As. "I'd never had straight As and wanted to see if I could do it," explains Pete. "It took a lot of discipline, a lot of saying 'no' to fun stuff. But when I focused, it worked. I once again saw what happens when you work hard and apply yourself. I got straight As in those 300 and 400 level classes. I was really proud of that moment."

After leaving college on a high note, Pete landed his first adult job at Dechert, Price and Rhodes, a law firm where he joined the accounting staff. He loved working there and being surrounded by smart, driven people—especially, one in particular. It was at the firm that he met his future wife and the love of his life, Marielena. "She was the most beautiful woman I've ever seen," he gushes. "The rest became history."

The two married in 1994 shortly after Pete had gone on to work at another law firm where he received the life-changing lecture from one of the partners. Since then, the two have had a fantastic partnership raising their children and balancing each other's personalities. "We're complete opposites," Pete muses. "She's been that natural governor to keep me from being too Type A. I can just go, go, go and work, work, work, but she is a stop and smell the flowers kind of person." Today, Marielena stays home with the kids. It is an arrangement Pete appreciates as it has given him more freedom to devote himself to work while making sure never to prioritize it over them. "When you marry your best friend, you can talk about anything. It makes things so much easier and fun," Pete smiles. He considers his wedding ring to be his most prized possession.

Around the time he met his future wife, Pete also had the transformative experience of participating in a Dale Carnegie course where he confronted one of his biggest fears—public speaking. Despite being continuously pushed out of his comfort zone over the 12-week program, he really enjoyed the program. In fact, he enjoyed it so much that he's gone back three times to help teach the program. He's also a member of Vistage, the world's largest executive coaching organization for small and midsize businesses.

After leaving the second law firm, and graduating with a Master's in International Management, Pete moved to KPMG, where he stayed for almost one decade. While there, he met one of his most influential business mentors—Doug Moll. Doug was brought in during the midst of a crisis that was affecting the team both professionally and emotionally. Pete's partner on a major project died suddenly and unexpectedly, and Pete was left picking up the pieces as he processed his grief over losing a friend.

It was a high-profile project for the Department of Justice, and the client was demanding results. Doug came in and began putting things in order. "He arrived, and there was an immediate sense of calm," remembers Pete. "He gave instructions to each team member about what to do, and he gave me the tools to be successful. I learned a lot from him and did a lot of things I never thought I was capable of doing. We always go back and forth on who saved that project; he says it was me, but I say that I couldn't have done it without him."

Pete loved his time at KPMG & KPMG Consulting, but over the years, the tireless schedule began to wear him down. He realized the environment was no longer enjoyable for him. The culture was becoming more political and when the firm went public, the core principals changed. Pete was running a book of business worth $14 million while the average partner only ran about $5 million. It didn't seem right to him. It was then that he reached out to a friend who suggested INTEGRITYOne as a great place to work. Within nine months, the firm had won enough work to hire Pete full-time, and he made the leap.

As a leader, Pete considers himself to be consistent above all else. "The important thing for my team is that they know who they're getting every day with Pete," he says. "The people I work with don't have to worry whether Dr. Jekyll or Mr. Hyde will show up today. They're going to get Consistent Pete. I'm always trying to improve, and I try to lead by example."

To young people entering the working world today, Pete reiterates his commitment to continuing to learn and grow. "You need to be a relentless learner," he stresses. "You never know everything. You have to be voracious in learning new things. It's learning your job, but it's also learning the people part of your job. How do you work with people? How do you get along with people? You have to really make sure you're learning the people piece of the puzzle. So, stop and listen. When you're 22 like I was, you think you know everything, but you don't. You need to pause, pay attention, and listen to what is being said. Reduce the number of distractions around you. And don't forget good manners, they never go out of style. Say please and thank you. I learned the importance of that lesson the hard way. You have to get things done in business, but you get things done through people. And if you're a jerk about it, you're not going to get very far."

Dan Lender

Follow Your Instincts

Dan Lender wasn't raised with a silver spoon. He grew up in a rural part of West Central Pennsylvania, in the small town of Smithmill. His dad was a truck driver, and Dan and his three brothers often helped their dad with his trucks parked in front of the house. His mother worked at a clothing factory. The town was working class, and after high school, many went to work locally in the coal mines or lumber yards.

Everyone around him worked hard, but Dan knew that if he wanted a different kind of life, he'd have to excel. Both of his parents encouraged Dan and his brothers to dream big and prioritize their education. He buckled down in school and earned very good grades throughout his academic career. He earned his first dollars cutting grass and doing yard work for a wealthier family in town. Carefully, he put all his money into savings. Then he got his first real, W-2 job. It turned out to be a significant choice.

He'd just turned 16. Finally able to drive, he already knew where he wanted to apply. He had his heart set on becoming a pharmacist so he drove to the local pharmacy to ask for a job as a stock boy. With many in town mining coal and hauling lumber, Dan chose the pharmacy option because it stood out. It was a good, reliable job that paid well and wouldn't leave you with black lung or a broken back. It represented a major break from the past.

"I remember going to the pharmacy with my mom and thinking about how the pharmacist knew so much and was in control of so many things," Dan recollects. "I remember thinking, that's a neat job. There weren't a lot of white collar jobs in the area and the pharmacy seemed like a good job so I set my sights on that. When I started working there, I took the trash out, swept the floor, and did anything and everything I was asked to do. That particular pharmacy had an optical department and sometimes I would even work with the optician to help their patients. I knew I didn't want to sweep floors forever so I made the most of every opportunity I was presented. Sometimes I would help fill prescription vials, listen to the pharmacists work with customers, and talk to insurance providers and patients. I admired the pharmacists because they seemed to know quite a bit and everyone thanked them for their time and expertise."

Dan became a member of the National Honor Society in high school and started his collegiate career at Penn State University. Most people in the area who went to college went to Penn State. After a year at Penn State he transferred to the University of Pittsburgh to get a degree in Pharmacy.

At Pitt, he thrived. He became the President of his fraternity, as well as the President of his pharmacy school class. The curriculum was immersive and fascinating. He remembers walking past cadavers at the adjoining Medical school, happy to have selected pharmacy as his specialty. During the summer, he split his time between pharmacy internships and working for his brother's beer distribution company.

Throughout those months he lived something of a double life alternating between the physical labor of hauling kegs and the intellectual work required as a pharmacy intern. Pharmacy students are exposed to the various types of programming during their training. Dan interned in a community pharmacy, a hospital pharmacy, and a poison control center. Ultimately, Dan found the community pharmacy to be the most appealing since it allowed for a more diverse client base and since it provided more freedom on the job.

Dan graduated in 1986 and became a registered pharmacist. He'd done what he'd set out to do. He left small town Pennsylvania for a more urban life in Pittsburgh while also pursuing a trusted position in healthcare. But still, life called to Dan. He enjoyed working in a pharmacy but over time found he was yearning for something more. Within a few short years, he was on to his next career working as a field representative for a pharmaceutical company. This position would allow flexibility in his daily schedule and provide him the opportunity to use his knowledge as a pharmacist. While working full time as a pharmaceutical rep, Dan also worked part time as a pharmacist.

"People ask me how my career has taken so many twists and turns," smiles Dan. "How did I get from being a pharmacist to where I am now? And the truth is that I like to try different things. I don't throw the past away, but I build on it. I want to learn and be good at different things. If I see a new problem that needs to be solved, I want to try to address it."

Since his leap from pharmacist to drug rep, Dan has continued to display his talent for adaptation. Today, he's about a million miles from his past life in pharmaceuticals, founding and running Golden Rule Home Watch and Concierge.

Dan founded the business in early 2018. He and a friend had been looking at various concepts, and the home watch business was the one that stuck. By this time, Dan also had an extensive background in IT and cyber security, and the marketplace seemed ripe for the services he wanted to offer.

Golden Rule caters to clients who leave town and their property for extended periods of time. They often tend to be wealthier people who go south or west for the winter, or the super-wealthy migrating between homes, across the U.S. and the world. Golden Rule also works with clients (families) who find themselves responsible for the home of a loved one who has passed away or has had to leave for various reasons. These clients often live in another part of the country and until they decide what to do, the house may sit idle for months or years. Golden Rule ensures that client homes are monitored and well taken care of. "Our goal is to be the trusted eyes, ears and feet on the street for our clients when they are not around.

Dan or one of his contractors come by the house before the owner leaves to understand any compelling events or interests of the owner. While walking through the house and property together, Golden Rule carefully notes the unique character of each home and any possible issues to watch out for. They locate the gas main and water main, check the roof, and perform a detailed check of the home from top to bottom, interior and exterior. Once the homeowners are gone, Golden Rule checks in on the house according to what the homeowner has requested. Usually, clients opt for once a week or twice a month. Golden Rule uses high-tech tools like moisture meters and laser thermometers to confirm any problem or validate that the home's systems are working correctly. Any issues are extensively documented, photographed and sent to the client with recommendations.

"We have a very comprehensive electronic reporting template that is customized for every home," describes Dan. "It's time, date and GPS stamped and will tell the homeowner exactly when we were there, what we did, and will include any photos and necessary details. If there is an abnormality, we will certainly include that information. This is more than a neighbor looking in on your house on a best case effort. We provide peace of mind to our clients knowing that we are experts and are licensed, bonded, and insured for such things. Our clients want to know that someone trustworthy is in their home and monitoring it." If there is an issue then Dan has a network of well vetted partners that he can call upon or introduce to the homeowner.

Dan's wife, Amy, keeps the books for Golden Rule. Amy, like Dan, grew up in a working class family. Her mother was a home economics teacher, and her father was a postal carrier. She and her two sisters were raised outside of Pittsburgh. And like Dan, she always had ambition. The two met when he was a pharmacist in Pittsburgh, and Amy was working as a nurse in a Cardiac ICU. Dan considers their partnership crucial to his success. "She has incredible common sense," he notes. "If you ask your friends and family about an idea, they almost always say, 'That's a great idea.' They tell you what you want to hear. Amy is a fantastic sounding board; she'll tell me if something doesn't make sense. She doesn't always tell me what I want to hear. But she does always tell me the truth."

Dan considers the birth of his and Amy's two children to be among the most defining moments of his life. "As a young adult, you're mostly focused on 'me'," he reflects. "Then you get married, and it's two people. But the really lifechanging moment was when we had our first child and suddenly you've gone from first to second to third in the blink of an eye. You keep falling in the batting order," he smiles. "In my opinion, as a parent, a good parent, you do anything for your kids. You're more concerned about their needs than your own needs. As soon as a child is born, you are changed forever."

This perspective is one he inherited from his mother. Once her boys were born she never considered buying herself a new dress but would spend every dime to make sure her children had everything they needed. Though the family wasn't wealthy, they always had enough to eat. She would often sew their clothes. Dan was the youngest by 11, 7, and three years and remembers that nothing was thrown away. Clothes were often patched and handed down.

From his father, Dan feels he got his work ethic. He was frequently hauling clay or sand for local companies and taught his boys to work hard and, treat everyone honestly and fairly.

Dan's family lived in the house that his maternal grandfather built. There were several barns on the property, too, and the boys loved to play in them. Growing up they had chickens roaming around along with cats and dogs. They were only about a half mile from town. "When I went to college it was a common practice to ask where others were from. To gauge the size of the town, people would normally ask how many stoplights the town had," laughs Dan. "Well, there were no stoplights. In fact, there were probably more cows than people."

The whole area had been deep mined, and while Dan was growing up it was strip mined. Many in his family had been a part of the mining industry. His grandfather and some of his uncles would come home completely black from head to toe after a day of working in the mines. Unfortunately, many of them had black lung disease or some other related health issue at some point in their lives. There were closed mine shafts all over the area and kids were always warned to stay away from them for safety reasons.

"My dad would work in all kinds of weather," Dan recalls. "My parents wanted my brothers and me to have a better life than they had and always emphasized the importance of an education. They didn't want us to follow in their footsteps in that line of work. My brothers and I all aspired to get an education."

Dan and his brothers loved to play baseball in the community. The family wasn't rich, but their childhood never felt lacking. Hunting and fishing were big in the area, and riding in trucks with dad was always a special treat. They didn't have a pool, but they swam in the local dam during the summers. "Playing ball and swimming were daily activities," remembers Dan. "Back then, you'd leave the house in the morning, and the rule was to come back before the streetlights came on."

Dan did well academically in high school and also played baseball and football. His parents, and especially his father, rarely missed a game. He graduated in the top 10% of his class before going on to college.

After several years as a pharmacist, Dan made his first big leap after a chance conversation with a drug rep who often came by his pharmacy. She mentioned her company was hiring in Pittsburgh, and Dan got the job. For about two years, Dan successfully navigated the work of a pharmaceutical rep before another pivotal event put him on a new path. He was approached by a well-known biotechnology company specializing in monoclonal antibody technology and was offered a position.

For about a year and a half, Dan worked as a clinical study monitor. He was collaborating with physicians and hospitals on the best practices for utilizing the ground breaking biologics. Unfortunately, the company did not gain FDA approval for its lead product, and the organization dissolved its workforce. Dan had had a taste of something more exciting and didn't want to go back to a conventional role at a pharmaceutical company. Not sure what he wanted to do, he returned to the pharmacy world. He was thankful he had the foundation from his education as a pharmacist.

Even though he returned to the world of pharmacy, Dan always had an eye for opportunities. While a pharmacist, Dan and a colleague who was a registered dietician and exercise physiologist launched a new business. Both had encountered many people who suffered from chronic health problems and weren't improving with treatment. "People would come in with high cholesterol, heart disease, uncontrolled diabetes, or perhaps they were unable to lose weight. They would often get another prescription for a symptom, but they would never get any better," Dan describes. "We saw an opportunity to work with people on their nutrition, exercise profile, and general health management. When people played a more active role in their own healthcare, they got better. We had great results, but it was not reimbursable by insurance. As a result, people did not follow through over the long-term. Our service was a great concept, but the market was not ready for it."

Five years after Dan's return to pharmacy life, he received another life-changing offer. A friend he'd met as a pharmaceutical rep called him and asked whether he'd like to quadruple his salary. "He kept talking about IT, and at the time, I didn't even know what IT was," laughs Dan. "But my friend knew of my work ethic and character and encouraged me to move to Northern Virginia where he promised he would teach me what I would need to know. So I put my things in storage, packed a couple of suitcases, and moved to Northern Virginia in 1998. Everybody thought I was crazy."

Dan became a salesman of enterprise software and that role eventually turned into work in cyber security. Along with a small group of colleagues, he jumped from business to business over the next few years. He was hired at McAfee which was then bought by Intel. He was very successful at McAfee and won national awards and notoriety. He became a master of putting together large deals. The secret to his success in sales came down to one word—honesty. "I've been through a lot of sales training," Dan remarks. "You can employ all the tactics that you are taught, but if you don't treat people fairly and with respect and aren't honest with them, they won't trust you and won't do business with you."

With the desire to do something different, he left McAfee to go to a small, innovative company that specialized in cloud based cyber security and cyber threat intelligence.

The work was rewarding and lucrative, but it was also stressful. "Cybersecurity is very exciting, has a lot of intrigue and there are always new threats," observes Dan. "There was always a new crisis that needed to be addressed."

"I remember the first large transaction I did, and the commission that I earned," says Dan. "Big deals don't happen easily or quickly so it took a long time to get that commission. When the deal was finally done, and I received the big commission, it was kind of hollow. I realized that money did not make me happy. Money is nice, it allows you to get the things you need and want, but it doesn't buy happiness." In 2017, Dan decided to leave the cybersecurity world and find out what he could build on his own. Thus, Golden Rule was born.

As a leader, Dan stresses the importance of setting clear expectations. "Whether you are a kid or an adult, everyone likes to know the rules up front," he asserts. "Sometimes people don't know or leaders don't say exactly what they want and expect. People need to know right away, what's good, what's bad, and what's expected. So I try to set those very quickly. Asking questions and communicating is good because people don't know what you're thinking. Just be open and honest, and treat people with respect."

Dan has a strong Christian faith and is a Deacon at his church. Dan and the other deacons work together to help members of the community who are struggling with their bills and who aren't getting enough food, clothing and other aspects of daily life. "No one in NOVA should have to worry about having enough food," reflects Dan. "I have also taken my daughter on Missions trips. I think it's important that young people learn to help others."

As his father did throughout his childhood, Dan stresses the importance of a good education to young people. "Don't go to college just to go," he encourages. "Get an education that's going to serve you well. An education that you'll be able to get a job in or that will sustain you until you find the right opportunity. Remember that it's okay to change careers. Internships are a great way to try something and confirm whether it is something you like. You'll either realize you are still passionate about it or you'll learn that it's not what you want to do. You can't lose. So listen to the voice in the back of your head; it's almost never wrong."

Luiz Lobo

New City, Small Town, Big City

When Luiz Lobo was growing up in Brazil, a black and white picture was on his wall of a man he did not know. One day, at the age of nine, he asked his father whom the man was, assuming it was some distant relative. The picture was of U.S. President Abraham Lincoln, Luiz's father's hero.

Luiz's father grabbed the picture and sat with Luiz on his bed. He told Luiz the story of Lincoln—his values, his life, and his legacy. Luiz's father was a Mason, belonging to the local lodge and doing community work through the organization; he liked that Lincoln and the other Founding Fathers had been Masons as well. From that time onward, Luiz felt connected to the United States.

In school, Luiz did very well, and he decided to figure out how to get to the U.S. At the age of 16, he applied to a competitive foreign exchange student program called AFS Intercultural Programs (AFS).

"There were 169 candidates for only five spots within the regional chapter," recalls Luiz. "It then became a national competition.

AFS began as the American Ambulance Field Service, a volunteer ambulance corps created in April 1915 by A. Piatt Andrew. It was transformed from a wartime humanitarian aid organization into a groundbreaking international secondary school exchange, volunteer and intercultural learning organization with a noble vision: to help build a more peaceful world by promoting understanding among cultures. "As drivers became friends, they decided to send their kids to live with each other's families because they didn't want something like this to ever happen again," explains Luiz.

As part of the competition, Luiz had to master history, reading and writing tests, and successfully debate other challengers. The contest lasted over a year and a half before Luiz was finally admitted as an exchange student to the U.S. and sent to tiny Plainview, Minnesota.

"I was asking, Minne-what?" laughs Luiz. "I had heard of New York, Los Angeles, Chicago, and other big cities but was not aware of the state of Minnesota. What I learned when I came here was that it wasn't at all as you saw in the movies. There was that aura of the Heartland that I really believed in and the values I learned when I came here. The people in Plainview were honest and hardworking."

Luiz has written his own American success story as founder and CEO of Lobocast Communications. His career has included stints as a photographer, reporter, news anchor, producer and more. Today, he calls on the communications skills he honed during his journalism career to help individuals, corporations and organizations with their strategic communications needs.

Lobocast offers a variety of services. Individuals can use the firm to improve their verbal, non-verbal and vocal skills. Executives often seek them out ahead of important conferences and presentations. Corporations use Lobocast for crisis communications services; in other words, when a firm needs to represent itself well in the media, they turn to Lobocast to manage and guide their public presence.

Additionally, Luiz uses his years of experience in video production to assist companies with promotional or informational video projects. Firms approach with a project in mind, Luiz gathers a crew, writes the scripts, and serves as Senior Producer/Director of the final product.

Finally, he's established himself as a masterful event coordinator who can be counted on to pull off genuinely massive events. "I handle hard-to-accomplish events," Luiz explains. "I've been involved in global affairs that had over 240,000 people attending within four days. I was brought into that project about eleven months beforehand, and everything was chaotic. I like trouble shooting.

"I like to help people, organizations and governments struggling to accomplish what they were tasked with. They hire me to come in and get the house organized and tell them what they need to prioritize and focus upon."

The last three major projects Luiz worked on were all for the UN, including the world's first Indigenous Peoples' Games, which took place in both Brazil and Canada. Indigenous athletes from over 38 countries competed, including the U.S. Organizing the event involved directly liaising with the then-President of Brazil, the embassies, the U.S. Department of State and stakeholders worldwide.

Luiz has had a passion for journalism and communications since childhood. He was born in Brasilia, also referred to as "New City," in 1966. The city was new back then. Brazil had been contemplating moving the Capital inland from Rio de Janeiro for some time, and in 1960, they found Brasilia to be a strategic place. Today, it's home to over four million residents, but at the time, much of the city was still empty. Luiz remembers the city in the early 1970s as a Wonderland-like adventure park for a young kid. Everywhere he turned, there was construction, bulldozers, empty pipes and undeveloped open space. The dirt in Brasilia was red, and Luiz remembers coming home or arriving at his grandmother's house covered in the bright soil.

When he was only six years old, he received a tape recorder as a gift. It ignited his passion for interviewing. "Well, it was actually my mother who got the tape recorder as a gift from my father," laughs Luiz. "But right away, I decided that tape recorder was mine. I went around and interviewed everyone in the family, including my sisters and cousins. I asked them questions such as what's your name, how old you are, and what you like doing the most? I'm sure we still have those tapes somewhere."

Luiz's father was a pharmaceutical salesman while he was growing up and would often be on the road for long periods, sometimes a month or longer. He drove across the country in an old VW Beetle. Luiz's mother, meanwhile, was primarily a homemaker, but over time began a side business making cakes, sweets and other baked goods for parties, weddings and birthdays. Although it was the 1970s, she showed a flair for entrepreneurship, and women began showing up at the house to take her culinary lessons.

When Luiz was nine, his father took him on one of his long business trips which became another wonderful memory for Luiz. He has three younger sisters, and he notes that his home life was very matriarchal. He had a seemingly infinite number of aunts and female cousins. Some male bonding time with dad was exhilarating.

Luiz excelled academically, and on the athletic side, he became a strong sprinter for the track team. His exchange year in Minnesota began after graduating from high school in Brazil, meaning he repeated his senior year. He wanted to finish high school in the U.S. and use the opportunity to learn English, with which he was only passingly familiar before his trip.

Adjusting to a new country, new home and new language was hard, but Luiz was equal to the task. His host parents were working-class, simple people, not upper-middle-class and certainly not wealthy. His host father was a farmer, and his host mother did hair out of the home, somewhat reminiscent of his own mother's entrepreneurial skills. Some of the other kids teased him, particularly about his language skills and accent, but he found a mentor in his English teacher, Mr. Gerzevske.

Mr. Gerzevske was tough, and most of the students were afraid of him. He loved Shakespeare and addressed students formally, referring to Luiz as "Mr. Lobo." On Luiz's first paper, Mr. Gerzevske gave him an "F." Another time, he tasked Luiz to write a report about the book *The Old Man and the Sea*. Struggling with the text, Luiz wrote his report about the movie adaptation instead, which he had already seen. Mr. Gerzevske asked Luiz to stay after class, but instead of punishing him, he offered his help. "He told me if you want to learn English the way we speak it in America, come to my office every day after school," remembers Luiz. "I'll teach you anything you want to learn." So he did; he mentored me. He even taught me slang and curse words. At the end of the year, he invited me to have dinner with him and his wife. I was probably one of the few students who ever went to his house. I graduated with an A- in his class."

While in Minnesota, Luiz wanted to make some extra money over and above the small stipend he received from the exchange program and was able to get a job in the news industry. He walked into the local newspaper's office, announced that he was a photographer, and the paper hired him at $20 per photo they used.

After his year in the AFS exchange program, Luiz returned to Brazil. With his improved English language skills, he spent a year teaching English in a private school before moving on to radio broadcasting. He liked the work but wanted to return to the U.S. Luiz reached out to a friend, Matthew Garber. Matt was also an AFS student, who had lived with Luiz's family in Brazil. Luiz went to San Francisco for a year before Matt's parents invited him to stay with them in Corydon, Iowa.

Matt's hometown was tiny—even smaller than Plainview, Minnesota. Once again, Luiz found himself back in small-town America. "Matt and I played the guitar. I taught him and he is now much better than I am. We used to play at home gatherings and parties. Luiz began working at a grocery store and later as a bartender in a small Italian restaurant. His new host mother—whom he refers to as "Mama Garber"—owned beehives and produced honey. Luiz helped develop a logo for her business and traveled to other small towns to sell and deliver her honey products to nearby stores.

After some time in Iowa, Luiz returned to Brazil to start college. He entered a radio broadcast journalism program. At the age of 20, he did his first national story for television, a biographical piece about a Holocaust survivor, Stanislaw Szmajzner. "Szlomo" was one of 58 known prisoners to escape the Sobibór extermination camp in Poland successfully. Inspired by his story and legacy, Luiz remembers this interview well. At around this time, he also married his first wife.

With some experience in the journalism field under his belt, Luiz returned to the U.S. to begin a communications program at the University of Iowa. Shortly after, he started his graduate work in Multimedia. Luiz took a job as an executive producer for PBS Iowa. At PBS, he began co-producing fascinating documentaries about nature and history. The U.S. Department of Education awarded Luiz and his team a $4.5 million grant to develop interactive videos and other multimedia educational projects about the Mississippi River. "With that and another local grant, I was about to develop a three-and-a-half-year project," nods Luiz. "I became something of a pioneer in digital television and produced the very first 16x9 broadcast in the U.S., working with engineers."

For 14 years, Luiz remained in the U.S. His two daughters were born in Iowa. He spent time in Atlanta and Chicago, continuing to pursue a successful career in TV journalism, before realizing he would return to Brazil. His youngest sister, 31, had just passed away. His parents were distraught. Luiz felt the need to be closer to the whole family. A year later, his mother also passed away at the age of 62. Luiz was divorced by this time.

"When I went back, I began producing stories for networks, including CNN International," Luiz relates. "When they needed a story in Central Brazil, they would often call me. I would produce interviews and stories in English, and they would air it here on CNN or CNN International. I also did pieces for Discovery Channel and was a local producer on a show for the History Channel, called "Searching for the Truth," a series where we went around the world to find the truth about the history of different places."

He also continued his focus on environmental topics, spending more than four years working on a documentary project about the Amazon Rainforest with four friends from Iowa. "Partly because of that and because of my other experience, I got a phone call," recalls Luiz. "It was from one of the most famous anchors in Brazil, Ana Paula Padrão. She asked me to come to Sao Paolo and fill a position at the station as a weatherman and special assignment environment reporter."

For the role, Luiz was sent to exotic, far-flung locations to report, even doing a series on Antarctica where he visited the scientific stations of U.S., Chilean and Brazilian researchers. Then one day, Ana had another question for him. "She told me she was exhausted and needed to take a break," Luiz describes. "She said she needed someone to replace her and that I had to get in the studio right away. So I became a national news anchor in Brazil just like that."

Around this time, Luiz's daughters often visited Brazil and decided they wanted to move full-time for a while. They were still young—12 and 14. Their decision to come live with their father provoked another move. Luiz decided to return to where he was born, Brasilia, where he still had extended family. He knew that while he worked his high-powered job, he wouldn't be able to keep a close enough eye on his girls in fast-paced Sao Paulo. He went back to Brazil's Capital, the once-New City.

The girls stayed in Brazil until it was time to graduate high school; at that point, Luiz insisted they go back to get an American high school degree. He stayed behind for several more years to finish out some outstanding projects, including the UN's massive Sustainable Development Conference, Rio + 20. Lobocast was up and running, and Luiz had already expanded into the events space. He also produced several corporate videos, working with private and government agencies.

In the process of planning the First World Games of Indigenous People in 2015, Luiz came to D.C. Almost immediately, he fell in love again with a large city and knew he wanted to stay. "I visited the State Department by invitation of the U.S. Embassy in Brazil to talk about the UN endeavor with the Games," Luiz recalls. "This is where I knew I wanted to live," he said.

Luiz remarried a few weeks later in Brazil, to his wife, Cintia. Soon after their marriage, the couple relocated to the D.C. area. "I met her through common interests, such as ice cream," says Luiz with a smile. "But that is another story. She is a significant influence and inspiration in my life. Everyone in her family is very successful and hardworking.

Both of his parents have also been important role models in his life and career. "My father is hardworking, is very ethical and is devoted to the family," Luiz describes. "And from my mother, I got tenacity. She was a fighter; she was a cancer survivor for over 23 years before she ultimately died from it. She was writing a book about her life, and when she died, we published the book. I get through tough times with faith, friends, family, love and prayers. I always look up to the memory of my mother and how well she fought. I admire her optimism and positivity."

As a leader, Luiz considers himself strategic, with a coaching mindset. "I want to make sure everybody on the team gets what's best for them," he reflects. "I try to get everyone in the place where they belong. One of the things I've had to do many times in the various roles I have filled is to build strong teams. I love building a team and seeing them work together."

Luiz emphasizes that young folks entering the working world should focus on quality over perfection and continue developing a skill set. "Whether it's your first day or whether you're a senior executive, everyone needs to continue to develop their communications skills."

Today, Luiz is happily settled in Washington, D.C., and as a bonus, he could finally bring his father to see an important landmark—the Lincoln Memorial. "He was so proud, he cried," smiles Luiz. "Whatever kind of connection he has with Lincoln, it's strong. I feel that connection with the U.S., as well. The most important place to me is where my heart and values are. And that's here."

BERNHARDT

WEALTH MANAGEMENT

Francesco Marra

Heart of a Champion

Francesco Marra grew up in beautiful Naples, Italy, where the sun always shines and the kids spend as much time in the water as on the land. At the age of 21, he had already been a professional water polo player for more than five years, working his way through several of the major and national leagues and winning tournaments and championships along the way. In Italy, playing professional water polo wasn't necessarily a way to get rich, but it could certainly be a livelihood; several of Francesco's teammates recently retired in their early 40s.

Francesco credits his mother with teaching him the resiliency and tenacity needed to succeed. Her positive disposition, emotional support, and consistent encouragement were the exact type of emotional education that enabled the Marra brothers to realize their goals in life. Francesco's parents had divorced when he was only ten, and his mother and her new beau (an American citizen) chose to marry and move to the United States. Francesco's younger brother went along with her, and within a year, Francesco, ready for a big change, felt compelled to move, too.

The decision, like many others he has made throughout his life, was a bold one. He went from being a successful and prominent person in the community he loved to being a stranger in a strange land. He couldn't speak the language, didn't know the culture, and hadn't gone to any sort of business school. He had a few years of culinary education, but without English, he had to start from the very bottom as a prep cook in an Italian restaurant. But he did bring one important asset with him: the heart of a champion.

Demonstrating the same commitment and focus that had made him a star water polo player, Francesco set his mind to succeeding in his adopted country. For 12 months, he intensively studied English every morning until 1:30 and then went to his job every afternoon at 3:00. He completed homework assignments on the metro and still found time to go out and have fun with his younger brother Emiliano in his new city.

As his English improved, he also learned Spanish since he was working in kitchens where most of his coworkers were from Latin America. "For a while my Spanish was better than my English," laughs Francesco. His aptitude for languages and for showing up worked in his favor. "I was the guy who would come in two hours early to see how a certain piece of meat was cut," remembers Francesco.

His dedication was noticed, and in a short span of time, he went from Kitchen Porter, to cooking on the line, to making pasta and entrees, to becoming sous-chef, to finally being promoted to Executive Chef within a mere three-year period. He was even featured in the *Washingtonian* as one of the best up-and-coming chefs in the DC area. It was a shockingly meteoric rise.

Despite the many challenges he faced, Francesco's boldness still wasn't exhausted. He finally found himself earning success and credibility in his community, and once again, he found himself thirsting for something more. He had been told he would be able to buy into the restaurant where he worked, but when that fell through, he knew he had to think about the future. He talked to Emiliano, and once again the pair decided to leave their relatively stable life behind for a new adventure.

The brothers founded a food import and delivery company, starting out with a single van and driving to New York City once a week to pick up the goods and deliver to DC restaurants. The decision was definitely a pay cut; Francesco had gone from a cushy $80,000 a year gig as an executive chef, to, in his words "barely paying rent." However, he and his brother were thinking long term. "I knew I had to take a step backward, to go forward," explains Francesco. "I knew it wouldn't be as much money right away, but I had to take the risk. I knew I had the commitment, the focus, and the work ethic. I knew long-term, this was going to pay off."Today, Francesco says his most prized possession is his old business card from that first business; it reminds him of how far he had to go, and how high he has climbed. Over time, they rented a 1,000 square foot warehouse, their first; by the time they sold the business in 2014, they had acquired a 24,000 square foot warehouse and ten trucks on the road. They also boasted about 40 employees and peaked at over $7 million in annual revenue.

Through the 2007 economic recessions while running the food distribution business, the brothers decided they'd like to diversify into importing equipment and vertically integrate the opportunities with their existing food distribution clientele. Around this time, Francesco's older brother Vincenzo, came over from Italy with his family so he could reunite with his family and join the business. The brothers sensed a good business opportunity with brick ovens and began importing ovens from a certain manufacturer in Italy. Soon thereafter, however, they began receiving feedback from their American buyers. They were told the ovens were outdated and didn't have the technological innovation of some of the other modern options. So the brothers approached the Italian manufacturer with ideas for improvement. "We told them their product is antiquated and that it's not up to the standards of American manufacturers. They said 'no, we've been doing this for three generations and we're not going to make any changes'," recalls Francesco. "That's how our company, Marra Forni, was born." The brothers founded an oven company with Francesco as the President and CEO, Emiliano as VP of Sales, and Vincenzo, as the COO.

Today, Marra Forni handcrafts beautiful ovens with teams of masons and exquisite personalization. The ovens range in price anywhere from $10,000 to $60,000, because the final product is a one-of-a-kind artisanal piece of architecture and art. Everything on the oven is customizable, from the base to the tile. Marra Forni even offers on-sight masons who can build the oven inside a restaurant or kitchen if moving the oven into the space would be impossible. "They are made to spec," affirms Francesco. "We only have two machines in the masonry department. The rest are made by hand by our masons, and we only produce on demand. Today, we manufacture an average of 400 commercial ovens annually, have eight figures in revenue and are growing double digits every year. We are also planning to start our residential division by 2021."

The company was co-founded by the Marra brothers in 2011 as a builder of brick pizza ovens with some of the components being imported from manufacturers in Italy. Today, they import only the raw material from Italy; a proprietary refractory brick stamped with their last name and made with special materials to help retain heat. It is rated for over 2000 degrees Fahrenheit which allows it to cook very efficiently, consistently, and at a much higher speed.

The real turning point came in 2014, when the brothers chose to sell the food distribution business. It was then that Emiliano decided to depart the family business and go into business on his own. Francesco and Vincenzo decided to focus more fully on developing the oven business and expanding their capabilities. That year, they created the first rotating deck oven with a touchscreen controlled smart oven that allows users to customize the rotation of the oven anywhere from 15-280 seconds. "This is extremely important for a chef," explains Francesco. "If a chef wants to put processes in place to eliminate some of the errors in the kitchen, you can customize the rotation. If your perfect pizza heats in 95 seconds, you can set the rotation to 95 seconds and it's ready. The oven has the same footprint as a regular oven but can probably do double or triple the business. We have customers who have done as many as 250 pizzas in one hour, just with one oven." Marra Forni is the only company in the U.S. that offers the rotating deck oven.

Although they began making ovens for local mom and pop restaurants, today Marra Forni's clients include high ranking restaurant groups, boutique hotels, large chain hotels (Hyatt, Hilton, Marriot), stadiums, colleges, universities, hospitals (Johns Hopkins), retirement homes, and more. They have been the preferred oven provider for Whole Foods (almost 150 installations) and Wegmans for the last two years, and have also sold to Shop Rite, Balducci's, and other grocery stores. The list does not end there, they have also established good business relationships with large food service companies like the Compass Group, Aramark, and Sodexo, as well as outfitting the VIP club in the Washington Redskins' stadium. "People think a brick oven is just for pizzerias," points out Francesco. "But it can be utilized for any style of cooking—braising, roasting, searing, or baking. You can use it to make bread in the morning or you can slow roast overnight. I always say, it's not just a pizza oven, it's a brick oven cooking solutions. I think we've done a phenomenal job being recognized as a pizza oven. However, there are 70,000 pizzerias in the U.S. and about 700,000 restaurants so we're going to start to change the focus and change the perception of what people have for our brick ovens."

Francesco's aspirations for Marra Forni are high. The company has expanded to a 27,000 square foot of space for manufacturing and storage, which brings their total square footage to about 51,000. They now have about 60 employees and have sold ovens on 5 continents and in 23 countries. Still, the bulk of their business is in the U.S., and Francesco plans to expand that. "We have four business developers in the U.S., two in Mexico for the Latin American market, and one that lives in Milan doing Europe and the Middle East," says Francesco. "We want to become a truly worldwide company whether that's by opening up manufacturing somewhere else or by acquiring companies strategically." Additionally, he wants to expand into residential ovens in 2021.

The brothers' goal in launching the business was simple: they just want to enable restaurants and chefs to meet their potential. "I'm in this for the best interests of the customer." affirms Francesco. "I want our customer to be very successful. We make a great product so they can be successful in their story, in their life, and in their careers. I've been there, I've suffered, and I've had my own restaurant that closed after seven years in business. I don't want anyone to go through what I have experienced. The restaurant business is probably the industry with the highest failure rate in the country. With our product, we hope we can help people with their operation, with their production, and with their cooking technology."

Amazingly, Marra Forni Ovens isn't the only venture Francesco is running. The brothers also have a catering business that contracts with the Italian embassy to provide food for the ministers and important personages passing through. As the only embassy with a full restaurant on Massachusetts Avenue (the triangle of the world's most prominent embassies), it often attracts world leaders from nearby embassies, particularly the English, Brazilian, Japanese, and Swedish officials. Their contract with the embassy was just renewed for another six years, and they plan to expand their catering services further.

Additionally, they're running The Pizza University and Culinary Arts Center, a self-funded pizza school that they are in the process of turning into a non-profit business. "In Italy they have over 1,000 pizza schools, and Italy is the size of Florida!" exclaims Francesco. "In the U.S., they teach all kinds of culinary classes but nobody teaches pizza. So in 2018 we decided to open the school. All we want to do is give back to the community that made us successful. We want to help people get into the business and make sure they have the tools and information to do so successfully." The school offers courses three days a week, and students learn every step of the process of making fantastic pizza—from choosing the ingredients, to understanding the difference between types of flours, to learning to stretch the dough, and to learning how to properly use the oven. "We're hoping to have a Pizza University in every region," nods Francesco. "And we're getting some huge endorsements from industry leaders and food and beverage companies. I'm also working with Veteran's Affairs, to start doing pizza classes to help rehabilitate veterans. We want to give back and pay it forward."

The brothers have certainly come a long way since their childhood in Naples. Although their home was beautiful, their lives weren't always easy. Their father had some bad habits, and after Francesco's parents divorced, the boys spent little time with him. It was a defining moment for Francesco to experience the departure of his father and to watch the suffering his mother went through. "I decided at that moment I really wanted to be a better person," he remembers. "If I was ever a father, I knew I wanted to be a role model and to give my kids what I didn't receive from my father when I was young. I realized that family is everything and that you have to support each other. I promised myself that I would be a better human being and that I wouldn't make the same mistakes my dad made."

Francesco's mother and her three boys were taken in by family—Francesco's maternal grandfather and his beloved uncles. Without their care and support, the family would've been out on the street. Francesco loved playing with his cousins, and came to think of his uncles, and especially his grandfather, like fathers to him. He remembers wonderful family trips to nearby Sorrento and remembers learning to cook from his grandmother. She taught him to make typical Neapolitan dishes, from fresh pasta, ragu, seafood dishes, and Italian desserts. "Nonna gave me inspiration to become a chef," smiles Francesco.

Francesco's sense of focus was always one of his greatest strengths. He is also admired by his colleagues for his innovative and unique approach to both business and design. He loved playing in the water and followed in his uncle's footsteps to embrace water polo. By the time he was 15, he began playing with the First Division Team. In the meantime, he was also accepted to cooking school, where he began studying and planning for his career beyond water polo.

"I was playing water polo seven days a week on several different teams," recalls Francesco. "I made a lot of sacrifices every day because I loved what I was doing. When everyone went on vacation, I was training with the Italian National team. I was really focused. When I do something, I really devote my time and commit to it. If I do it, I've got to do it really well."

Francesco found mentors among the older players and coaches, and eventually, after joining the military for a year of compulsory service, he made the Italian National Military Team. With them, he travelled to St. Petersburg, Russia for the World Cup, where they won the Finals and became World Champions. He had held his own against the absolute best.

When his mother and brother made the big move to the U.S., Francesco knew it was time for him to try something new, too. He was already a champion, and he knew he could do it all over again and perform at a championship level. It was then that he picked up stakes, started over in the U.S., learned English and Spanish, and started washing dishes in restaurants.

Over the years, Francesco owned other businesses outside of the food distribution company. He co-founded with his brothers and a few other friends an Italian restaurant in 2007, the one he mentioned failed after the Great Recession. But he was fortunate and smart to have diversified his resources enough to be able to pull through that period of time.

In 2003, Francesco met Ana, the love of his life, who had also immigrated to the U.S. at the age of 11. The two married in 2005, and since then have had three children—Sophia, Francesco Lorenzo, and Luca. Ana is a brilliant, professional woman who works as a CPA. "She's an auditor and she audits me every day," jokes Francesco. "She's an amazing mother, a wonderful companion, and a great partner. Without her sacrifice, I couldn't have done what I have done. I especially admire her integrity and feel blessed to have her by my side." All three of his kids are active, with the boys choosing to play soccer, and Sophia practicing ballet three hours daily. Sophia hopes to go on to become a professional ballerina.

As a leader, Francesco reflects that he is equal parts democratic and autocratic. "It depends on the situation," he elaborates. "I'm not the kind of person who decides that what I think is the only solution. I'm collaborative. I like people to share their thoughts and ideas. I listen and take into consideration their comments and suggestions. As far as vision goes, I have high aspirations. I want to be a worldwide company. We're very committed to being a leader in our industry."

To young people entering the working world today, Francesco advises having a strong work ethic. "There's no secret to success, and success is not an accident," he says. "You need to work extremely hard. You need to be focused and committed, consistent and persistent. You need to be willing to sacrifice. Without all of those things, success could be difficult to achieve. I came here without any detailed and specific training. Yes, I had some culinary training, but it was insufficient. I had to learn. I had to start from the bottom. I was an immigrant who didn't know the culture. That is why my first business card is valuable to me. It represents my journey from 1,000 square feet to 51,000 square feet. You can achieve anything if you're really committed."

He also stresses that a little competition never hurt anyone. "I don't see it as a threat," he smiles. "It's great for business because it drives you to do better every day. There's space for everyone. At the end of the day, the best company will prevail." To finish he evokes to the new generation, there is only one thing you cannot buy in life and it is time, so don't waste any time!

Anne Meltzer

The Magic Happens Out There

Anne Meltzer comes from a long line of strong women. Her grandmother worked in a children's clothing store while she was growing up, and Anne remembers playing behind the counter, learning to use the register, and dressing in high-end dresses bought with the employee discount. Every Friday night, she would go to her grandmother's house for dinner. "She was tiny, but you didn't mess with her," laughs Anne. "She was feisty and fiercely independent, but she was fun to be around. We were very close." Anne considers an Afghan her grandmother handknitted for her to be one of her most prized possessions.

Anne is just as close with her mother, a teacher turned real estate agent turned VP of Marketing of a Title company. "She helped that company explode," recalls Anne. "She was so good at what she did. In her role, she planned parties and events, and helped create an image for the company that led to extraordinary growth." She remembers that her mom led by example as a working woman and inspired her to be ambitious in her career. Anne even wrote an essay about her mother when asked to write about her hero in school. In a later time, Anne believes her mother might have gone even further. "Mom once told me a story about a meeting of her friends at the country club," recalls Anne. "They were discussing whether they'd rather be born when they were born or now. My mother was the only one who said she'd rather be born when her kids were born. She felt that she could have been anything if she was born later. When she was young, if a girl went to college, she got a degree to teach, to be a social worker, to be a nurse, or to be a secretary. Girls weren't pushed to have high ambitions. But my mom was tough and a hard worker. In fact, she worked until just a couple years ago. She inspired me to be like her."

It's no surprise, then, that Anne has followed in the footsteps of her grandmother and mother and has become an unmitigated success in her own right. Today, she is the Managing Director of Tucker & Meltzer Valuation Advisors, a business she started in May 2006 along with partner Brooke Tucker.

Anne and Brooke met in 2000, after both of the accounting firms they worked for had been acquired by American Express. Brooke decided to leave and start his own firm, Tucker Capital Advisors in January 2004. That same year, Anne took her second maternity leave. Upon returning, she found her workload had been drastically reduced and felt underutilized. She briefly took a job at a small valuation firm, but less than a year later, a major event shook her sense of stability.

"My older son was about to start kindergarten, and my husband was told by his cardiologist that heart surgery was necessary," remembers Anne. "His mitral valve was regurgitating. In that moment I realized, 'I'm not doing this anymore. I'm not working for other people anymore.' I called Brooke because we were still close and told him what I was planning to do. I told him that I was planning to start my own valuation practice."

It turned out to be a fortuitous phone call; Brooke was doing M&A work but a global law firm was sending him more valuation work than he could do alone. He was busy selling five or six businesses and had seven or eight valuations to get done for them. Anne started her own firm but helped Brooke with those valuations. By the following year, Brooke decided he wanted to pull the valuation practice out of his M&A practice. "He said to me, 'I'm going to start Tucker Valuation Advisors,'" smiles Anne. "I told him I thought it was a great idea, but it has the wrong name. I wanted to be a partner. I also pointed out that it would immediately provide me with more credibility if we were partners as opposed to me being an employee. Plus, we were already splitting the fees as if we were partners. He agreed."

Thus, Tucker & Meltzer Valuation Advisors (T&M) was born. In 2007, they hired their first part-time employee, a fellow mom with a flexible schedule. In 2008, they began doing valuations for Employee Stock Ownership Plan (ESOP) clients. "When a business owner decides they want to sell all or part of their business to an ESOP, the ESOP will hire a trustee, and the trustee will hire a financial advisor. We act as the financial advisor for the trustee," explains Anne. Today, about 50% of T&Ms business is ESOP valuations (both annual and transactions), 35% is Estate, Trust and Gift valuations, and the remaining 15% is other types of valuations to support purchase price allocations and 409a valuations, to name a few.

Over the nearly 14 years since its founding, T&M has consistently grown, but they did encounter a major speedbump when Brooke Tucker sadly, passed away from lung cancer in 2016. "We found out he was sick in January, he had surgery in March, and he was expected to survive. He passed away in June, Anne says. "We weren't ready. He had said he was going to stop working at 70, but he was only 65. We had been planning T&M's ten-year anniversary and had to cancel everything."

Suddenly, Anne found herself the sole proprietor of T&M with four strong employees. She had taken on little pieces of the company's business development work over the years, but now she was tasked with taking over everything. She quickly brought on a past employee who she knew was familiar with their systems to help with production while she began evaluating how to move forward with the business. "It was a pivotal moment going from a company with two owners to a company with one owner, me," remembers Anne. "I stepped away from the technical work and flourished in the BD role. I put a lot more systems around the process in an effort to grow the company, and I loved it. I loved meeting with people, talking to people, leading the organization, and managing people. In fact, I thrived in the new environment. Some people are easier to manage than others, but I really enjoy working with each person and understanding what they need to make them more successful."

In 2018, Anne promoted a young employee, Donni Engelhart, to become her new partner in the business. Donni was essential to T&M, and rival firms were already trying to recruit him. Anne knew it would be much more difficult to poach a partner than an employee and offered him the opportunity to buy in. Like Brooke, Anne believes in mentoring. "Donni wanted to grow," she observes. "He was very bright and was making a name for himself, and I knew we needed to keep him. He has been a key player in the success of the company."

By the time Brooke passed away in 2016, T&M had around 30 annual ESOP clients. Today, the team of six staff has 51 annual ESOPs. In three years, the practice has doubled. Besides being active in ESOP trade associations and attending both regional and national conferences, Anne is also active in four estate planning councils and is currently the Past-President of the Baltimore Estate Planning Council. The company is earning 60% more today than it was in 2016.

Anne considers her team at T&M to be a second family to her. "I joke that I manage it like a Jewish mother," she laughs. "I have two families—my family and T&M. I'm so lucky that I get to work with them. We don't track our time at T&M because everybody just gets their job done. We don't track our vacation time because people take their vacations when they need to and work when they need to. Everyone takes professional and personal responsibility which is part of our culture. And we all like and respect one another."

Growing up, Anne always knew she wanted to do something with numbers. From the time she was a girl learning how to count change at her grandmother's cash register until college when she majored in accounting, she loved math and numbers. She spent her childhood years in Baltimore, where both her father's and mother's family came from. Her dad's parents had died when she was very young, and her maternal grandfather passed away when Anne was 9, so she grew up particularly close with her maternal grandmother and her grandmother's father who was 102 when he died.

Hebrew school was a big part of Anne's upbringing. She went to Hebrew school on Sundays, and after school on Mondays and Wednesdays for six hours a week of studies. Anne has an older sister, and the family moved twice within Baltimore before she was in fourth grade. They ended up in Pikesville where they found a strong Jewish community, and Anne attended many bar and bat mitzvahs in her adolescent years. In the summers, Anne went to sleepaway camp for four weeks during the summer and then came home and played tennis and golf at a local country club.

It was during high school that Anne realized she loved working. As soon as she got her driver's license, Anne got a job working 16 hours a week at a local department store. She continued to work all through high school at various jobs but never less than 16-20 hours a week while still achieving a high GPA.

While Anne had hoped to go to University of Michigan, for financial reasons, she ended up attending University of Maryland, College Park. Anne got into the business school right away and planned to double major in chemistry and business. However, after nearly failing her freshman Honors Chemistry class, she decided to focus on business and major in accounting. She pledged a sorority where she thrived and became Philanthropy Chairperson and later, the House Manager. "It was very good for me, because it gave me leadership opportunities," she reflects.

Meanwhile, she continued working 16-24 hours a week throughout college and tried to be strategic about her jobs. During her junior year, she got a job working at a women's clothing store where she knew she'd be able to get a discount on business clothes for future interviews. After her junior year, she landed an internship at Ernst & Young. While she received a post-college job offer from E&Y, she did not find the work interesting and decided to accept a position at Wolpoff & Company, a large local accounting firm in Baltimore.

Wolpoff immediately saw potential in her. She was put to work as a consultant in the long-term care practice and did some work on the marketing side as well. "I was 23 years old and going to state and national conferences where I represented the firm and tried to market our long-term care practice," remembers Anne. "From the start, I knew I wasn't the type to sit at a desk all day." Although Anne liked Wolpoff, she was still young and restless. Less than two years after she started her job, she came home with a proposal for her roommate and tried to convince her they should quit their jobs and go to Europe. Anne had just started dating her future husband, Richard, but she wasn't thinking about marriage yet. Besides, she knew she might never have an opportunity like this again to see the world. Anne and her roommate, Aileen, packed their suitcases, updated their resumes, and left for their adventure.

The experience was life-changing, but after six months, they were ready to come home. They had found jobs in London as waitresses but the wages were meager and people didn't tip. They were tired and out of money when Anne's mother played a little trick on her. "She told me she'd run into my old boss from Wolpoff, and he wanted me back to work," laughs Anne. "So we came back home, I called him, and he said, 'I have no idea what you're talking about.' My mom lied to me to get me to come home. But he did give me my job back!" Anne stayed with Wolpoff for six more years until the business was bought out by American Express in 1998. And two years later, she and Brooke were fatefully brought together.

In the meantime, Anne and Richard were married, and he has been a constant source of support ever since. "Richard was also raised by strong women so he's not afraid of strong women," she reflects. "He is an exceptionally supportive person. He supported my decision when I wanted to quit my job, give up a nice income, and take a risk to go out on my own. I like to cook dinner and be a mom, but I'm not married to a man who has 'expectations' that he's going to have all of that taken care of for him. We're equal partners in everything. He's creative and a great problem solver. When I do run into issues, he is without a doubt one of my first sounding boards that I go to. He even created the T&M logo!"

Anne's prized afghan also has a special relationship to Richard. Her grandmother had made Anne and her sister each an afghan during their childhoods and promised to make them a second as a wedding gift. Anne's sister married young and got her second afghan, but Anne was still single when her grandmother was getting ill. Anne asked if her grandmother would go ahead and knit a second afghan for her since she was unsure whether she would be alive to see Anne's wedding. A week after her grandmother died, Anne met Richard. "I think my grandmother sent him to me," Anne smiles. "The afghan is heavy, beautiful, and big enough for a king size bed!"

As a leader, Anne stresses the importance of collaboration. "I don't make any decision in a vacuum," she affirms. "If the decision is going to affect other people, I want their input on that decision. Another big thing for me is that I don't get worked up anymore. Every problem has a solution and that solution is usually easier to find when you stay calm and thoughtful."

To young people entering the working world today, Anne advises them to pursue a career they enjoy. "Do something you like doing," she asserts. "Don't look to be a partner somewhere, don't look to your endgame yet. Enjoy your job while you have it and take as much from it as you can. In addition, put yourself outside of your comfort zone. Push yourself and push the people around you. If you want to attend a meeting, just ask. A friend of mine who's a therapist always says, 'The magic happens outside of your comfort zone so don't be too afraid to go there.'"

Shariq Mirza

All Walls Have Doors

In July 1991, Shariq "Sharick" Mirza came to America from Karachi, Pakistan with $250 in his pocket. His maternal uncle, Sami Uddin Mirza, gave him the $250 on the day he left for the US and played a key role in Sharick's family support structure. His paternal uncle, Anwar Mirza, provided the fuel for Sharick's rocket to escape the gravitational force with a trajectory toward anywhere he dreamed. Anwar purchased Sharick's ticket to the US, gave him an old beater car and helped him pay for a semester of tuition at University of Houston and another semester at Houston Community College. Sharick spent the first month at an aunt's place and then with the paternal uncle for four months. After that, Sharick was on his own—completely independent in a totally new world.

It was hardly an easy transition. At one point, Sharick found himself sleeping in his car in the heat of the Houston summer. He practically worked around the clock, attending school by day and hardly sleeping three hours a night. Some years he worked the graveyard shift at a local 7-Eleven, where he was held up at gunpoint more times than he can remember. "You know what they say in books and movies, that your life flashes before your eyes when you're about to die?" asks Sharick. "All of that happened to me. It was like a movie started playing about my life. I knew I was going to die. This guy was holding a gun to my face, and I was calm. I was really calm. I had no sense of panic at all and was just thinking about my family."

Around this time, Sharick also developed a hacking cough that never seemed to go away; much later, he discovered that the cough was merely a side effect of his severe exhaustion. The cough finally went away after four years when Sharick started his professional life.

"My plan was to be self-sufficient," reflects Sharick. "I had an aunt, uncle and cousins all over, and all of them were self-financed. Nobody gave them charity. All of them worked very hard, and I knew I would have to, too, once I got here. Every summer I used to lose 30 pounds because I would be working 100-hour weeks when I wasn't in school. My mother would get very upset if she saw pictures of me!"

It took Sharick seven years to graduate from college. In that time, he transferred from the University of Houston to Southeastern Oklahoma State University where he completed his Bachelor of Science in Computer Information Systems. He wasn't particularly drawn to computers at the time; instead, he chose his major with an eye toward survival. He knew computer technology was bound to be crucial to the future economy, and he set himself up for success by absorbing everything he could about the field.

It's no wonder Sharick's motto is "All Walls Have Doors," meaning no matter what life throws at you, it's up to you to find a way through. Today, Sharick's success would likely astonish his younger self. As Founder and CEO of Assurety Consulting & Solutions Inc., Sharick guides a 63-employee business that has helped transform government and industry for more than 18 years.

Assurety began in December 2003 as Sharick's personal consulting firm, although he quickly began to expand and hire additional employees. His brother, Tariq Mirza, joined Assurety in 2006, and the brothers worked together to grow the company. His first client was IBM, but he diversified his income by contracting his brother to a previous employer, players in the mortgage industry and Emory University. "We were doing all kinds of things," recalls Sharick. "Then, about eight years ago we decided we need to have a clearer message and strategy about what we do, and we started focusing on the postal, parcel, ecommerce, and logistics industry. Now, our company leads the data governance for the entire postal and parcel industry. Anybody who's sending anything to your home—whether it's Amazon, eBay, JC Penney or Bank of America—those transactions happen through data specifications that Assurety manages today." Assurety's work is so game-changing that the Smithsonian Institution recognized the organization for their transformation of the entire US postal and parcel industry ecosystem. Among other things, Assurety solves complex business and technical problems and provides business consulting, technical and professional services, BI and analytics services to mid-size and large enterprises. Assurety also provides software solutions to automate and streamline workflows, optimize transportation efficiency, provide customer insights, address analytics and profiling, and postage optimization software to the commercial mailing and shipping industry.

As with most start-ups, it hasn't always been smooth-sailing for the firm. Several years back, the company lost a major contract unexpectedly; Assurety had been working sole-source with the USPS when their contracts went to compete. They partnered with IBM, as their work was combined with IBM's tasks, and they lost several tasks on price to a smaller firm. "That was a very stressful time for everyone," remembers Sharick. "But within three months, we were able to find work for 11 of the 13 people who had been on that contract. It was a risk to try to keep them all on our payroll, but I asked them to give me time and promised them I would find work for all of them. We lost money, but we kept nearly all of the employees. And it paid off. Within seven months, we got all of our work back. The small company that won on price could not deliver. So not only did we come back, we grew out of it and doubled the size of the company. Again, all walls have doors, and integrity is critical. My brother Tariq played a key role, and continues to play a key role with his relationships to work with me to win work. And that's why people were willing to help us because we showed goodwill and high integrity and had a legacy of solving their complex problems. People saw that and it has really paid off for us."

At this juncture, Assurety is looking to expand beyond postal logistics and ecommerce work, with an eye toward government contracting for agencies' logistical needs. "We can solve complex logistics, fraud, marketing and operations problems in any industry. Hopefully, we're going through a rebirth," smiles Sharick.

Sharick comes by his commitment to integrity and hard work honestly. Growing up in Karachi, both of his parents served as role models for him and his younger brother. Sharick's father, Asif Mirza Baber, was a professor of philosophy and political science, and promoted an environment of intellectualism in the home. "I would say one of the biggest things he engrained in us was a lot of quotes from philosophers," reflects Sharick. "One of the biggest that he would repeat often was from Emmanuel Kant: 'There is nothing good in this world but goodwill toward others.'"

Sharick's father was smart, educated, wise, humble and highly respected in the community and was often found in the same starched white kurta-pajama. Before Sharick's birth, his father had the traumatic experience of being imprisoned in China on suspicion of being a CIA agent, and afterward suffered psychological problems including PTSD and schizophrenic episodes. As a young child, Sharick remembers that his father was too ill to work, and instead stayed home with his children. But that never lessened his sons' admiration for him.

"My father helped out the neighbors, the elderly and anyone he could help," Sharick relates. "He was incredibly principled. At one point he was offered a position as Minister of Communications, a position accompanied by a thousand acres of land by the newly elected government of Bhutto (PPP). It was offered to him because, as a student, he had already won two national student union elections on his own in Pakistan. He was one of the key founders of DSF (Democratic Students Federation). He led many changes for the students in the country including student discounts on public transportation and led the movement against the army dictatorship. He always spoke his mind, and they wanted to quiet him. He turned them down."

Those principles were the key lesson Sharick's father passed on to him. One time, Sharick found money on the ground and brought it home. His father walked with Sharick to where he found it and told him to leave it there explaining that the owner of the money would most likely return looking for it once he discovered it was missing. It wasn't his money which meant it wasn't his to take. The experience stuck with Sharick throughout his life.

As Sharick got older, his father recovered sufficiently to begin teaching again, offering philosophy lessons to adults and returning to university. He went back to school at the age of 60 and earned a law degree which taught Sharick to never give up learning, but to continue to set goals for self-improvement and always look for the next step on both professional and personal levels.

In the meantime, his mother, Fozia Talat, had been the family breadwinner. She was something of an anomaly in that era, a college-educated woman in Pakistan. She had been lucky; her older sisters hadn't been allowed to pursue a higher education, but they advocated for her schooling to their older brothers and parents. After receiving her undergraduate degree, she demonstrated a natural knack for entrepreneurship, opening a school in Sharick's childhood home and charging tuition to neighborhood kids. Sharick attributes his business sense and entrepreneurial spirit to the example set by his mother. Among other things, she taught tailoring and oil painting. She was an accomplished artist, and Sharick considers the two paintings of hers hanging in his house among his most prized possessions.

He also keeps with him some of his father's diaries. His father journaled religiously, keeping a daily diary throughout his life. By the time he passed away, he left behind stacks of his writing about the fascinating life he'd lived. Unfortunately, some of the books were lost during the family's move from Pakistan. Sharick's father happened to pass away during a visit to the US, and his mother decided to stay with him which meant it was several years before Sharick could travel to retrieve his father's belongings from a storage unit. But those that he was able to preserve are priceless artifacts of his father's life.

Sharick grew up in a neighborhood that was largely migrants from India known as PECHS (Pakistan Employees Cooperative Housing Society). The atmosphere was intellectual; most of the residents were highly educated, professional and middle-class Muslims. The family home was always busy and was frequently packed with people. It was a three-story house with renters on the first floor, a teacher at St. Patrick School Master Bruno Lucas, and another Christian family (the first floor was split into two apartments). His grandparents lived with his parents and brother on the middle floor, and an aunt and cousins on the third floor. The aunt's husband, Sharick's uncle, who was a high-ranking officer in the Air Force had been tragically killed outside the court during a trial in a politically-motivated murder, so the family moved in as was typical in Pakistan at the time. Having so many cousins and extended family around was usual for the time and place, but Sharick feels grateful to have grown up with so many great connections and the influence of his older cousins, many of whom ended up in America, as well. It was like growing up in a free Montessori school system.

"Growing up, our veranda would be full of kids in the afternoon, for my mom's school," smiles Sharick. "She was doing that since I can remember. They would come around 1 or 2 in the afternoon, and stay until 5 p.m. She would help them with homework, tutor them in math, English, science and help with whatever they needed. When she wasn't teaching, she would tailor and sell clothes." Her brothers and a paternal uncle helped out the family financially, too.

As a kid, Sharick loved playing sports with the other neighborhood children. Most of it wasn't formalized; it was simply kicking the soccer ball around. But Sharick had a talent for both soccer and cricket, and went on to play both in school. He also won high jump titles and became a champion table tennis player. To this day, he plays semi-professional table tennis at local clubs, including at a Maryland table tennis club that is ranked No. 1 in America.

Sharick had an enjoyable childhood, but he still knew he wanted to get out of Karachi. As he put it, he needed to find the door in the wall. His desire to come to America drove him to achieve in school, earn high grades and prepare for a move abroad. An older cousin, Imran Khan, visited Karachi during that time. He still lives in San Jose, is a nuclear scientist by profession and works on nuclear physics, astrophysics, cosmology and inner-core geology as a theorist. He was a role model for most of the kids in the family, a super-genius individual. He gave Sharick 1,200 rupees to take a computer science course, and encouraged him to pursue the field.

Despite considering schools in Australia and the UK, Sharick ultimately chose to attend The University of Houston because he knew he could rely on family in the area as he got on his feet. Still, Sharick was quickly supporting himself on his minimum wage jobs. "It was credit cards and $5 and $6/hour jobs that got me through school as an international student," nods Sharick. "I think I lost a lot of my life expectancy during those years!"

The punishing schedule meant it took longer than usual to finish his degree, but he finally graduated in 1997. By then, he'd already been working at Microsoft for two years in Dallas, which meant he regularly commuted between Dallas and Oklahoma. After graduation, he relocated to Roanoke, Virginia, where he accepted a job at Hollins University as a Programmer/Analyst.

Unsurprisingly, he had heard about the opportunity through another cousin, Kamran Khan, who was the CIO there, and mentioned the job opening to him. Sharick looked into the opportunity and decided to apply. "What I liked about Hollins University was that they had the most advanced technology but didn't have personnel to manage it," describes Sharick. "During my two years there I rarely went home on the weekends. Rather, I worked hard and learned everything I could." Within six months, Sharick was promoted to Project Manager because many folks left Hollins in a short window.

After two years in Roanoke, Sharick decided to make a move to Northern Virginia, where he accepted a role at Conquest Systems. He recalls choosing Conquest because, again, they had the most developed data mining technology in the field. There, he met his most important career mentor, Ron Clark. Ron was known for being abrasive and hard to work with, but for some reason the two of them hit it off. Sharick attributes it to his work habit— that of someone who didn't mind being challenged as long as it meant learning—and with what he was taught to respect his elders.

"He beat everybody up," laughs Sharick, describing Ron's conservative and old-school management style. "But unlike most people, I would go to him willing to take his abuse, which I considered golden nuggets. But because I wanted to learn from him he accepted me more than most. I learned things from Ron that I would never learn in school or at work from anyone. He was highly experienced in management, leadership, and soft skills."

Around the time of his move to Northern Virginia, Sharick also married his wife, Sarah. The marriage was arranged by the couples' families, and the match has turned out to be a happy one. "She's an extremely loyal person," describes Sharick. "She doesn't care about material things, homes, cars; that's not her priority. She is committed to me, our kids and the relationships that are important to her. That comes through every single day, in every single thing she does. Family is a lot more important to both of us than business. I have learned from her that small things and time with kids and family is more important than anything else.

She also supports Sharick's adventurous side. He recalls that on the couple's 15th wedding anniversary, he took Sarah out for a surprise in Ocean City, Maryland. She realized they were heading toward the airport and surmised they were travelling somewhere. As it turned out, Sharick had gotten tickets for them to go skydiving. "They started giving us things to sign, and she asks, 'What's this?!'" laughs Sharick. "Then she realized we're going to jump from a plane. She panicked at first, but then she jumped, and now she says it was the best thing she has ever done. And she wants to do it again. So we're planning to do it again."

Sharick, like his father, stresses the importance of goodwill as a leader. "I like to trust people," he reflects. "I'm more of a hands-off manager. I rely on people to get their jobs done instead of doing their jobs for them. I'm focused on developing systems and routines and giving people the opportunity to learn."

To young people entering the working world today, Sharick advises continual learning. "We die when we stop learning," he emphasizes. "Read a lot of books and find a mentor. The only way to grow is to continue reading books. Find the profession that will continue to interest you 10, 20 or 30 years from now. Never give up on your learning and remember: all walls have doors. If you come up against a wall, create your own door. You should never be stopped by a wall."

D. Scott Montgomery

You Can't Do It Alone

Scott Montgomery prides himself on putting his relationships first. Valuing the people around him is both a path to professional success and a closely held personal value.

Growing up, Scott saw firsthand the way bad relationships can have ripple effects on others. Five years after being born in Daytona Beach, Florida, his family moved to Valley Forge, Pennsylvania. His parents divorced when he was nine, and their separation was far from amicable. As a result, Scott witnessed years-long estrangement between loved ones. Scott manifested this familial chaos by causing disruptions in school. Most of his teachers considered him something of a problem child, although there were exceptions. One teacher in particular treated Scott with empathy and kindness. He always appreciated her and recently reconnected with her over FaceTime through a classmate who ran into her in Scott's hometown.

The first place he was able to build functional relationships and find mentors wasn't at school, it was through work.

In 9th grade he got his first job at Burger King, then quickly moved on to a local grocery store. On his first day, he was told to wear a white shirt and tie. Ever the troublemaker, Scott showed up in a grey shirt. That's when he got his first real taste of discipline. "They sent me home, and I had to change and come back in a white shirt," smiles Scott. "It was the first time I realized that I don't get to break the rules at work like I had in school. It clicked with me that I wouldn't have a job unless I listened. My manager was forgiving and I went to work every day thereafter with a white shirt and tie. The grocery store staff really clicked with me. I met my first mentors, and I realized that relationships could be very fulfilling and satiating. Results were mine to deliver, and I appreciated that. It gave me money and a little bit of structure. It was the grounding I needed to launch my understanding of business."

For four years, Scott moved up the ranks at the grocery store, going from bagger, to cashier, to the bakery department. Ultimately, he ended up as a deputy to the boss of the bakery department before realizing upon graduating high school that he did not want to be a baker professionally. Thus, he pivoted from a service-oriented career to a business-oriented one selling insurance.

Scott was hired by National Liberty Insurance, where he quickly topped the salesman leaderboard. However, again he felt the work wasn't for him in the long run. He felt uncomfortable with some of the sales he was asked to make, especially those to elderly folks who needed insurance. Determined to make a good living and live a good life, Scott moved on and found a more permanent home with Bell Atlantic.

Scott was brought on to Bell Atlantic, later Verizon. His first role was in selling office supplies, and in this, he met quota every month and in general overachieved. Once again, it was a positive relationship with a mentor that propelled him forward in his career. After some time, Scott's manager insisted that Scott should be part of the team that would help open up a new ISDN office in Virginia Beach. Over the objections of a couple of other managers, Scott's mentor got her way, and Scott was on his way to Virginia Beach.

With just three other salesmen and two managers, Scott successfully got the Virginia Beach operation up and running over the course of six months. While there, he impressed the higher-ups enough that he was offered a job in the corporate Verizon office. "They told me I was gregarious and knew the systems well," he recalls. "They said they needed a guy like me on that part of the team. So I accepted the offer and moved to Arlington, Virginia where I doubled my salary. I couldn't believe my good fortune. I didn't have my four-year degree and yet was working with people who had their Master's and doctorates. They also assigned a few junior managers to me to manage while training me how to be an effective leader. Then they promoted me again to senior management. I was handed a department and a call center, and I had to pinch myself to make sure I wasn't dreaming." I was fast-tracked to upper management quickly.

Scott may have shocked himself with his success, but it was hardly shocking to those around him. He acquired a reputation as a personable go-getter who was both deeply competent and loyal. He bought a house that he quickly flipped, bought two more houses, and also paid down some debt that he'd accumulated after high school. While at Bell Atlantic, he also made another important connection. He met his future wife, Katelyn.

After 12 years with Verizon, Scott decided it was time for a new adventure. One of his former bosses had started a small consulting firm and invited Scott to join the business as the third employee. Scott jumped at the opportunity and also decided to go back to school full-time. Scott registered to begin taking college classes at Northern Virginia Community College. He graduated from a 2-year program in one year with honors and earned his Associate's degree. Scott had now achieved a good deal of professional success and completed his first level of higher education.

Underneath all of it, he most cherished his time with his family. He and Katelyn had their first son, followed by twins two years later. He knew that only by setting out on his own (launching Worldgate) would he achieve the kind of flexibility he sought to have in order to be hands-on with raising his children. "Being a father and being a husband are my two most important roles," Scott affirms. "So for me, the desire to be self-employed is personal."

He co-founded Worldgate in 2002 with Katelyn, but it was quite some time before the vision and mission of the business would coalesce. At first, it was just a name on a piece of paper. Scott briefly experimented with turning it into a real estate business and obtained his real estate license while still working. In the meantime, Katelyn ran some consulting contracts through the company. "For seven years, Worldgate sort of morphed and rolled around," describes Scott. "It was 2009 before I finally told myself that I was going to make it happen and turn Worldgate into a career. Initially, it felt risky. Katelyn held the family finances in order through her billable consulting jobs, and I reached into my Rolodex to find people that needed a nimble firm that was able to understand them and meet their needs. A few contacts working in public school systems expressed interest. We decided to develop Worldgate around the notion that we could support school districts."

"When it was time to go to market with this model, I reached out to folks at school districts where I had worked earlier in my career," Scott recalls. "Again, the relationships tied it together. They confirmed that they could use our help. After in-depth conversations with them, we learned what they needed and determined what we could offer and how we could satisfy their needs."

Eleven years later, Worldgate has had great success with this model. In December 2009 we got started with our first contract with a significant school district and from there went on to win major contracts with several of the top ten districts in the country. Worldgate helps K-12 public school districts meet their IT needs and offers everything from staffing, to project management, to technical expertise, and more.

Our proven track record has meant increased investment in Worldgate's services over time. "If a school system doesn't have the resources to develop software, to train staff, and to roll it out to the teachers and administrators, we can add a lot of value and help them," explains Scott. "Being a small business means we can be more nimble and more flexible in cost, unlike a lot of the larger consulting organizations. We are a relationship-based firm, we care about getting the work done, and we care about being on point for our clients. And by the way, many of our employees once worked for 'the big 6 consulting firms' and feel more engaged with our mission and the culture of Worldgate than their bigger firm experiences. The bottom line is that we have talented people and our customers are getting great value. It's a win for everyone."

Scott's career in ensuring children are adequately resourced at school is a poetic full-circle moment for the kid who never engaged much in his own schooling.

Unsurprisingly, Scott's title today is Chief Customer Officer. He's responsible for marketing the business, bringing in the clients, maintaining relationships, and making sure everyone gets what they need. One anecdote in particular sheds light on Scott's commitment and loyalty to his clients and friends. Scott really likes to tell the story of winning their contract with a prominent public school district. During the bidding process, there was a mandatory meeting that Scott's team couldn't make due to an emergency. In this scenario, most businesses would be withdrawn from the bidding process. Worldgate took a different approach. "I instructed my lead salesperson to go into the school district, knock on procurements' door, and simply apologize for our inability to make this meeting," says Scott. "I wanted our sales person to shake their hand, look them in the eye, and say we are here to help them when the opportunity presents itself again. Shortly thereafter, we got a call back from procurement advising that we were able to continue in the fair bidding process. In the end, we were awarded the contract. I think that was in large part because of the integrity we showed by showing up, looking them in the eye, and letting them know we're here to help. They were really impressed with us. We create partners and relationships with our clients in order to maximize our value and satisfy their needs."

Scott has not forgotten his childhood and the role that it played in forging the hardworking, successful man that he is today. Soon after his parents divorced, his father moved back to Florida, where Scott spent summers. In Florida, his fondest memories are of attending minor league baseball games at a local stadium. "The stadium was the Jackie Robinson Ballpark and was where the Astros played," Scott reminisces. "On Tuesday game nights I would indulge myself in the hometown baseball experience. There were a lot of cracker jacks and promotional items that were given away." Scott kept one piece of memorabilia in particular, a plastic orange trumpet with a noisemaker. Today, he considers it one of his most prized possessions, because of what it represents.

"I've had it for 38 years, and it'll never get thrown away," Scott laughs. "When I was learning to drive, I would place the orange trumpet in front of the car with an egg on it. The goal was to get the car as close to the trumpet without knocking off the egg. So the trumpet represents the good times I have had and the work I did to achieve things. Nevertheless, being at the ballpark gave me a sense of freedom. If I was not with a parent, I could breathe and have the freedom to run around and have a good time on a beautiful Florida night. I basically was in a big playground."

Now a parent himself, Scott is committed to giving his kids the same freedom. Aside from organizing his schedule so that he always has time for them, he's also committed to being a positive role model. To that end, he's also heading back to college. He prides himself on being a continual learner. Right now, he's enrolled in pre-requisite courses in order to apply to the University of Virginia's bachelors program. "On New Year's Eve, I was in Charlottesville with some friends, and we went to watch a UVA basketball game," Scott says. "One of the things I noticed with that team was that the kids were helping each other up when they were getting blocked or knocked down by the opposing team. Their assists far exceeded the other team's assists. It wasn't about the score; it's about how they were playing as a team." Scott was inspired; he called the school to ask about their programs, and they were eager to help. "Last night I was doing my school work on the couch while my kids were doing theirs," smiles Scott. "I felt like I was teaching them about the value of education. That's what it's all about to me. Role modeling is important, and Worldgate offers me this opportunity."

Through it all, Katelyn has been an incredible partner in both marriage and business. "Katelyn is 50%, if not more," nods Scott. "This wouldn't be half as rewarding without her. We say that I'm the kite and she's the string; we compliment each other perfectly. I'm the visionary and am always looking forward for the next opportunity. She's conservative, tactical, and oriented toward making sure it all stays stable. She's grounded, and I need that. It completely works for us."

As a leader, Scott emphasizes collaboration. "In team meetings, as issues are discussed or problems that need to be solved are brought up, I ask for team inputs on how to fix the issue we are discussing," relates Scott. "I own my own spot at the table, but I give everyone else their spot or opportunity to contribute. There is no 'I' in team."

To young people entering the working world today, Scott reaffirms his commitment to his relationships. "You can't do it alone," he urges. "You don't know what you don't know. If you come out of college with a 4.0 GPA thinking you know it all, you don't. You still don't know what you don't know. I've been doing this for 35 years, and even I still have to look to others for their input and feedback. It'll be easier to move forward if you can come to grips with the reality that others can contribute and can teach you things."

Tamara L. Nall

Fulfilling Her Destiny

Tamara Nall wasn't like other 12-year-olds. She did well in school, enjoyed playing with the other kids in the neighborhood, and sometimes argued with her sister. But she was also running a business, and it was pretty far from a lemonade stand.

Tamara was born in Toledo, Ohio and lived the early part of her childhood in Bessemer, Alabama. Her father was an Administrative Manager at a well-known soda bottling company in Alabama and instilled a business mindset in Tamara simply through leading by example. When Tamara's father later moved the family to Atlanta, Georgia so he could attend Divinity School, he worked as Vice President of Human Resources at a meatpacking company in the city. Occasionally, Tamara accompanied her father to work. It was there that Tamara noticed the operations did not seem to be as efficient as they should, which in her young mind presented an interesting business opportunity.

Strewn through the hallways were what seemed to be limitless boxes of invoices. Tamara remembers asking her father what would happen if someone had a question about what they ordered. Her father replied that clerks come out and they just keep looking until they found the invoice. Tamara, who thought the system could not possibly produce good results, asked, "Can I put together a proposal about how I would organize this? Because this is not productive," she asked. Her father, perhaps admiring her ambition, told her to put together the proposal, and looped in his boss. Tamara pitched to her father and a Senior Executive at the company, and she won a contract to do the work.

After school, when her homework was done, Tamara would crack open some of the boxes of invoices her father brought home in the evening. On the weekends, she would go into work with him and organize all day. Eventually, she brought her younger sister, Rachel, onto the project. However, Rachel tired of it pretty quickly. "I think she quit, but to this day she says that I fired her," laughs Tamara. "I'd see her face when we went in on the weekends, and she was so upset at the lack of order. She saw chaos, but I saw profits! It was Heaven!" Tamara made $30,000. Her father helped her declare the income and file taxes on it. Rather than spend the money, she saved it until college, when she used it to go on her first big trip to South Africa, a lifelong dream.

That enterprising kid grew up to be an even more enterprising adult. Today, Tamara is the Founder, President & CEO of The Leading Niche, a business she started in 2007 while still working full-time for Booz & Company, the commercial side of Booz Allen Hamilton.

The Leading Niche (TLN) is a contractor primarily focused on data analytics, cyber security, and other IT solutions in the fields of financial services and public health. They're a respected global business with employees and contracts in the US and abroad. "On the data analytics side, we concentrate on fraud, abuse, and forensics," Tamara explains. "Once we started working with the federal government, we started supporting agencies to build algorithms to analyze unstructured data and conduct research that combines strategy and data intelligence."

TLN has worked on international public health projects, particularly with HIV as well as less common diseases like Zika and Ebola. "We do lab work and non-lab work," says Tamara. "We feed information back to our customers so they can make informed decisions about how to allocate budgeting for new projects."

The name "The Leading Niche" was actually chosen by Tamara's late mother, whom she speaks lovingly of as kind, artistic, and creative. "Leading" is meant to convey the business's technological capabilities; Tamara was set on ensuring as much automation as possible. "The idea was that we are going to lead the industry in what we're doing; we're going to be the best at analytics," affirms Tamara. "And then I also wanted us to have a niche. I didn't want to be all over the place. I didn't want to be one of those companies that says, 'We can do program management, and we can do janitorial work, and we can do advanced planning.' No, we focus on what we specialize in." To top it all off, TLN is also Tamara's initials, giving the name a personal touch. The logo is shaped like the globe, representing its international reach.

Tamara cannily launched TLN two years before leaving her job with Booz, allowing her time to get a feel for the marketplace and make connections. Although she worked long days, she would burn the midnight oil working on TLN after work and on the weekends and holidays. Additionally, she knew that when she began meeting with clients, she didn't want to call TLN a "start-up," preferring to have a couple of years of experience and revenue under her belt to show potential customers. She took on small contracts whenever she could get time away from her labor-intensive job, which sometimes had her working as many as 20 hours in a day. In 2009, she hired her first employee—an assistant. That same year, she won her first major client.

The client was SkyBank, a regional bank in West Africa. The opportunity was M&A work. SkyBank had lost market share, and they wanted to know how to gain it back. Tamara put together a proposal, informing them that they needed to either acquire or be acquired by another bank, and offered likely candidates for the merger. As to how she got this contract, Tamara confirms, "It's all about relationships. This was through a colleague I'd met at a summer program at the Harvard Business School years prior. I reached out to him and it turned out to be perfect timing. SkyBank had asked him to do this work, but he only had three analysts on his team. He needed someone to partner with him."

At this point, Tamara moved quickly. Booz was in the midst of a round of layoffs, and after Tamara resigned her position, she quickly called around to former coworkers who were suddenly unemployed. Fortuitously, she now had a pool of about 50 qualified people looking for work. She ended up bringing 18 on for the project, which TLN and its partner won, beating out even world-famous McKinsey for the contract. TLN had committed to hire one-third of the staff on the project locally, train them, and develop them as well. Suddenly, TLN had gone from a one-woman show to a legitimate contender.

Tamara doesn't take her blessings lightly. The guidance she received from her father, who is a retired pastor, and her mother, who constantly read to her from the Bible, taught her to trust in God's plan. "I believe God created me to be an innovater and to employ people," Tamara said with thoughtul affirmation. "I wake up every day and I'm grateful to be an employer. I love that I can help people to feed their families, pay their mortgage, and create something. I don't think I was made to do anything else. Being an employer is my God ordained Destiny. Both she and the business certainly do their part to give back; TLN contributes 10% of its net earnings to the community, while Tamara herself gives 10% of her gross salary to tithes, offerings, and the community.

She comes by it honestly. Her father, the aforementioned pastor, was also a practitioner of tithing, and his congregation knew him as the type to give away everything if he wasn't reigned in. Along with her time sorting invoices at her dad's office, she mostly remembers being in church. It was a small church of about 100 members, but their commitment was large. "On Sundays, my dad had to go visit everybody," she recalls. "He would go pray with everybody, so we wouldn't get home until very late; the church was my second home."

The Nall girls did not grow up wealthy, but they did not want for anything. Their parents taught them to be grateful, patient, and kind. "My mother's thing was, if it's not nice, if it's not true, if it's not necessary, don't say it! And I would say, 'Well it was true and necessary, how about two out of three?'" laughs Tamara. "My mother constantly prayed, and she was slow to speak because she considered everything so carefully. She always had to pray over things, and sometimes that frustrated me. But she was like the calming ocean. I honestly think my mom was an angel that was sent here on Earth." In fact, Tamara considers her mother's Bible to be her prize possession. "It has a tan leather cover and a picture of the family in it," she describes, tearing up. "Of course it has all of her highlights and underlines in it. She taught us to turn to God, and that's where I get my comfort, my strength." Although Tamara's mother was very educated, with multiple Master's degrees, her main goals were to follow Christ and rear her two girls.

Tamara's parents were married for 45 years, but her father loved her mother for 52; he had to chase her for the first seven. "My mother said she'd never marry a military man or a preacher," smiles Tamara. "She'd always joke that God has a sense of humor, because she married my dad, and then he became a preacher!" Tamara remembers their relationship as loving, with her father constantly catering to her mother—something of a lifelong infatuation before she passed away several years ago.

Her parents' lack of attachment to material things is particularly on display in one anecdote. Tamara's father had been accepted into Theology School at Emory, and the family was packing up to move from Bessemer, Alabama to Atlanta, Georgia. "My mom picked me and my sister up from school, and we saw all these kids going by on bikes, roller skates, carrying things, and we thought there must be a carnival in town," Tamara laughs. "We pull into the driveway, and basically, our parents had taken all our stuff and put it in the yard. They said you can keep one toy; the rest we're giving away. God had blessed us abundantly, so we had to bless others. I took one doll, my Baby Alive (which she still has to this day) and that was it! We cried for days but to no avail. We were moving to Atlanta with few material items."

The girls tried to adjust in Atlanta leaving behind a few more little businesses, like babysitting and opening their own mini-library for the neighborhood kids from their book collection. They adjusted to the public schools; in Bessemer, they'd gone to a small, private Christian school. But with their father back in school himself, there was no income for private education. Tamara and her sister were the first African-American students at one of their private schools in Alabama. The Nall girls were part of a bussing program in Georgia called M2M, or "Minority to Majority," which meant that minority students who lived on one side of town would be bussed to schools on another side of town that had a predominantly white student population. For Tamara and her sister, this also meant that they had to get up at 5 or 6 in the morning to ride to their school. It was a long day, and while Tamara made friends enough to sit with at lunch, she wasn't invited many places.

Still, she threw herself into her own success and thrived in both academics and extracurricular activities. She was involved in everything, including being one of the school announcers. She even notes that her younger sister, Rachel, was often referred to as "Tamara's sister," much to Rachel's frustration. She kept her GPA high and notes that she did so without much external pressure. Her parents encouraged her to work hard, but they never demanded high grades. "They expected us to do our best," reminisces Tamara.

Her father graduated from Emory and began pastoring a congregation of only five members. He quickly grew the attendance and moved from preaching in a banquet room at a hotel to a brick and mortar church that was paid for in full.

By the time she graduated high school, Tamara had a 4.2 GPA and was fourth in her class. Her mother had taken a job as a secretary at Emory some time before, which meant Tamara could attend the university for free. She already had her heart set on a business degree, but during her first year of school, an intriguing program caught her eye. The program was a dual degree program with Georgia Tech. Students completed their work at Emory, then went on to get a second degree at Tech in two more years. She went to her academic advisor to speak to her about the program, citing her interest in chemical engineering. "I was told to not do it because females, particularly minority females, should only major in liberal arts," remembers Tamara. "I said, 'Thank you very much, you've been so helpful.' and then I went home and applied for the program! I'm the kind of person that, if you're gonna try and close the door, I'm going to knock down the roof!"

Tamara ended up completing the dual degree program in 7 years—opting to stay an additional year so she could check out some non-degree courses like Chinese—with a business degree from Emory and a chemical engineering degree from Georgia Tech. Right away, she was a hot commodity on the job market. She was recruited by several of the top management consulting firms, but Booz was far and away the most impressive of the bunch. They flew her out, invited her to all their parties, promised to mentor her and embraced her as their own. She was excited and knew she'd found the right fit.

Moving to New York City brought Tamara a level of freedom and breathing room she had never had back home in Atlanta, where she was often recognized around town. "I was so used to being the preacher's kid. I always had to live the perfect life," recalls Tamara. "New York gave me freedom. I could finally get away from that pressure. And New York has so much opportunity. I just love New York!"

Tamara was a hit at Booz, quickly rising in the ranks. "They liked the fact that I had the business side and the engineering side," observes Tamara. "That shaped my career. They would put me on the hard healthcare projects because a lot of people were good with analytics, but not equally so with strategy. A lot of people were good with strategy, but they couldn't communicate the numbers to clients in a digestable bite." She also had an ingenious little trick for acquiring mentors. She would often approach people she admired and thank them for inspiring her and mentoring her from afar. From then on they were happy to step into the role.

Booz paid for her to attend Harvard Business School, entering a program she chose as she observed that most of the African-American principles and partners at Booz had gone there. In her eyes, to be a partner at Booz meant only one school, so HBS was the only MBA program she applied to. It was all or nothing. Her time at Booz prepared her for the rigor of business school. She had already trained to process large amounts of information and filter out the relevant parts quickly.

As much as she loved her time with Booz, entrepreneurship called to her, and she left 3-4 years short of becoming a partner. "I think of entrepreneurship as opportunity," says Tamara. "My father got laid off when I was young, and our lifestyle changed. My friends whose parents were business owners didn't have lifestyles that changed. I saw that and wanted the same kind of security, that kind of freedom. I truly think if you're smart, and you put in the work, and you build the relationships, it's going to happen for you." Additionally, she found that as she rose through the ranks at Booz, the pay was higher, but the workload never seemed to decrease. She knew she didn't want to work 20 hours a day for the rest of her career. "I wanted to work smarter, not harder," notes Tamara. Thus, The Leading Niche was born.

As a leader, Tamara considers herself to be, above all, collaborative. "I love innovation and continuous improvement," she explains. "So I try to be very fair. I'm a collaborative leader that wants us to get to the solution together."

To young people entering the working world today, she advises building your network—an ingredient just as crucial to success as intelligence or work ethic. "Never underestimate the power of the person sitting next to you," she instructs. "They might look like they're not anything special, but try to be a giver before you're a receiver. In my network, there are very few people who would not help if I called. Likewise, I would bend over backwards to help my network. I'm always trying to connect with people."

Katie Nelson

Creating Win/Win/Wins

Although Katie spent most of her childhood in Arizona with her father and stepmother, she was born in the DC area where her mother and maternal family remained. After college and a few years working in the southwest, Katie turned to her new husband Adam, and asked, "Why don't we try somewhere new?"

"We thought we were footloose and fancy free. We had no kids and nothing tying us down anywhere so we could throw a dart on the map and move," Katie laughs. "Then we looked at each other and said, 'We are not good at darts and could end up in a remote part of Saskatchewan.' We knew that wasn't a good plan. We did it the smart way and actually wrote down the places where we would want to live and where we knew people. That led us back to Virginia."

Moving across country was a big change because for the first time, Katie decided to think seriously about what she wanted her career to look like. She began applying to jobs in the DC area and was open to whatever new opportunities might arise. "I had an interdisciplinary degree in communications and sociology which means my degree was not marketable," Katie jokes. "I'm not a doctor, a teacher, a lawyer, or anything that had a clear career path. In the weirdest turn of events, I looked at my family and work history, where I came from, and what I loved to do and decided I would go into sales. I would have never predicted that before our move. I applied for sales jobs. It was a defining moment because until that time I never thought it was something I would do or be."

She took a commission-only sales job selling office supplies for Miller's Office Products. It was a woman-owned small business, and the job allowed Katie a great deal of freedom to set her own schedule as long as she hit her goals. Katie took to the work and realized that she loved the products and building relationships with clients. She learned how to cultivate customer relationships and spoke with them at length to determine what problems Miller's Office Supplies could help them solve. She also discovered the joy of residual income. "If you need paper this month, you will need paper next month," Katie explains. "If I build a strong relationship with you, you're not going to another company next month to buy paper. In a sense, there was an aspect of guaranteed income, if you could maintain that relationship."

After 12 years in sales at several different companies including two where she was the minority owner, Katie was finally tired of selling and making money for other people. She grew tired of being the one bringing in customers, building relationships, and building a client base, without reaping all the benefits of ownership.

"I had met a woman once who assumed I owned my firm, but I told her I was a minority owner and only owned a small piece. She viewed me as the gal Friday who got everything done and who brought in the business. She told me, 'That's what I do, and I own my own company.'"

"She asked me a question that changed my life," Katie recalls. "'If you had your own company, what would you really want to do?,' she asked. "I told her three things—I didn't think I'd be able to own my own business, what people want is for me to sell for them, and I was exhausted of having to vet someone else's dreams and integrity before I would sell for them. I then told her that I would love to teach people what selling is really about and how to do it. She said, 'Okay, go do that.' But then I pushed back—telling her, 'No one wants to be taught something like that. They only want me to make them money.' She thought my defensive nature was funny and told me she would hire me to be a sales coach. And my response was simply, 'What's a sales coach?'"

After this eye-opening exchange, Katie immediately started researching what services a sales coach might offer and how. Within a couple of weeks, she found that the career she envisioned for herself was a real possibility and that the marketplace was hungry for coaches with a skill set like hers. Thus, in August of 2016, Sales UpRising was born.

The name is important to Katie. She wants salespeople and business owners to feel proud of their work and empowered to build their sales in mutually beneficial ways. As Founder and CEO of Sales Uprising, Katie and her team work with small businesses to quickly and intelligently expand their revenue. Their ideal client is a service-based business that's been operating for about three years and has yet to break $250,000 in revenue. "At $250,000 in revenue you know this is a good quality idea and there's proof of concept," explains Katie. "But there are some foundational business pieces they need to understand to take it to the next level and one of those is selling. If you haven't hit $250,000 yet, you haven't mastered it yet so let us help you."

The focus on elevating businesses above the $250,000 threshold has provided Katie with a guidestar for growing her own business, and it has paid personal dividends as well. "It's gratifying to see someone get over that hump," smiles Katie proudly. "And while I work with both women and men, seeing women achieve that success point is so special, being that the success rate for women business owners is currently very low."

Clients of Sales Uprising can be from any sector or any industry. The principles they teach are universal. Katie's team analyzes clients' business needs, works to create a more efficient sales process and pipeline, and helps create a business strategy with a sound and profitable structure. For the first couple of years, Katie was the sole employee of her firm, but in year three, she began to bring on additional staff.

As a businesswoman, Katie stresses the importance of relationships that serve all the players involved. "When a salesperson helps a customer, it should never be to the salesperson's detriment or the customer's detriment; it should be a win/win," she explains. "I had years of experience working with government contractors. And in that case, I had a client, and the client had a client—the government—so I had to make sure they are also winning. Ultimately in sales you're looking to create win/win/wins."

Although she'd never seriously considered sales as a career before her move to DC, she has roots in the industry on both sides of her family. Her maternal grandfather, a Captain in the Navy, went into commercial real estate after his retirement. His wife was in residential real estate. Katie's mother was in retail, a buyer for Macy's, while her father was in insurance and real estate. Meanwhile, her stepmother, Sally, worked for her family's business selling guardrail, fencing, and highway signs. "Everybody in my life sold things," reflects Katie. "But I never thought I would do it as a profession when I was a kid."

Katie had an unusual childhood. Her parents divorced when she was four, and her father was able to get full custody of her and her younger sister, Meagan. At the time, Katie's mother was suffering from alcoholism. But after her children moved to Arizona with their father, she was able to get and stay clean and sober. Throughout her childhood, Katie and Meagan would fly back to the East Coast to spend a month with their mother over the summer, or several weeks during the Holidays.

Katie remembers a little bit about the first few years of her life in Arlington, Virginia, particularly spending time with Nana, her beloved maternal grandmother. Arizona was an adjustment—some good and some bad. Her father had to take on more parenting responsibilities. "My dad is 6'3" with massive hands, and I remember him French braiding and putting pom poms in our hair, if you can imagine that," she laughs. She enjoyed being near her paternal grandparents and extended family and getting to go to the pool all year round.

Her elementary school was down the block, and she could safely walk through the community to her babysitter's house when her father was at work. After several years of single parenting, Katie's father met Sally, and the two eventually married. Sally had two children of her own—Nicky and Toby—and blending the families wasn't always easy going. "Sally and I had a really contentious relationship for a long time," remembers Katie. "There was nothing wrong with her. In fact, she was lovely. And she was 100% different from me. We butted heads a lot through high school and part of college. And we developed a great friendship later in life."

Now, in retrospect, Katie is unendingly grateful for what she calls the "north, south, east and west of parents," referring to her mother, father, stepmom Sally, and stepdad Francis. "I was so lucky to grow up with the whole compass," she reflects. "There was a purpose for each parent, and I'd go to each one for different things."

Katie remembers that her mother was always her emotional support. When she needed advice, she could always call. She learned hard work from her mother who had a 25-year career with the post office after entering sobriety. Meanwhile, Sally was a whiz with finances, and a responsible role model. She kept the house in perfect order, made floral arrangements, reupholstered couches, and generally modelled successful adulthood for young Katie. Francis, himself 51 years sober, imparted the importance of value, meaning, purpose, and direction as a former Staff Sergeant in the Marine Corps. And from her father, Katie says she got her positive attitude. He always taught the kids that no matter how tough things get, you keep your head up and keep going.

Katie enjoyed school but more for the socializing than for the academics. She had trouble focusing in class and preferred to chat and giggle with her many tight-knit friends. In fourth grade, she changed schools and met Margo, the long-time best friend who was a bridesmaid in her wedding. To this day, they and their friend Erin have virtual Zoom happy hours each week. Katie recalls that she may not have been the class clown but she was "the one encouraging him." In middle school much to her teachers' dismay, she recalls that she was often reading fiction in class instead of her textbooks.

Katie's parents emphasized activities and community involvement, so Katie was constantly being shuttled from one extra-curricular to another. She played soccer, softball, and tennis. She sang in the choir, played viola in the orchestra, and participated in Campfire Girls—a girl-scout like program that taught wilderness skills. By high school, she was very committed to tennis and made the varsity team as a sophomore. Through it all, she continued to make friends. "I was the person who could get along with anyone," smiles Katie. "I hung out with all the different groups—the jocks, the nerds, and the emo kids. I was a little bit like all of them and still am, truth be told."

Being immersed in diverse social groups and community activities brought Katie a love of interaction, and she soon gained a reputation as a straight-shooter. Ever since adolescence, Katie's friends have called her for her no-nonsense advice, knowing full well that all her insight comes from a place of love.

As a teenager, Katie decided she wanted to have her own money. She first got an under-the-table job at a local florist shop before she was old enough to work (legally, and not as a babysitter). At the age of

15, she got a part-time job at a call center over the objections of her dad and Sally. "We were not well-off people and didn't have a ton of cash given that they were raising four kids. If I wanted something, I didn't want to have to ask for it," says Katie. "But looking back on it, that call center job was hysterical. I was a 15-year-old girl coming in with her viola and backpack after orchestra and sitting in a cube next to a guy who's around 40 years old smoking a cigarette! I loved that job. I made around $420 every two weeks and saved most of it."

During her junior and senior years, Katie began focusing her energy on trying to get out of applying to college. She wanted to work and not spend four more years in school, but her parents wouldn't hear of it. Finally, they compromised; Katie agreed to try out a local community college. After a year, there she transferred to Arizona State University where she moved into the dorms even though the campus was nearby. She got a job at the campus deli for about three months where she "created the best sandwich ever." But she soon realized she hated the food service industry. She then took a job working for her dad at his machines company selling wire stripper blades. At school, she spent two years taking courses in various fields, but nothing was quite resonating with her yet. After her junior year, she decided to take a break. "I told my mom and dad that I loved them, that I tried it their way, and that I'm done now," she remembers. "I told them that I would go back to college when I was ready to get my degree but that I wanted to work and make money now. They weren't happy with me."

Katie scored an inside sales job in posh Scottsdale, AZ for Club Med, where she sold all-inclusive high-end vacations to tourists looking to go abroad. Although her family had been reluctant to support her decision to leave school, they had to admit that the commissions and the perks that Katie was receiving were nice. With her excellent sales record, she was able to send her brother on an all-expenses paid trip for his honeymoon and take her mother to the Bahamas. She loved every minute of it, and in her three years working there, she ended up the number one salesperson in the company.

After Club Med, Katie hit the road with her boyfriend Adam. He was in the radio frequency world and helped Verizon set up their first national digital network. This involved travelling across country running computer programs; Katie was the driver. After three months of that, she decided it was time to go back to Arizona State University to complete her degree.

For the first time, she actually met with a career counselor to talk about her degree. "I showed them the credits I had and asked about a course of study," she laughs. "They told me I was one year away from two different degrees. I had enough credits to get a degree in either communications or sociology. I didn't want to make a choice, so they helped me set up an inter-disciplinary studies degree. I loved it so much that I got a 4.2 GPA in my final year of school."

After graduation, Katie took a job at an Anheuser-Busch distributor where she quickly found a model of sales she did not want to emulate. The business was sexist; women were expected to market by putting on skimpy clothing and going to bar parties sponsored by Budweiser. She was ready for a change; and after she and Adam got married in the fall of 2003, they decided to take a risk and move to the East Coast. "He stayed in Arizona to sell the house," she notes "And for the first year of marriage we didn't live together!"

After four years at the office supply company, she was being aggressively recruited. After turning down the recruiter several times, he finally told Katie point blank that there were five companies who wanted to hire her and that she should at least come in and meet with one or more of them. One of the businesses was a small, friendly staffing firm called Prism, and Katie felt at home there right away. Over the course of several years, she became their Business Development Manager. Her mentor, coincidentally named Bill Gates, at the firm asked her to go into business with him.

It was the first of two businesses where Katie owned a minority interest. But after her second experiment with minority ownership went bust, she knew she needed to try her hand at something else. That something else eventually led to Sales UpRising. And no one was more supportive of that decision than her husband, Adam. "I told him that I thought I needed to start my own business and warned him that there might be no income or lower income at times. I even told him that I wasn't sure what I was selling yet. His response was an emphatic 'It's about damn time,'" Katie remembers. "He knew I made a lot of money for the people for whom I worked and asked me if I knew that. He has been supportive of every crazy thing I've done. He has worked for the same company for over 16 years and has consistently grown with them. So we're sort of 180 degrees different. He is the anchor that holds down my fly-away-ness!"

Katie always tells those who attend her seminars, "Sales is my love language!" It's a mantra that she strongly adheres to, especially when see sees colleagues or clients doubting their own ability to sell. "People should be proud to be in sales: you're providing a solution to someone in need, and that's nothing to be afraid of or ashamed of," she exclaims!

As a leader, Katie says she embraces a servant leadership style and prefers to be at the back of the pack helping stragglers and strugglers than at the front taking credit. "For me, it's not about a title or a position or what's on your business card," she says. "It's not about any pomp and circumstance. It's not about the paycheck that comes with it. It's about being able to stand 100% in who you are, taking care of your people, and living and walking in integrity. That's the leader I aspire to be."

To young people entering the working world today, Katie encourages patience and openness. "You may or may not get it right on the first try," she points out. "Don't worry about it too much, you'll figure it out. College is amazing, but that doesn't mean it gives us everything we need for the rest of our life. We have the ability to make our story different if we want it to be."

Guy O'Brien

Music is in My DNA

In high school, Guy O'Brien started DJing to earn some extra cash. Money was tight, and he knew his mom needed him to help make ends meet where he could. As he got older, he was covering his clothing and personal expenses and was relying on his mother only for food and shelter. This allowed her to spend more money for her bills and his younger siblings, Celeste and Leo.

It was the late 1970s, and rap music was a young, as-yet-little-known art form coming up in New York City. Although Guy lived in New Jersey, a short bus ride from the City, at the time it felt like two different worlds. One night at a party, he watched another DJ, Mark, talking over the music. "I went up to him and said, 'Why are you talking over the record?'" recalls Guy. "Mark said, 'Listen man, it's rap. It's what they do in New York.' I thought, I better learn this so I can keep up. Since I was a drummer, I could hear the beat in my head. I heard it as beats, and I heard it as poetry. I thought of it as rhythmic poetry."

Pretty soon, Guy found he had a natural talent for rapping. He began writing lyrics and performing a little around town. Then one day, fate intervened. He was walking with a friend out of a local pizza place when they noticed a car out front. In the car were a few acquaintances and some friends of Guy's friends. Also in the car was Sylvia Robinson, the famous R&B singer, who was then at the top of her career. Guy's friend was quick to bring up his skills. "You gotta listen to this guy," he said, and got them an invitation into the car. Guy sat down next to another young man who was also auditioning for Sylvia, and the whole group headed off to her mansion up the road.

The other boy's name was Hank, and quickly, both Hank and Guy started to put on a show for Sylvia and her friends. The two were competing, thinking that Sylvia would only want to work with one of them. Then suddenly, one of the quiet friends in the group stood up and announced that he, too, was a rapper. His name was Mike, and he wanted to audition as well. "He starts doing his thing, and she's like 'Oh, wow,'" remembers Guy. "'You know what? Three's my favorite number,' she exclaims! 'I'm not going to choose between the three of you, I'm going to put the three of you together. That's how we were discovered.'"

Guy (known as "Master Gee," his stage name), Henry Jackson (Hank) and Michael Wright (Mike) became the Sugarhill Gang, a world-famous rap group best known for the monster hit "Rappers Delight," which was the first ever commercially successful rap song. It was the first rap single to become a Top 40 hit on the Hot 100, and the three men, only teenagers at the time, quickly became teen heartthrobs on the ride of their lives. "I couldn't stay onstage after a performance because there were people pulling me off stage," remembers Guy of their first tour. "You could not hear me talk. It was pandemonium anytime I opened my mouth to talk in public. I was like any teen idol you've ever seen in your whole life. I couldn't leave a venue or walk down the street in public without a security detail around me. I experienced the whole nine yards as a teen heartthrob. Girls would cry or faint in my presence. We did a European tour and travelled all over the world. And we put out several more records that were also hits."

Fame hit the boys fast and furious, but like so many other young artists without guidance in the industry, they were exploited for their youth, talent, and relative naivete. The three signed to a five-year contract with the record label with terms that left little on the table for them given how much the Sugarhill Gang pulled in for the label. On top of that, Guy wasn't used to having any significant amount of money; he was 18 and quickly fell into the trap of spending money on cars, girls, clothes, and apartments. He didn't know anything about investing and didn't think about saving for the future. One day, at age 23, he woke up and realized that he was completely broke.

It was a major turning point for Guy. All his life he'd loved music, but his years in the industry had taught him a lot of hard lessons. Not only that, he now had a young son. "I never knew my biological father, and I wanted to be a good dad," nods Guy. "I remember one day I was at the store with my son, and I had $5 in my pocket. I was praying the whole time he wouldn't ask me for something worth more than $5. It was at that moment that I said, 'I gotta do something. I can't have my son growing up in this environment.' I didn't have a high school diploma, and I had no job experience. The only thing I'd ever done is tour the world and make women scream!"

From 1985 through 2005, Guy completely left the music business. He turned down another world tour because he had a steady job. His label replaced him with a new "Master Gee." Many of the fans hardly noticed the difference. The label would have the stand-in rap over Guy's backing track at shows. Then, in 2005, another fateful event took place. Mike called Guy and asked him to get back into music. Mike, too, had left the record label after being fed up with how they treated him. "Without any question, that phone call was a defining moment in my life," says Guy. "I made a decision for the first time in over 20 years to do what I wanted. Before that I was doing what people wanted me to do, what they needed me to do, or what I had to do. I had a wife and two other children by then. I had people that worked for me. I was on the Board of Directors for several organizations. But at the end of the day, music's in my DNA."

Guy decided to begin performing with Mike again, but getting the Sugarhill Gang back together wasn't that easy. The record label still owned the rights to the group, and Guy and Mike fought endless legal battles with the record label over the next ten years. Finally, in 2016, a key figure at the label passed away and his brother was charged to settle the estate. The brother wasn't interested in continuing the feud with the Sugarhill Gang. Instead, he sat down and worked out an agreement with them. Since 2016, Guy and Mike have been performing as the Sugarhill Gang again, and they're more appreciative than ever that they have the opportunity to do what they love.

"I fought for many, many years to do what I do on this level today," reflects Guy. "A lot of tears and a lot of blood have gone into me doing this. I have a responsibility to my legacy, and I also have a responsibility to the millions of Sugarhill Gang fans all over the world. Our fans have been listening to our music since the beginning and have turned their children onto us. I have a responsibility to do it right. Music is my thing. Not very many people get a chance to do their thing at this level. Most don't. I might walk down the street and pass a man playing the guitar, and in his heart of hearts he's dreaming of being on the stages where I perform. So I feel like I have a responsibility to that guy. It's a privilege to do what I do! And I truly appreciate what I've been given the opportunity to do."

Guy grew up around music. Born in Manhattan, his earliest memories are of his maternal grandparents who owned an audio equipment store called Crazy Eddie's in Brooklyn. "My grandfather, Peter, would always have new microphones and speakers," recalls Guy. "He was the first person to show me how to be successful and how to carry yourself. I didn't know what wealth was back then, but I thought everybody had a store. I thought everybody would fly to Jamaica every couple of weeks!" Guy and his mother lived in a nice apartment next door to his grandparents, in a swanky building with a doorman for several years. However, the relative peace of those early years didn't last.

Guy's mother had had him when she was 16, which was much more taboo at the time. As a result, she had a strained relationship with her mother. She eventually met a man and moved away from her parents with Guy. She had a second child, Guy's younger sister Celeste, and endured poverty, violence, and abuse at the hands of her boyfriend. By the time Guy was seven, the two had split up, and his mother was dating the man she went on to marry. The man who would become Guy's stepfather. The family moved to Englewood, New Jersey, where Guy's younger brother was born and where they settled.

Guy had a complicated and troubled relationship with his stepfather. "Dad was a pilot, he taught flying, he was an accordion player and trumpet player, he could take apart a sports car and put it back together. He was phenomenal, he was a quintessential renaissance man," says Guy. "He was an amazing person and was one of the most intelligent people I've ever met in my life. But he had a terrible mean streak." Guy's stepfather was physically violent and abusive to his wife and the children.

"I was afraid all the time," remembers Guy. "I was deathly afraid in my house. The only relief I'd ever get would be when I'd leave the house. Anytime I was home, a situation could go from bad to worse at a moment's notice. The way I am with my children is a direct result of how he was. I never wanted my children to have that feeling of living in fear of me."

Still, Guy looked up to his stepfather in a lot of ways. He would bring Guy to the airport and take him flying in the plane he co-owned with a friend. He taught Guy how to work on cars. And most of all, he introduced Guy to making music. Music and musicians were everywhere in their home, and Guy would spend hours with his stepdad in the studio where he was a recording engineer. "In every studio, there's a piano and a drum set," explains Guy. "I liked to bang on things, so I was drawn to the drums. Whenever he would go in there, he'd find me on the drums. One day he says, 'You like the drums? I'm gonna teach you how to play.' So he signed me up for lessons, he encouraged me, he got me a drum set later that Christmas. He'd make me practice and would encourage me, but I still lived in fear knowing that he might punch me in the face if I didn't do one of the assigned chores right. It was a weird situation in which I loved him and hated him at the same time. He had a positive influence on me, as well as a negative influence."

By the time Guy turned 15, his mom and stepfather split up and left the family struggling to make ends meet. Regardless, throughout all of the hard times, Guy always remained close with his mother. "Anything that anyone would admire in me, I got from my mother," asserts Guy. "I admired her ability to be able to handle whatever was in front of her. She was a true soldier. She dropped out of school to have me. She taught herself bookkeeping and got a job as a bookkeeper. I have no idea how she was able to do it, but she ended up being in book publishing. She always figured things out. She put food on the table for three kids as a single mom. She was abused physically, but she figured it out. She always landed on her feet, no matter what happened. I admired how bold she was. And in a room full of people, she always stood out. She had a huge influence on me."

It was after their divorce that Guy decided to start earning some extra cash from DJing, and the rest, as they say, is history. He left high school to go on tour with the Sugarhill Gang. After a whirlwind few years at the top of the industry, Guy found himself broke and looking for a job, any job. Like most people did at the time, he started by checking the classified ads in the newspaper, and one ad caught his eye.

It was a job with a magazine subscription company. The ad read, "Free to travel. No experience necessary. Representing lead publications."

Guy called the number and was asked to come in for an interview. The manager told him he'd be sent on the road for weeks at a time and would have food and housing covered. Being embarrassed about his financial state, it was exactly what Guy had hoped for. He wanted to get away from New Jersey for a while. He accepted the job and ran back home to get a few things and borrow $10 to get back to New York. With nothing but an old overnight duffle and a garbage bag, Guy hopped in the back of his new boss' Buick, and rode up to Springfield, Massachusetts to start his new career.

Almost immediately, Guy was recognized by one of his roommates; it was a situation he'd hoped to avoid. And within a day, word got out to the rest of the staff; his roommate immediately began spreading the word that they were working with Master Gee. But Guy kept his head down and focused on learning the business. His job was to sell subscriptions door to door, but his job training didn't exactly inspire confidence. He was matched with another salesman, who immediately left to smoke a joint in a nearby park. Then he would get a drink at a local bar before he finally visited a home, sold a magazine, and stole some of the money from his sale.

"Someone eventually came back to pick us up, and the trainer tells me, 'Hey man, you'll be all right. You're ready to go out on your own.' And I'm saying to myself 'What do you mean I'm ready?! I saw a guy smoke weed, drink a beer, and steal $5!' Fortunately, I always had the ability to adapt," laughs Guy. "I grabbed a credential and at first I kind of struggled through it." He managed to make a couple of sales on his first day, which he learned later was unusual for a new recruit. The next day, his boss noted his success in the field, and Guy quickly rose in the ranks. Before long, he was promoted to field supervisor. He began making real money, and the business owner wanted to invest in Guy. "He told me, 'Show me you can save $10,000, and I'll give you five of my people to start your own business,'" recalls Guy. "He was my first real mentor. Eventually, I got to that point, and I built that business from five people to over 50 people. I went from getting a $7 advance when I first walked through the door to making millions doing it."

Eventually, Guy's old boss made the decision to retire and sold his customer service business to Guy as well. By this time, Guy was on the Board of Directors for the National Field Selling Association, had a house in Chicago and Los Angeles and was, by his own account, "quite the corporate guy." He had created a new life but something wasn't right. "I was highly successful. I had all the trappings of success, but I was miserable," Guy admits. It was then that Mike called him and asked him to take the leap back into music.

Guy doesn't regret the years he spent building his business career. On the contrary, he did what he did for his children and is happy to have been able to give them the stable life he never had. In fact, he considers one of his prize possessions to be a painting his daughter made for him for Father's Day when she was in Montessori school in 2007. "It says, 'To the best dad," Guy smiles. "I used to carry it with me but now I have it on my nightstand. I always wanted to give my children the greatest life that I could possibly give them. I left music, I left what I love, to take care of what I love."

To young people starting their careers today, Guy advises care when building your team. "Create your team before you do anything," he warns. "Talent with no team is no talent. Get somebody that can help you manage your team and get somebody else who will give you legal advice. Always know what you're good at, and be honest about the things you're not good at."

These were lessons Guy had to learn the hard way, but thankfully, through decades of work and struggle, he ended up right back where he needed to be, with the Sugarhill Gang. "I'm fortunate, I'm successful, I've got cool stuff, but that's not what's important. The trappings of success are just a byproduct. The performance is the greatest thing. It's amazing! When I cross the threshold of that stage, I'm Master Gee," smiles Guy. "There's always a point in the performance where I transition to Master Gee and am no longer Guy. I'm not thinking about what I have to do. I'm just Master Gee, and I'm rocking the crowd."

Dr. Sam Pappas

A Cultivated Mind in a Disciplined Body

Sam Pappas was born to two Greek immigrant parents and was raised with a respect for the wisdom of the ancient Greek world. In the birthplace of modern medicine, Sam's forefathers always stressed the importance of "a cultivated mind and a disciplined body" for maintaining good health. The lesson stuck with Sam.

The more time Sam spent as an MD, the more he observed that the advice doctors typically offered their patients was lacking. "A friend of mine got me started looking at research in the integrative health world," he explains. "I was looking at this data and thinking, 'Man, this research is confirming what my grandparents said.' I go back to Greece occasionally, and I see older people thriving. I took a deep dive into the literature of Greek medicine since I have always been fascinated by warrior cultures. I was also fascinated by health through a historical lens. So I started to teach myself lifestyle medicine."

Sam's colleagues were less than enthused about his studies. Many dismissed the idea of integrative health and encouraged him to focus on prescribing pills and getting the patients out the door. There was enormous pressure to treat as many patients as possible, as quickly as possible. This didn't incentivize the behavior—spending time getting to know your patient—that Sam has found so important to improving patient outcomes.

"I spent more time with people than my peers did," he explains. "I asked them about diet, stress, work, meaningful friendships, spiritual outlets, etc." And the patients responded. Within a year or two, his reputation had spread across the area with mothers in North Arlington singing his praises as their doctor of choice online.

After some time, Sam ended up in charge of a practice, where he was named a top doctor by the *Washingtonian* magazine. He had a long waiting list of patients who knew him by reputation only. And yet, for the medical establishment, there was only one metric that mattered. That metric was money. "They were shaming me and comparing my daily patient visits for a month to the average of other doctors. I saw 14 patients when others were seeing 30," he recalls. "I would counter that I have the best outcomes, my patients have fewer hospitalizations, my patients were raving about me, I was a *Washingtonian* Top Doctor, and other things that I thought would be metrics a doctor's practice would want. But obviously, those weren't the key metrics they wanted."

Seeing the writing on the wall, Sam began to put together an audacious plan. He'd start an integrative health practice, out of network, with concierge services. Patients could choose to pay a flat annual rate of $2,500 to $3,000 a year and get full access to Dr. Pappas in-person or remotely via Skype whenever they needed him.

Sam's hospital was shocked and claimed the move came out of nowhere. Sam's wife, Joyce, was nervous. "She was very worried," he recalls. "She felt that going 'out-of-network' was risky and wasn't sure concierge services would be attractive to patients. But I assured her that

I know how to take care of people and that my work ethic and sweat equity will make it work. I told her, 'If we do this, they will come. I don't know how it'll all work out, but I want you to partner with me.'"

Joyce was trained as an ICU nurse—a "fantastic" one at that notes Sam—who had given up her career and plans for medical school to move to New Jersey with Sam and raise their kids. But she was also blessed with incredible organizational skills and a head for business. She became the co-founder of Pappas Health and today takes care of the back office and operational side of things. "I'm more of a 30,000 foot kind of guy," explains Sam. "Joyce is hardworking, knows finances, and is very much synergistic with my approach. She's the one meeting with all of our business advisors and professionals and handling all office matters. I'm really blessed that she can do all of those things and allow me to serve our patients."

Today, along with Sam and Joyce, Pappas Health employs three other staff members. The practice is small but thriving. Sam estimates he has about 1,000 patients in total, not to mention a few thousand more who subscribe to his emails. The practice fuses traditional medicine with Sam's passion for integrative health which ensures that patients receive the best of both worlds along with a hefty dose of one-on-one attention. "I say that we are both high tech and high touch," describes Sam. "We use tools like telemedicine as well as email. Many people in the concierge world will spend an hour with you and tell you to take a pill. We're the opposite. We'll text and email you, see you regularly, and take deep dives into your biochemistry. It's a unique mission. I'm proud to be the only *Washingtonian* doctor that has a focus on both traditional medicine and integrative health and wellness."

Sam's faith in himself, as well as his hypothesis that his ability and reputation would follow him to his new practice, proved correct. Since Pappas Health was launched in 2016, they've never spent a dime on advertising; all of their clients have come to the practice via word of mouth. He even counts many doctors as clients; some of the formerly skeptical doctors see the better outcomes Sam is able to produce and have come around to integrative medicine as the best way to care for themselves. "Initially other doctors thought I was crazy," Sam laughs. "But then the patients realized that I was simply recommending lifestyle changes in most cases. Things like exercise, taking vitamins, and changing the diet. The other doctors were scratching their heads, but the patients were coming in droves. We got better results for them, and I quickly became a doctor to many doctors."

Sam started considering medicine at a young age. His mother saw something in him that she wanted to encourage; something that led her to believe he was cut out for the field. "My mom was kind of like a GM for a sports team," Sam laughs. "She would remind me that I like to communicate, that I was a good student, and that I should consider this field. So I was pushed in that direction in a very loving and nurturing way."

Sam is an identical twin, and his brother, Tom, had other talents. The two of them were inseparable throughout childhood and adolescence. They even shared a bedroom up until they went to college. They were best friends. "We were attached at the hip," smiles Sam. "We'd always go out together and we had many of the same friends. We got along very well and looked out for each other. Basically, we were thick as thieves. I was the oldest by 15 minutes but was always more shy growing up than Tom! And since Tom was more outgoing and we had a lot of common friends, we were very synergistic. Basically, we grew up in a wonderful environment. We also never complained because as twins we attracted a lot of attention!"

Sam, Tom, and their younger brother, Bill, grew up in New Jersey, where their mother stayed at home with them, and their father went off to work at his produce business. Their Greek heritage was a huge part of their upbringing. Both parents came to the U.S. as adolescents when Sam's mother was 13 and his father was 17. The boys were raised attending the Greek Orthodox Church, which was very central to the community. They attended Greek schools, learned to speak and read Greek, and would even take trips back to the motherland for vacation.

Sam's father had been a semi-professional athlete in Greece who played soccer on a small 1st division team in Athens before moving to the U.S. Once here, he started in the restaurant business and worked his way up the ladder like so many other Greek immigrants before eventually switching from restaurants to produce distribution. "He said, 'I'm going to get a truck and start selling to these Greek businesses' since they had a cultural connection," Sam explains. "His love of history and geography meant that he connected with all these people from different parts of Greece. So he had a wonderful business but put in a lot of blood, sweat, and tears. In the summer times, my brothers and I were a part of that business. It was a relationship business, so I really got an appreciation for the importance of relationships from him."

Sam's mother, meanwhile, came over with her parents in 1960. Sam's maternal grandfather was a huge influence on him growing up; he was, in Sam's words, a "larger-than-life" figure, who told them stories of picking up a gun to defend Greece during the civil war. "From him we learned about our history, our culture, and the importance of stories," Sam affirms. "I would say I grew up with one foot in the Greek world and one in the American world."

Both academically and athletically, Sam thrived. He was competitive, and both the twins were driven to try to best each other in the classroom and on the field. "It came easy to both of us, but I was always a little bit better," winks Sam. Their father passed along his love of soccer and would take the boys to see the Cosmos, a team in the North American Soccer League. When they were younger, the twins played soccer and baseball, but as they grew older they developed a love of basketball thanks to the influence of their coach and mentor, Mr. George. Mr. George ended up moving from their middle school to their high school where he continued to cultivate their skills and push them to be better. By 10th grade, Sam was named all-county and one of the top 10 sophomore basketball players in New Jersey. He was also voted the best player on the team.

Through it all, Sam's mother continued to push him. "If I came home with a B, she'd say, 'Is this the best you can do?'" recalls Sam. "She was a great role model as a leader. She was tough, but I learned a significant amount from her. We had some really formative discussions. My dad was more of a quiet leader so early on I saw different leadership styles. He led by example, but she was hands on and would push and cajole. She was the disciplinarian and would exude tough love. So we were pushed to excel and as a result we all had high expectations for anything we did."

By junior year Sam had gotten his first job outside the family business. "I don't remember ever being paid by my dad," he laughs. "I think the payment was free room and board!" At his mother's encouragement, he went out and got a job at McDonald's and learned firsthand the rigors of the food service industry. Then, she pushed him on a possible healthcare career. "She asked me what I thought about healthcare," Sam remembers. "I said, 'I'm interested in it, just because I love biology, I love sciences, and I love serving.' So she said, 'I recommend you go talk to some doctors.' I was so impressed by them and that calling."

Through his conversations with doctors, Sam found out about an opportunity working in the State Medical Examiner's Office in Newark. He worked on the second floor there and processed body parts and fluids for examinations in cases with autopsies. "I was the low man on the totem pole, but I became a fan favorite of the doctors there," Sam says. "I was a young kid who was interested in medicine professionally and would ask questions and help others out. It was a very moving experience. They loved me, and the science part was really cool." He continued to work there in the summers throughout college. The doctors there were proud to learn he'd gone on to successfully get his M.D.

Sam's parents' combination of leading by example possessing a strong work ethic, and pushing them to excel paid off. Tom and Sam were both accepted to West Point. Ultimately, though, Sam decided the military wasn't for him. By then, he had decided to become a doctor, and becoming a doctor in the military meant a commitment of 16 years of service. Instead, he headed for Lehigh University in Pennsylvania, and the twins were separated for the first time in their lives. The transition was a tough one. "We had a clean break," says Sam. "As a result, college was not easy for me. I learned it was tough to fly solo and not have my brother for support and encouragement! My best friend was no longer with me."

But Sam buckled down and focused on his studies through college. He didn't have the typical partying experience a lot of kids have since he knew he needed top grades to go on to medical school. His intensity paid off. He was accepted at several schools but fell in love with Penn State University in Hershey, Pennsylvania.

"Once I was in Medical School, I became a lot more balanced," Sam says. "I realized it was okay to be in the middle of the pack and get a 90%. All of my peers were very smart." The second half of medical school involved doing rotations with different specialties. But unlike most students, Sam decided he wanted to travel. He was able to work in different parts of Pennsylvania and also went to the prestigious Cleveland Clinic for six weeks. "That was my best experience," Sam nods. "It is a great hospital, and someone there gave me the best advice—the Cleveland Clinic doesn't have a lot of hands-on work for residents but nearby Case Western Reserve has one of the best residencies in the country."

Sam considered everything carefully but ultimately decided to return to Cleveland for the Case Western residency. It was destiny calling for it was here that he met Joyce who had been working as a critical care nurse. They had planned to stay in Cleveland for some time, but soon after they married, Sam's mother fell ill with ovarian cancer. Thinking she had only months to live, the couple relocated to New Jersey where she happily lived for six more years.

Sam took a job at a community hospital where he did both clinical and academic work as a teacher working with medical residents. There were only four faculty members (larger schools have more like 100) so he became a "jack of all trades." He taught, saw patients, and helped with administration. It was there that his interest in integrative health began to be piqued.

After about four years there, Sam accepted an opportunity that quickly turned out to be the wrong move for him. A mentor of his had offered him a position at the University of Medicine and Dentistry of New Jersey. It would be a significant pay bump and more administrative work. "I thought it would be awesome, but it was perhaps the worst decision I have ever made," admits Sam. "Within a month I knew I had to leave. I learned that I left for the wrong reason—I left something rather than moved toward something. I made plans to leave after one year when my contract was up. Looking back, it was the worst year I have ever had professionally, but it was a fabulous life lesson. I also learned a lot about my health. When you're not happy, you have a long commute, you're overworked, and you never seen the sun, you can't be healthy."

While planning his departure, Sam spoke with an old friend, Patrick, from medical school who invited him to come to Arlington, where he was running two successful practices and looking to expand. In 2004, the Pappas family relocated to the DC area, and the new job was a much better fit. "I warned Patrick that I was a little different. I liked to spend more time with patients and practice integrative health," recalls Sam. "Patrick was okay with it as long as I billed for my time. So he gave me a lot of freedom."

The partnership went well for a time, but ultimately Patrick began to have personal issues that were interfering with his work performance. The hospital where the practice operated offered to buy out the practice under one condition; Sam was to be in charge. The two parted amicably, and Patrick decided to go his own way. It was as Sam became more enmeshed in the large hospital system that he began to chafe against the counter-productive metrics being pushed by the administrators which then pushed him to launch Pappas Health.

As a leader, Sam says he believes in "we." "I'm very much hands on and very much believe in getting to know someone and connecting with them," he reiterates. "I don't micro-manage. I get to know people and put them in my family. Whatever I've done, I've always been able to connect with people. I've learned to give people goals and get out of the way."

To young people entering the working world today, Sam advises an appreciation for adversity. "Cultivate a biography of meaning," he encourages. "Serve others. Have mentors and learn from them."

"I'm fascinated by leadership and strategy," Sam says of the future. "My next chapter is going to be about that. I'm still learning, I'm 50 years young, and there are a lot of opportunities. My twin brother and I are avid readers, and we've been talking about putting together a website, cultivating some of our readings from health, to history, to religion. I think we need to share wisdom. The dynamism of the future with the traditionalism of the past. Looking forward and back. It's an exciting new chapter."

Michaela Pratt

Never Work a Day in Your Life

The work of drug and alcohol prevention has special meaning to Michaela Pratt; she grew up almost entirely with her mother, as her father was an alcoholic throughout her childhood and through the end of his life. Back then, the reality of her fathers' struggles with his addiction brought shame to Michaela and her older sister. They saw the fathers of their friends being involved with their kids and wondered why their own dad couldn't do the same. They didn't know what alcoholism was. "Today we talk about addiction as an illness," she points out. "It's not a character flaw and it's not a choice. But back in the 1980's, it wasn't like that. And as a child, you viewed alcoholism as your parent picking something over you. It was easy for us to question why we were not enough for him."

Michaela's mother was a working single parent who did everything she could to fill the void where her father was missing. The two had separated before Michaela was even born, and they divorced soon after. In Stockholm, Michaela's mother and her two girls lived in a communal type of housing, where residents had their own apartments but shared a communal space, kitchen and occasional cooking duties. Every Saturday, one floor would cook breakfast for the rest of the building. There were 22 apartments in each building and six buildings overall. The environment gave young Michaela a real home and community, and she became close with her many neighbors. "For my mom it was the perfect set-up," she explains. "We had instant friends in the building among all these other families. I remember being able to go anywhere and knock on neighbors' doors. Everybody knew each other, and neighbors might even offer you apple pie or something. We'd have big carnivals together. It was a great place for a child to grow up since there were so many people and everyone watched out for each other."

In the summers, Michaela and her sister would spend time with their father in the northernmost part of Sweden near the border with Finland. In fact, the border was just a short ride down the road. They had extended family—paternal grandparents, aunts, uncles, and cousins—there, and they enjoyed their time with their dad. "My dad was very smart and was like an encyclopedia of knowledge," Michaela smiles. However, such trips were also fraught with disappointment and broken promises. "I remember we'd do things like make him sign a contract that he'd take us fishing in the morning," she recalls. "The next day we'd show him the contract to try to get him to stick to it, but he'd be too hungover to go.

Despite his struggles with getting sober, Michaela knows that his inability to be there for his daughters was something that affected him deeply. After he passed away, she found a letter he had written to her, her mother, and her sister. Today, that letter is one of her most prized possessions because it says a lot of things that he was never able to say to them in life. "He wrote about his struggle with alcoholism and his disappointment with himself. He wrote about seeing himself at a turning point and that he was going to be better from now on," she says. "It was from when he was in treatment. When I got older, I had it laminated once I realized the power of that letter. To me, it gives me motivation in the sense that it gives what I do professionally a meaning. He wanted more for himself, and he wanted to be better. He realized the pain that he caused to his family without ever telling us."

Today, Michaela works to spare other families that pain by investing in the prevention, treatment, education and research around substance use disorders as the Director of Development for Second Genesis Foundation, a non-profit that provides financial support to organizations and institutions in this space.

Second Genesis' roots in the Washington, DC area run all the way back to 1969, when world-renowned psychiatrist Dr. Sidney Shankman founded the nonprofit to serve individuals and families in the throes of addiction. The organization utilized the therapeutic community model, a more holistic approach that focuses on the patient's overall lifestyle rather than simply encouraging abstinence from addictive substances. Second Genesis expanded to serve families throughout the mid-Atlantic region—serving nearly 300 adults and 100 adolescents in residential treatment and another 250 in outpatient programs daily in 11 treatment centers throughout Maryland and Washington, DC—before shuttering in 2014 due to financial difficulties and continued cuts in government funding to its facilities. Before its closing, Second Genesis boasted an estimated 30,000 graduates from its various substance abuse recovery programs at a graduation rate of 68 percent, a notably high mark compared with similar programs. The organization also received worldwide praise for its work at the Second Genesis Melwood House facility in Upper Marlboro, Maryland, a facility dedicated to female patients that included children's services, career counseling, parenting classes and anger management workshops.

After its closing, Second Genesis' board sought to continue the vision of Dr. Shankman and thus began a foundation to steer funding from the sale of the organization's assets and new fundraising efforts to other worthy DC-area institutions with the similar mission of reducing substance abuse through prevention, treatment, education and research. Enter Michaela, whose role as Director of Development of the Second Genesis Foundation allows her to take advantage of her skills and past professional experiences to help achieve their mission—all the while driven by the passion derived from her own lived experience dealing with the issue she now works to combat.

Prior to joining the Second Genesis Foundation, Michaela served as President and CEO of Mentor Foundation USA, the US member of Mentor International, the leading NGO devoted to helping youth worldwide make healthy choices for their future. It was founded in 1994 by Her Majesty Queen Silvia of Sweden in partnership with the World Health Organization.

"2020 was a difficult year, in so many ways. The isolation and shutdown of communities has directly impacted everyone, but some vulnerable groups of society more than others," says Michaela. Since the COVID-19-related social distancing began, the frequency of alcohol and substance use has only increased. In fact, a recent study conducted by the Centers for Disease Control and Prevention (CDC) found the highest number of overdose deaths ever recorded in a 12-month period in 2020, numbers that suggest an acceleration of overdose deaths during the pandemic.

"Every year it's got worse and worse," she nods soberly. "In 2020, more than 80,000 people died of a drug overdose." Although many more Americans have died from COVID-19 than overdose, those who died from overdose were significantly younger.

While the nation and the world address the future spread of COVID-19 with effective vaccines, there is no vaccine for substance use disorders. The overdose epidemic existed before the COVID-19 pandemic and will continue after. Tragedies continue to mount as families and communities lose young people to overdose death.

Although Michaela considered her childhood wonderful and fulfilling, she knew from a young age that she wanted something more. And that 'something more' was a dream a 10-year-old girl had to move to the United States thanks to an unusual inspiration: the American TV show *Alf*, about a family who adopts an alien. She couldn't yet speak English, but she read the Swedish subtitles, and fell in love with the American lifestyle. "I loved that family," she laughs. "American families looked really, really nice. I loved the idea of everyone coming down in the morning for a pancake breakfast."

With visions of American suburbia dancing in her head, Michaela was intrigued when flyers advertising au pair jobs in the U.S. began popping up around her apartment complex. She was around 11 years old at the time, but she began to think seriously about how she could make her dream a reality. The biggest hurdle she saw was getting a driver's license. In Sweden, public transit is more readily available, and her mother didn't have a license and didn't have a need for a car. Michaela would have to save money to take classes before she could pass a driving exam, and such exams are more difficult in Sweden than in the U.S.

Still, once Michaela set her mind to something, she wasn't likely to back down. She began babysitting, started a popcorn selling business with a friend in the building, and ultimately landed her first real job at a grocery store at the age of 16. She began saving money for that time when she could take the driver's exam when she turned 18. "I wanted that American dream of a family like Alf," she remembers. "So it was either save money for the classes, or it's not going to happen. I wanted it to happen right after high school."

Sure enough, after graduation, Michaela came to Reston, Virginia for a year to work as an au pair for a family there. It was 2003, and that same year, she happened to meet her future husband. Still, at the end of the year, she felt she needed to go home. Her father had become quite sick, and she wanted to return to help take care of him. While spending time with her father, she spent the next year working with the agency that had sent her overseas doing the English evaluation and presenting the program to interested applicants.

Her father passed away after one year, and Michaela longed to return to the U.S. She had such a wonderful relationship with the family she'd served on her first trip that they invited her back to stay with them for free while she attended school. While there she befriended the new Swedish au pair who had taken her place and the two remain close to this day. Fatefully, Michaela also ran into her ex-boyfriend, Chris. The two got back together and married a year later.

Michaela started studying at Northern Virginia Community College before transferring to George Mason University. After graduation, she got a job at a marketing firm in Bethesda doing business management. Meanwhile, Chris was working on launching his own consulting firm and needed to relocate to Afghanistan to do so. When Chris set out for Kabul, Michaela returned to Sweden for another year, where she worked for Red Bull.

Her time at Red Bull was hugely successful. Her district, Stockholm, won best sales district with the most improved performance, and she was given a free trip to Italy and Germany as a reward. However, she chose to skip the trip to go join her husband in Afghanistan. "I felt it was important for me to go there to show my support," she explains. "He was making a big sacrifice for our family. If I really wanted to understand what he was doing and viewed this as an opportunity for me to do that." Michaela then began working for her husband's business and spent time in Kandahar, where she lived on the base, and Kabul, where they lived in an apartment building.

Chris has been a constant source of support since their fateful reunion. "We kind of grew up together," Michaela reflects. "I was 19 when I met him and 22 when we got married. We're very fortunate that we grew together instead of apart, because it can easily go the other way when you're married so young. He's the most driven and ambitious person I know. He's a fantastic father. Plus, his name is Chris Pratt. You would be surprised to know how much that helps in making dinner reservations!" The couple have two children now, a son and a daughter.

While working for Chris's company, Michaela did payroll and back office work and saw the business steadily grow to four partners and over 30 employees. But after a couple of years, she knew she needed to find her own way. "I wanted to miss him when I came home at night," she laughs. "Plus, your husband telling you what to do is cute for a hot minute, but then it gets old." She told Chris she'd begun looking for other work and stumbled into the Mentor Foundation. "I found them through the Swedish mafia," she laughs again. "I ran into two Swedish women at the ambassador's residence and started talking. I sent them my resume, and two weeks later, it landed on the Chairman's desk. She brought me in for an interview, and I spent a decade with that wonderful organization."

She was initially hired to do marketing and business management, but as the second employee of the U.S. operation, she did just about everything. "I had to figure things out and find solutions to anything in the office including technology matters," she remembers. "I had my fingers in Payroll, QuickBooks, project management, marketing, newsletters, design work, benefits, and many other things. I had the freedom to help find solutions that helped create a stronger future for the new organization. I thrive in that environment."

Fortunately, the leadership took note, and they worked with her to develop her skill set. "Sometimes it's easy for an organization to get comfortable when employees are running things well," Michaela notes. "I was fortunate that I was encouraged and continuously developed so I never felt bored. The leadership in the organization recognized what I was doing and helped me continue to grow professionally." Their faith in Michaela continued when the promoted her to President and CEO in 2017. Michaela spent a decade with the organization and helped hem build key partnerships and programs.

In April of 2021 she joined the Second Genesis Foundation as Director of Development, with a focus on fundraising and development to help grow the Foundations resources, partnerships and ultimate impact.

As a leader, Michaela works to embody that attitude and pass on opportunities to others. "I always encourage and give my team members the opportunity to prove themselves," she affirms. "I do not like to micromanage people or dictate to other people how to work. I'd rather provide positive reinforcement; I like to spot talent and develop it. I trust my team 100% as a professional and as an adult to do their job."

To young people entering the working world today, Michaela advises maintaining an attitude of humility and willingness to learn. "There's a lot of professional decorum that doesn't seem to be as well known by the younger generation," she reflects. "It's important to do things like send hand-written thank you notes. And to understand you can actually learn from somebody who's worked a lot of years!"

Michaela is excited about the new chapter in her career, where she can keep making a difference in the community. "I never envisioned myself working in the non-profit sector, especially not in the area of substance use prevention," says Michaela with a smile. "I think I subconsciously gravitated towards community service, as a way of dealing with our family history and grief. To me, what I do does not feel like a job. The saying is true, if you love what you do, you will never work a day in your life."

Ken Rochon, Jr.

Amplifying Hope through a Legacy of Smiles

When Ken Rochon Jr. moved from a small Midwestern town to Maryland as a teenager, he was unsure of what he wanted to do with his life. Being so close to the Nation's capital, he could smell success in the air immediately. "When I moved to Maryland, I had never felt so much opportunity in my life," Ken recalls. "I had just come from a place where there's no such thing as entrepreneurialism unless you count doing a paper route. I was working my butt off detasseling corn every summer, de-weeding the bean fields, and shoveling snow from driveways. All the jobs I had were manual labor. When I got here, I immediately saw an opportunity! You can do anything here and make a living."

Ken was only 17 at the time, but he had found not one but two successful businesses within the year. One was an entertainment company, and the other was a design company. Today, the former is known as Absolute Entertainment and the latter Perfect Publishing. They are both 37 years old and still thriving.

Few teenagers would have the wherewithal to build two profitable businesses from the ground up, but Ken had a natural talent for making connections and selling his talents to customers. His father taught him that a good name is everything- in life and in business, and Ken quickly built a reputation for providing only the highest quality services. "Absolute had an average five-star rating," explains Ken. "As a result, we charged almost $1,000 more for a DJ for a wedding than anyone else in the area. Then we put that money back into customer service. By 2002, we were doing about 1,400 big weddings a year. We were the second largest DJ service in the entire region with 23 high-end accounts."

As big as the business got, Ken almost lost everything when an embezzlement scheme was uncovered. An employee at Absolute Entertainment had, over five years, stolen over $150,000. DJ work is seasonal, and the theft was discovered shortly before a hefty tax bill was due. Ken was shocked, but as he began to take steps to right the ship, nine of his 11 DJs left. They started competing companies of their own, and the financial situation looked bleaker than ever.

"They thought the business was going to fail and didn't see any path for recovery," Ken reflects. "But I had two people who had been with me for 20 years and were willing to stay with me as I took steps to rebuild the company. It took three years, but we rebuilt it into the company we were before. Then I went on my very first vacation!"

Ken doesn't believe in quitting, and he's quick to attribute his attitude to another of his dad's lessons. It's clear he profoundly admires his father, with whom he's become even closer as an adult. "Playing baseball at age 12, I was assigned the catcher position, which I hated," laughs Ken. "When I told my dad I was quitting, he told me he'd never sign me up for anything else again in my life! That hit me like a ton of bricks. I never quit again, and I never quit another thing for the rest of my life."

Today, Ken is CEO of the Umbrella Syndicate and Co-founder of The Keep Smiling Movement, an international nonprofit mental and dental health organization. Both forge connections between people all over the world. The Umbrella Syndicate, founded in 2010, is a marketing and PR organization that amplifies good businesses and good causes. Through a lifetime of prioritizing relationship building and networking, Ken maintains a vast Rolodex of connections to help get the word out about exciting new ventures. Umbrella Syndicate now boasts thousands of connections, including business owners, writers, influencers, musicians, speakers, models and more.

True to form, Ken did not focus first on monetizing the Syndicate; he still had his successful entertainment business supporting him financially, and he knew that step one was building a rock-solid reputation. Instead, he began by offering his services to prominent clients in exchange for sponsorships. "I volunteered," he describes. "I would find the biggest events on social media and let them know I had a large platform and could get them exposure. All I asked in return was to be listed as a senior sponsor. They would look at my page and could see it was blowing up. I was getting 35,000 visitors a week, and they could see the potential exposure they would get. I did events at the White House and worked with the Ravens and Redskins. None of it was bringing in money yet, but it was bringing massive prestige. That became the door opener."

With little income flowing into the Syndicate at its start, Ken was able to use the work he'd done for movers and shakers to attract clients. Seeing the work he'd completed to date; Ken began to get offers for paid work. "I went through lots of years of looking at deplorable income statements, but in the market, I looked like a millionaire," laughs Ken. "People thought I was a millionaire! I'm next to all these big companies, proving that I'm worth $5,000 to $10,000 a day, or $2,500 per hour in some cases. Umbrella Syndicate wasn't started to be impressive financially; it was a relationship collateral investment portfolio."

Ken loved to ask his clients to name the most inspiring person they knew and then connect with that person. Along the way, he was always looking for purpose. "Every day, I was praying, not to make money, but to know what I'm supposed to be doing with my life," says Ken. "It took seven years, and then this 65-year-old Jewish man hands me a card that said, 'Keep Smiling.' I couldn't stop thinking about this card and what I could do with it. I talked to him that weekend and asked if I could turn it into a global movement. He said, 'OK.' That surprised me. I thought he would think I was crazy."

The man's name was Barry Shore, and for years he'd been on a simple mission—to keep people smiling. Since 1999, he'd been carrying "Keep Smiling" cards and handing them out to everyone he met. Ken loved the card and immediately saw the potential of The Keep Smiling Movement. "There's nothing more welcoming than a smile, no matter what language you speak," observes Ken. "This was God's gift to me, to have an impact on people this way. My son loves giving cards to people; you give the card to people, and they shift mentally. We call it 'shift happens.' Give the cards out, and you'll see how people change, how they're happier. Barry knew how powerful it was, he'd printed them in about 20 languages, and now we're up to 25. I'd like to have them in every major language."

Barry's work and life have been a major inspiration to Ken. Barry, a sufferer of Guillain-Barré syndrome, a disease that attacks one's central nervous system, woke up one day at 55, completely paralyzed. "He is a bit of a miracle because only about one in 10,000 people can get some mobility afterward," explains Ken. "Barry swims two miles a day. He attributes it to his attitude and mindset. His Rabbi gave him the 'keep smiling' card when Barry was struggling mentally and physically. He walks with a staff today, but he's mobile. He gets in the water swims two miles. Tracking his miles, he will tell you that he's swum from Australia to Los Angeles by now."

In the years between his injury and meeting Ken, Barry had handed out about a million cards. In less than five years, The Keep Smiling Movement has more than doubled with the loyal support of Dr. Andrea Adams-Miller, the Executive Director. "She turned my passion into a 501(c)3 nonprofit that 'Saves Lives with S.M.I.L.E.S by Creating a D.O.S.E. of H.O.P.E,'" Ken shares. "It opens countless opportunities to connect with others, sometimes personally and often professionally. The cards create smiles that invoke conversations. These conversations become motivational stories worthy of our Legacy book as they inspire readers that all is possible. These smiles, cards, conversations and books save lives, inspire hope and build a legacy. And abundance is created as a bonus."

Ken's father was undoubtedly a major influence growing up, but he credits his belated mother with his passion for a positive attitude. She always emphasized the importance of looking on the bright side of every situation. Ken's father was in the military, and the family rarely stayed in one place for more than a year or two. In fact, by the time Ken was 12, his father had been stationed in 13 different locations. The moves were rough on Ken, and often Ken would sabotage his friendships and leave his friends on bad terms when he learned they were moving. "My mother showed me the silver linings," Ken reflects. "She taught me that if you look for a problem with someone, you're going to find it. But if you look for the good in people, you always find it, too. My mom taught me how to believe in myself and other people."

Born in Rhode Island, Ken lived in Paris for two months and later in Hong Kong. When Ken's father was stationed in Vietnam, Ken and his mother moved to India to live in his paternal grandfather's home. His first memories are of New Delhi, where his grandfather taught agriculture throughout his career. He was the only white student at his school, but he recalls that he was easily accepted and never bullied. He learned to love Indian food, which he professes he could eat every day. He heard from his father in Vietnam via tape recordings sent in the mail.

The family's next stop was Germany, but in Germany, they moved between five different bases. "When I found out we were moving again, I'd just turn into the biggest jerk ever," remembers Ken. "I destroyed friendships and picked big fights. It was my way of not dealing with the pain of losing them. But my mom intervened when she saw what was happening. She taught me there was never a good reason to be negative. She always found a way to be happy."

After Germany, the family relocated to the US in a small town in Illinois. This area is where Ken spent the rest of his middle school and high school years. The adjustment to the US was huge. In Europe, Ken had, like most kids, been fascinated by soccer. He thrived on the field and excelled at the sport, but in America in the 1970s, soccer just wasn't an option. "Back in Germany, I thought I was going to be a professional soccer player," smiles Ken. "I was like a junior Pelé. I was 12 years old, playing with high school kids. I was an all-star soccer player. And then we moved."

Without soccer or any of his childhood friends, Ken spiraled into depression. It was hard adjusting to America despite the fact it was his native country. For one thing, the racism in Illinois shocked him. There was a black and white side of town, and Ken was called names for being kind to all the other kids, no matter their race. Some of the students teased him for being from Germany for coming from a foreign culture.

Finally, a friend of Ken's dad suggested that he try out for the cross country and thought that perhaps running would be a positive athletic outlet. "I hated life without soccer, and I was about two years into my depression," recalls Ken. "In my first 5k race, I killed it. I was in contention the entire race and was running with the top athletes. The high school coach was there and invited me to try out. In the 9th grade, I qualified for a spot at the state competition. I ended up being offered Captain of the Track team, Captain of Cross Country, and Captain of Indoor Track. And then my dad gets another assignment in Maryland."

His prowess at running was so sought after, all of Ken's coaches offered to let him live with them. They wanted him to remain in Illinois and complete his high school running career. Ken was also an accomplished artist and had already been awarded two art scholarships to Illinois State University. His art teacher also extended a similar invitation. But Ken knew that as important as his community had become to him, his family was more important. "I was 17, and I had to reinvent myself yet again," Ken remembers. "It was hard. But I didn't sabotage relationships this time, and I was committed to earning in Maryland what I lost in Illinois. It was the first time I had something to prove—prove that I could do it again."

Ken earned two small cash art grants to study Medical Illustration at Anne Arundel Community College. The degree was a mixture of art and science; Ken realized it was a way to earn money while embracing his love of art. "I had a love of anatomy," says Ken. "I was studying Leonardo da Vinci's anatomy drawings when I was in the second grade." His love of science, meanwhile, was spurred on by a harsh third-grade teacher, Mr. Engel. "He was strict," Ken grins. "He ran his science class like a military school. No matter how hard I worked, I couldn't get more than a C- in his class. But as demoralized as I was, when I went on to 4th, 5th, and 6th grade, I was always the top student in science all because of Mr. Engel."

Despite his love for art, Ken quickly realized that medical illustration was not at all creative. He decided he wanted to make a difference, particularly to kids in his community, finishing college with a degree in education. He knew teaching paid very little, but he enjoyed influencing young minds, and he was making money with his DJ business. His teacher's salary served as a supplement rather than his only income stream. "The idea of teaching came from my mom," Ken states. "My mom taught for 22 years before she was diagnosed with dementia."

Ken spent a few years teaching in Prince George's County before realizing that as much as he wanted to change his community for the better, the education system wasn't built for real change. "I was naïve to think I could make a difference in that system," admits Ken. "If a kid worked in my class and put forth an effort, I would give them a minimum of 70%. But the principal I worked for didn't see things the same way. His focus was to cash the check and go along to get along."

In 2005, Ken's mother was diagnosed with Alzheimer's, and he devoted himself full-time to assisting his father with her care. It was a new dimension to the relationship between father and son. "I'm the oldest, and my younger brother and sister never gave him any trouble," describes Ken. "I probably gave him 50 times more trouble than both combined! I was rebellious, and that didn't fit well with his military background. But when my mom got sick, I was the one who dropped everything. For three years, I minimized everything else I was doing to help him. My dad and I became super close because of that situation."

After his mother passed away, Ken followed through on a lifelong dream of publishing a book. "She had always wanted to be an author, and she left without getting to do that," relates Ken. "I committed to not letting that be my story. A year after she died, I published my first book, *Becoming the Perfect Networker*."

Around the same time, Ken's future wife, Nelly, entered the picture. She was patient with Ken's devotion to his mother during her long illness, and he loved that she understood the importance of family. The couple has one son together, Kenny. "She's a rock-solid mom, wife, and homemaker," he observes. "She makes sure home is home. When I enter the door to our house, I don't bring problems or issues with me. We have rules about that. My phone gets docked, and I'm 100% present with Kenny and my wife."

Ken's commitment to family is evident in the pride he speaks about his young son's achievements. "He can be a scientist, an engineer, a leader, or anything he wants to be," Ken beams. "By age three or four, he was already doing 8th-grade problem-solving. He's learning sign language; he knows 50 flags and 50 different chemicals and their application in the world." Ken's favorite object in the world is the self-published book he and his son worked on together, *Kenny's Favorite Jokes*. "It's the first thing we've done together," reflects Ken. "And we are going to continue building on this foundation."

As a leader, Ken describes himself as a chameleon. He's both a visionary and a team player. He stresses the importance of democratic management—empowering rather than dictating to his teams. "I don't want to micromanage," Ken says. "I was always working for someone who told me how to do things. I'd rather just tell you to get something done and let you come up with the best way to do it."

To young people joining the working world today, Ken stresses relationships above all else. Relationships are, after all, what got Ken to where he is today, which is part of his reputation. "You have to build partnerships," reflects Ken. "And you have to learn how to bet. One of the defining moments of my career has been during the pandemic. I would have had 99% lost income if I didn't know how to pivot, but since my pivot, I earned my doctorate and I've done some of my best work."

That best work included the two compilation books *HOPE is DOPE* and *D.O.S.E. of HOPE*. Two multiple book editions devised to showcase inspirational stories of resilience to give others a reason to smile. "The feedback has been a beautiful thing as we have had people say that they had given up," relates Ken. "And The Keep Smiling Movement gave them the dose of hope they needed to stay positive. That result is what I desire, a world where others are inspired and motivated to be resilient while they leave a legacy. With that, their SPH increases, their 'Smiles per Hour,' and when you increase your SPH, you're happier, healthier, and more abundant."

"Personally, I have embraced the sentiment 'We Amplify Goodness,' which you will find on the back of every keep smiling card, as my mission and purpose for a living," Ken states. "What a way to live life and tip the Happiness Index. Therefore, I challenge you to test this

SPH Factor phenomenon to increase your smiles and leave a legacy towards a life you love that inspires others."

LaJuanna Russell

Trust Yourself

To her classmates in high school, LaJuanna Russell seemed to have it all. She was pretty, popular, and academically successful. She was also a dancer and was captain of the drill team. She was always on the move and seemed to know everyone. But on the inside, LaJuanna was suffering from low self-esteem. She didn't know she was pretty or popular. From her perspective, she was just doing what she had to do—throwing herself into school and work, and keeping away from home.

LaJuanna has always been close with her mother, but as a child and teenager, she avoided the family home where her then-stepfather tyrannized the little family. He was physically, emotionally, and verbally abusive, and hardly a day went by that LaJuanna didn't hear insults and ugliness thrown her way. "He would call me dumb, stupid and ugly all the time," she recalls. "I didn't have any self-esteem for a long time because of that abuse. I think that's why it was important for me to succeed."

Tired of living under such circumstances and knowing her stepfather would never help fund her college education, LaJuanna legally emancipated herself at 17. That summer after high school, she began crashing with various relatives as she saved money to pay for her first semester of college. She'd had little guidance and wasn't aware that she wouldn't be able to "pay as you go" once she got to school. Suddenly, she had a huge tuition bill that she was unable to pay, and her education depended on her coming up with the money. She was able to borrow about $1,500 from an uncle to get through that first semester, and from then on, she completely paid her own way.

Against the odds, LaJuanna thrived and succeeded in college. After graduation, she began working in marketing and later graphic design. She quickly realized she could make more money as a 1099 contractor helping various groups with their design needs than she could as an employee of a company.

A few years after graduation, LaJuanna was successfully running her own business. She had moved into international business development and was coordinating trips between the U.S. and the Caribbean. Everything was going swimmingly when she heard a familiar voice in her head, and her old insecurities kicked back in. The voice was telling her she wasn't good enough. She, therefore, decided to leave her successful business because she needed to pursue an MBA. "I decided I needed a degree to do the thing I was already doing!" LaJuanna laughs. "In hindsight, I'm glad I did it, but I now wonder how I was able to convince myself that I needed a degree to do what I'd already been doing. Why did I need a piece of paper to give me confidence? I needed that external validation of someone telling me I was good enough."

LaJuanna finally hit a major turning point in 2013. She had founded her company, Business Management Associates (BMA), several years prior, but sequestration had led to major financial difficulties. LaJuanna had always been behind the scenes doing operational work and didn't consider herself to be a salesperson. So she brought someone on to handle business development in 2008. By 2012, she'd realized this person wasn't really doing much of anything at all.

"When I let this person go, I thought 'well, at least I have a pipeline of business.' But then I called people 'in the pipeline' and they'd never heard of BMA," remembers LaJuanna. "I was hopeful that I could focus in 2013 and get things back on track, but then came sequestration. Revenue dropped from $3 million to $1.5 million. And I remember sitting at my mom's birthday dinner…crying. The bank was yelling at me, I was the primary breadwinner in my family, I had staff depending on me. Everything just seemed to be crashing down at the same time." Rather than give up, however, LaJuanna stepped up and took control. She knew there was only one person with the skills, passion and tenacity to right the ship and she was staring at her in the mirror. "I thought I needed someone else to do sales. I thought I wouldn't be able to do it," she reflects. "But who knew better what BMA was about, what it was capable of doing? When I was forced to 'sell,' I did it better than anyone else could.

"From 2013 through 2016, we grew from $1.5 million to $10 million in revenue, and it was all my change in mindset," LaJuanna says proudly. "I was doing all of the business development and sales, and was writing most of the proposals. It sort of goes back to that same feeling I had getting my MBA. Why did I need someone to tell me that it was okay for me to do that? Since that point, I've remained the primary rainmaker for the company and we've never been stronger."

Thanks to LaJuanna's business development skills, BMA is thriving. Currently they have about 80 employees and will celebrate 16 years in business in 2021. LaJuanna launched BMA while she was still working for a full-time employer. "I went to the president of that company and said, 'I'm going to make you a great offer,'" she smiles. "I'm going to quit, and you're going to hire me as a 1099 contractor for one year.

I'll keep working with you, and I'll develop my own business on the side." LaJuanna was so critical to the firm's operation that they quickly accepted that offer. They were eager for her to continuing helping them optimize their processes.

And that's exactly what BMA, a government contracting company, was born to do: process optimization. Who does what? How do they do it? Who oversees what workflows? How can projects be efficiently managed?

As the company grew, however, more and more clients asked for help on human resource (HR) related issues, and BMA transformed into an HR-heavy company. Today, about 70% of its work is in the HR space through federal contracts.

"We do all traditional HR work including things like creating policies, hiring, firing, classifications, helping people understand their positions, position management, etc.," LaJuanna explains. "We also help clients understand federal hiring—because it's very different—and help them hire to meet their organizational chart. We do retirement, retirement training, and we'll help manage payroll. From the strategic and operational side, we're doing workforce analytics with some clients now. One of the things I really love doing is workforce development, helping clients establish an effective career ladder. For example, what would a career ladder look like for a GS-5 to go to a GS-13? This helps employees understand where they can go and how they can get there. We do the whole lifecycle of the employee engagement and development."

Since the sequestration scare, BMA has focused on winning more prime contracts as these vehicles tend to be more secure in times of economic contraction. Today, BMA is a prime contractor on 90% of its contracts. Another result of the sequestration scare is LaJuanna's involvement with the Small Business Majority (SBM), a nonprofit organization that works with small businesses across the country and advocates for their issues.

SBM approached LaJuanna and asked if she would speak with an Associated Press writer for an article about the crisis. "From there I was asked to speak at events. I did a speech on C-SPAN that still runs to this day," she notes. "It was all about the impact of these shenanigans on small businesses. SBM helped me so much at that time and gave me something else to focus on. Today, I'm the Chair of their Board."

Between BMA and SBM—and a host of other targeted professional and industry involvements—LaJuanna keeps very busy. "Everyone thinks having your own business equals all this freedom. And there is a level of that, but between client work and staff needs and the demands of being a business owner, 'freedom' is defined a bit differently for each person."

That ability to adjust her perspective has been a critical success factor for LaJuanna and BMA. She is well known for her positivity and fun-loving spirit. In fact, having fun is a crucial part of the culture at BMA. LaJuanna strives to bring joy and humor to every situation. "If you're not going to have fun in a meeting, why go?" she jokes. "That's who I am, that's my personality, and that's what I want to infuse into this business. Things we have to deal with may not always be fun, but we're going to make it fun. We're not walking around with our heads hanging down. We laugh every chance we get."

LaJuanna attributes this fun-loving nature to her paternal grandfather—a man whom she admired and looked up to when her father was out of the picture and her stepfather was treating the family poorly. Her grandfather was a jazz drummer, a larger-than-life figure with a house full of friends and a big personality. "He was my best buddy in the world," she glows. "He was the kind of guy that if my grandmother went to the grocery store for a loaf of bread, she'd come back to a house of 30 people having a party. The thing he instilled in me was to make life fun."

LaJuanna was born in Alexandria, Virginia, and has lived in the area her entire life. Both of her parents were federal employees. Her mother worked as a secretary at the Department of Defense and her father worked for the IRS. The two divorced when she was only two years old, which meant LaJuanna's mother and grandmother played an even bigger role in her life.

As a young child, LaJuanna and her mother lived close to extended family. In fact, LaJuanna estimated the extended family in the area to be in the hundreds—and that was just the cousins. She could hardly walk down the street without being stopped by an aunt or uncle. Today, she never has fewer than 80 people over during the Thanksgiving holiday. As a young child, she was closest with her twin male cousins. They were slightly older and never lost the opportunity to torture her with games like 'shove LaJuanna in a hole' or 'tell LaJuanna to get in the sewer.'

"I remember so many times my aunt running out yelling, 'Leave her alone. Get her out of that hole!'" laughs LaJuanna. "They were always in trouble, but I loved it and loved them. Those were fun days."

LaJuanna was about six years old when her mother remarried. A few years later, the family moved farther out where it was more affordable so they could own a house rather than continue to rent. Unfortunately, the move meant that LaJuanna was no longer within walking distance of her beloved aunts, uncles, and cousins. Now, she was in the suburbs, and found the environment much more isolating. So, she threw herself into school and work and got a job at the local Friendly's when she was only 13. She loved working behind the counter and making conversation with customers. It was from her interactions there with other students and adults that she began to think about college.

As she got older, she landed a job as a receptionist where she was able to do her homework after school. From 3:00 to 9:00 PM she would work and study before going home to sleep. Sundays were reserved for church with her mother. Religion was often a comfort during the difficult years living with her stepfather, and LaJuanna strongly values her faith to this day.

Eager to get out of the house and prove herself, LaJuanna applied to Penn State and planned to study genetics. She had chronic asthma and wanted to devote herself to curing the disease. She was accepted through Early Admission and excitedly informed her mother, who wasn't nearly as enthusiastic about the news. She asked LaJuanna if she'd applied to any other schools. But LaJuanna had not considered the need to apply to multiple schools until her mother pointed out the cost of attending Penn State; clearly, it was not an affordable option.

LaJuanna's mother did some research and quickly came up with a solution. She went into her room and called the admissions office at Virginia Tech. Twenty minutes later, she told LaJuanna she was in as long as she completed the application and essay. "That's literally how I went to Virginia Tech!" marvels LaJuanna. She moved in with her godmother the summer before school and then into the on-campus dorms to begin school. Meanwhile, her mother finally left her stepfather a few months after LaJuanna left for college.

LaJuanna studied at Virginia Tech in between taking time off to work and make tuition money. She ultimately graduated with a primary degree in Communications Studies and minors in Marketing, Political Science, and English. From there, she got a job at the Optical Society where she did marketing communications and then moved on to the American Nurses' Association where she managed their exhibit program before moving into graphic design. It was then that she began to think about independent contracting and began her entrepreneurship journey.

While completing her MBA in International Finance several years later, LaJuanna landed a great job at Windstar Telecommunications. There, she worked about 30 hours per week in the finance department and was provided with stock options, which she used to purchase her first home. After leaving Windstar, she worked for two government contractors before ultimately deciding she could start her own business and do the work on her own. One particular mentor was Myles, her boss at the second contractor, whom she says gave her the confidence to start her own operation. His wife was also an accidental motivator. "I remember one night she came to the office around 8:00 PM. I knew I would have to be up until 2:00 or 3:00 AM to finish a proposal," LaJuanna remembers. "She walked in with her fur coat and told Myles they had to go to dinner. So they leave, and I'm there pounding out this proposal for six or seven more hours so we have a chance to win it. I finally realized that something was wrong with this picture and knew I could do this on my own."

Today, LaJuanna leads by example, and never leaves her own teammates working late into the night on their own. "Like last night," she describes, "we were working on a response. I was there with them in the conference room as we worked together. We had a bottle of wine and some food, and we all figured it out together. I'm not the type of person who is going to ask someone to do something I am unwilling to do."

As a leader, LaJuanna describes herself as 'free.' She doesn't micromanage; instead, she believes in allowing people the space to learn, develop, and grow into their roles. "Sometimes it works great, sometimes it doesn't," she admits. "Not every person can take that responsibility. I will tell you when the deadline is, but I'm not going to tell you how to do it. But I do expect you to get it done and figure it out. If I tell you how to do everything, you're never going to learn. If I find I have to micromanage someone, then we probably won't work well together because I need people to be as entrepreneurial in this setting as they need to be. But, with that being said, I will always be available to help teach and guide."

To young people entering the working world today, LaJuanna advises careful reflection before leaping, but also not to let fear keep someone form leaping. Two of her favorite quotes are "Never, ever, ever give up" and "What would you do today if you were not afraid," both of which she has displayed in her office. "Do not be afraid," she encourages. "Really think about what you want, then go for it. If you want to be an entrepreneur, just think carefully about why. Are you doing it because you think you're going to have a lot of freedom? Be ready to redefine what that means...again and again and again. Are you doing it because you think you're going to make a whole lot of money? Be ready for a lot of work before that happens. And even when it happens, be ready in case it evaporates overnight—think sequestration or a global pandemic—and be ready to work just as hard or harder to get back to where you were. Talk to people who have 'been there, done that' and really think about (your business) up front. And if that's really what you want, be fearless."

Guylaine Saint Juste

Investing Forward

As a girl growing up in Haiti, Guylaine Saint Juste lacked for nothing. She was surrounded by a strong family and community in Port au Prince. She remembers feeling safe in this strength and knew she had many people looking out for her. These early years shaped the woman she is today.

In fact, she says, "I would wish my childhood on anyone." Though they weren't materially wealthy, she had role models not many others had. Her grandmother, her grandmother's sister, her aunts and her mother made up a tight matriarchal group that lived closely within a space of a few blocks, and Guy spent much of her childhood at her grandmother's house learning to cook and sew. She learned a lot observing her older relatives quietly. "There were always people around," she smiles. "When we had a family gathering, we didn't need to invite anyone else because there were always 60 or 70 of us at every gathering. It was a strong family."

But just before Guy's 14th birthday, something drastic changed. Her beloved grandmother, the glue who held the family together, passed away suddenly. "I remember it like it was yesterday," she says. "She's been gone now 36 years, but I still talk about her in the present tense. She was an extraordinary woman, was humble, and was really a force of nature. She was the matriarch. You know the expression 'Standing room only?' Well, there was no standing room at all at her funeral. Even a half-mile radius from the church, people were packed along the street. You couldn't find a single person who wasn't wearing black. And they were from all walks of life—from wealthy businesspeople to people who sold shaved ice on the street. Everybody talked about the impact she had on their lives, and on that day I understood the meaning of the word 'legacy.'"

The death of her beloved grandmother, as well as the outpouring of support from her community, were experiences that stayed with Guy as she set about building her own life. It's no wonder, then, that she states that her most cherished goal—the reason she does the work she does—is to build a life of significance.

"I don't believe in the American way of saying 'giving back,'" she muses. "I don't think there's ever a way we can give back for all we've received. As an immigrant to this country, I've received so much. But I do believe in 'investing forward.' I believe we can do more to help solve problems by giving others the tools and the education to succeed. Investing forward, learning how to do that, is a challenge that appeals to all three dimensions of my being and I've decided to devote the rest of my career to trying to help solve it, or at least to have an impact."

That's why today, Guy is the Executive Director for the National Capital Region of Year Up, a program dedicated to furnishing young people with the skills they'll need to succeed in the working world. Year Up caters to the demographic that is commonly referred to as "at-risk," but which Year Up terms, "opportunity youth," recognizing that behind the difficult circumstances of poverty and discrimination, there are often talented, intelligent, committed youth ready to work hard and take on challenges.

Year Up is a national organization, with a presence in 21 cities and 17 markets. Through their year-long program, they prepare young people between the ages of 18 through 24 to take on roles at partner businesses. "They spend six months with us in training for roles that have career longevity and sustainable wages," explains Guy. "So we train for cyber, IT help desk work, QA coding on software, project management, business operations, financial operations, corporate sales, and more. We operate a very strong and robust training program."

In order to find recruits for the program, Year Up makes use of relationships with local schools, the foster care system, the juvenile system, and groups like the Boys and Girls Clubs, as well as good old-fashioned word of mouth. "We'll often get someone who says, 'I used to work with my friend at Chipotle, she completed the program, and now she works at Capital One,'" says Guy. "They realize that if their friend can do it, they can do it, too." In fact, Guy notes that 52% of their students are now finding out about Year Up via word of mouth.

The program is competitive, but for the students who do make it through the application process, the success rate is high. Approximately, 75% of those admitted to the program complete it and graduate. Students can currently choose between three area locations—Woodbridge, Alexandria, and Arlington. However, the Arlington location is currently being moved into Washington DC to allow for more geographic diversity. In two of these locations, Year Up partners with Northern Virginia Community College (NOVA) to provide a top-tier education that also counts as college credit for participants. Students learn not only a typical college curriculum, but also professional skills like being on time, dressing professionally, writing business emails, and other life skills.

Once the students graduate from training, they are ready to be placed with a partner organization. Year Up works with dozens of businesses across the area, including GE, Bank of America, Capital One, Verizon, Microsoft and JP Morgan. These businesses pay Year Up for the ability to access their pool of talent. At their placement, students complete the second half of the "Year Up" program, working as an intern for six months at their partner firm. "At the end of the six month internship, our partner businesses can decide to hire the intern as a full-time employee or wish them well on their job search," explains Guy. "You're talking about kids in Richmond making $65,000 to $70,000 per year. That is life changing."

The Capital Region branch of Year Up has been running for about 13 years, but since Guy took over 4 years ago it's grown precipitously. During her first year, Year Up impacted about 220 students with 48 corporate partners each accepting two or three interns. Last year, they almost doubled that number. They placed over 420 students among 62 companies that accepted five to ten interns each. And each student gets more out of the program, too. "We've grown our base, we've grown our revenues, we've created efficiencies, and we have pushed up wages," affirms Guy. "Wages were about $18 and change when I started, now we're at $23.73. We've also launched certifications for students, including an AWS certification, an A+ certification, and a cyber certification. We've included these in the program to increase their marketability. It's just not the same business we had four years ago."

The annual budget for the project is now $12 million with about 60 staffers across the region. Recently, a government-funded case study found that graduates of the Year Up program fared the best among youth workforce development programs. Students one year out and five years out were earning, on average, 52% more than a counterpart who hadn't completed the program. Surprisingly, even students who had participated in but never completed Year Up held a shocking 32% wage advantage over peers who never entered the program at all. It's clear that Guy is successfully implementing her passion for 'investing forward.'

She's come a long way since her childhood in Haiti, but she had the support of strong female role models like her mother and grandmother along the way. Growing up, Guy was always very close with her mother, and that closeness persisted until her death in 2001. She always had a positive relationship with her father, who was an entrepreneur and introduced her to the business world. Divorces were very rare at the time in Haiti, but her parents divorced when she was six. Because of this, she was able to marvel at her mother's strength and independence firsthand.

After the divorce, everyone, including Guy's maternal grandmother, assumed that Guy and her mother would be moving back home. It was almost unheard of for a young single mother to get her own place, but that's precisely what Guy's mother chose to do. "My mother was fiercely independent," smiles Guy. "I think I've inherited that. My mother was tough, and she decided she was going to raise her daughter by herself. She loved me and pushed me at the same time. Because nothing was ever too good for her daughter. She thought I deserved the absolute best, always." Guy's mother worked as a secretary at a bank to support them.

When Guy was 14, the same year her grandmother died, her father lost his business and left for the United States. It was a hard year, and a hard adjustment; with her grandmother gone, she noticed that her mother sunk into something of a depression. Still, Guy reiterates that her mother was "tough as nails" and she remained a caring and devoted parent. She made sure that Guy remained focused on studies and continued paying for Catholic school, piano lessons, and dance lessons. Each summer, Guy would travel to the U.S. to spend time with her cousins in New York or Florida.

Guy had always been a great student, and in high school she continued to flourish and was the President of the Student Government all four years. But around the time she turned 16, her grades began to slip. She'd met her future first husband, and suddenly she began to focus more on her social life. "He was at the University and he had a car," she laughs. "I discovered popularity because of that! Everyone wanted to be friends with me because I had guaranteed rides. His family was well-to-do, so he also had a few coins in his pocket, too."

She had finished high school and was prepared to sit for her baccalaureate exams—exams every Haitian student takes before continuing their education at the university level—when the political situation in Haiti suddenly deteriorated. Exams were cancelled, and on July 5, 1987, Guy left Haiti to come to the U.S. "I didn't say then that I had come to stay," reflects Guy. "But I think deep down, I knew I had come to stay. Some part of me knew. As a leader, I think I have immense propensity for change, for seeing how things could be better. And I think that's born out of the immigrant experience. I left everything I'd known my entire life. I left my friends, the food, everything I grew up with, and everything I defined as a part of my environment. And I started in a place where I didn't know anybody."

Both of Guy's parents agreed that she would be safer in the States given the unrest in Haiti, but Guy suffered tremendous guilt over leaving her mother behind. "It was more than difficult," she remembers. "In a way it felt like I had betrayed her because I had to leave her. But she knew that this was the best thing for me. She would never hold me back."

Guy came to Washington DC, where her father was working at Fannie Mae, and began learning English. She didn't waste any time; she arrived on the 5th and began working at a job on the 12th. Meanwhile, she looked into taking classes at NOVA and tested high in all the core subjects other than English. "I love numbers and did really well in math. I like numbers because numbers are universal," she nods. "I laughed and I smiled in class, but in reality, I felt lost. I remember seeing my classmates taking notes in Psychology class, but when the class ended I would cry my eyes out and think that I was never going to get this. I didn't think about going back to Haiti though. I'm the kind of person who considers things carefully and takes a long time to come to a decision. But once I've arrived at that decision, there's no turning back."

Despite her early struggles with English, she completed two years at NOVA in 1989. After graduation, she married her first husband, the high school sweetheart who had followed her to the states. Soon after, she went back to school at George Mason University to pursue a degree in International Relations. While at George Mason, Guy landed a job as a bank teller and would continue in banking until 2014.

In 1991, Guy had her first daughter, Joelle, while still in school and working. After graduating from George Mason in 1994, she moved from her teller job to a job at SunTrust Bank. Five years after the birth of Joelle, Guy had a second daughter, Jessica, but by then her marriage was beginning to falter. "I was growing and my then-husband was not," she recalls. "I learned that I can deal with a lot of things, but mediocrity probably isn't one of them."

The couple separated when Jessica was 18 months and Joelle seven, and Guy focused on her career and the girls. Her mother took early retirement and moved to Washington DC from Haiti to help care for them. She supported Guy as much as possible in the years before she passed away, on January 25, 2001. "She died in my arms," says Guy. "She was fighting because she knew she was going to leave me alone as a single parent to two daughters. I climbed into her hospice bed and told her that her entire life had been about me, and that now it was about her. I told her that I knew beyond a shadow of a doubt that I was going to be okay, and she needed to let go. Within two hours of that conversation, I lost my mom. It was one of the hardest things I've ever done, and one of the most glorious things I've ever done, to help my mother die peacefully."

For several years Guy did manage to raise her two daughters by herself and advance her career. SunTrust paid for her to complete a graduate degree in Retail Banking Management at the University of Virginia, which she completed between 2005 and 2007. Then, in 2007, she had the blessing of meeting the love of her life, her husband Jacky. The two were married in 2008, and today he enjoys a wonderful relationship with Joelle and Jessica. "I'm eternally grateful to him," glows Guy. "He's the person who made me believe that I, too, was worthy and deserving of investing in myself. He's a very kind and generous person."

Given the challenges that come along with being a single parent, Guy remembers both of her daughters' college graduations as two great moments of celebration. Joelle graduated in 2013, and Jessica in 2019, both with no debt. "Both of them saluted their mother publicly on the day of their college graduation in words that I will never forget," remembers Guy. "Joelle thanked everyone for coming and she handed me her diploma, and said, 'This is yours. I can't imagine a life without you in it. I can't remember a moment in my life that you weren't there.' And Jessica made a collage of all of her moments with me on her graduation cap. At her dinner she said something similar; it surprised me from her. She said, 'I know you don't know how much I love you because I don't do a good job of showing you!' Those were two glorious experiences of fulfillment. I always told them, 'They're not the center of the universe, but they were the center of *my* universe.'"

In fact, Guy's love for her daughters is what motivated her to devote herself to investing forward. When she realized Jessica was about to go to college, she had a sudden revelation—she'd spent her adult life caring for these two girls. Now, she needed to find significance another way. She had risen to become a Senior Vice President at Capital One Bank, but she was ready for something new. It was soon after she had that thought that she was contacted by the headhunter for Year Up.

As a leader, Guy says she considers herself to be 'tribal.' "Everybody talks about teams; a tribe is deeper than a team," she elaborates. "There's a pride associated with it. I'm not formal, I'm probably one of the least formal people that you'll meet, but I am about tradition. I respect and value traditions. And I think tribes have ways that they do things that are very distinct. There's a sense of belonging, like you're part of something bigger than yourself."

To young people entering the working world today, she advises them to be true to their values. "Be very clear about what are the three or four core values that define who you are," she encourages. "For me, it's truth, love and harmony. Make sure you live consistently in alignment with those values. The truth of the matter is that when you lay your head down, there is a higher truth."

BERNHARDT

WEALTH MANAGEMENT

Peter D. Schwartz

The Leadership Journeyman

Peter Schwartz's parents were deeply religious. He grew up Catholic, went to mass, attended Catholic schools, and even believed that he might go on to become a Priest. After visiting a seminary for a weekend and noting that the lifestyle was more stark than his relatively modest upbringing, he decided against the vocation. But he remained an active participant in the church until high school, when he began to have questions and doubts.

"The Franciscan brothers who taught us would give me dogmatic replies," Peter recalls. "I rebelled against it. I intentionally flunked religion in a Catholic high school my junior year. Keep in mind that I was a National Honors Society student at the time. My parents were not happy with me." Although he had rejected organized religion, Peter's impulse toward spirituality never dampened. Instead, taking his curiosity and love of learning, he embarked on a spiritual journey of his own.

Peter began to explore other world religions, past and present. "I took a mythology course in college, and I was so fascinated by that," he describes. "It was a great way to immerse myself in how the Greeks and Romans dealt with the spirit. I ended up minoring in mythology and ancient history. Along the way, I heard about Joseph Campbell, who had a huge influence on my life. I read everything he wrote. Interestingly enough, *The Hero's Journey* is highly correlated to leadership development. It's about the death of a "current self" that is needed to give rise to a more "evolved and complex self"; that's leadership development."

Peter refers to himself as a "leadership journeyman," someone who doesn't prioritize the destination over lessons learned along the way. Recently, he completed the famous Camino de Santiago pilgrimage, walking for 34 days straight across northern Spain to Santiago de Compostela. As he walked, he reflected on the choices that have guided his life, the lessons gleaned from others, and his commitment to his work.

On the pilgrimage, participants receive a "pilgrim passport," a fold-out document on which a pilgrim collects stamps along the route. Peter considers this to be one of his most prized possessions. It reminds him of both the physical and emotional journey he took. "To me the pilgrim passport is a visual representation of the concept of a leadership journeyman," he reflects. "It's nothing more than a series of stamps on the way to Santiago de Compostela. Santiago was a wonderful place, but those stamps are really what tell the story. It's the milestones along the way that represent the joy and hardship of walking to each one of those places."

Peter relates the three phases of walking the Camino—physical, spiritual and soulful—with the three stages of leadership development—expertise, achievement and impact. The physical stage represents the learning done in the early parts of a career. The spiritual is the phase of achievement. And the final, soulful phase is similar to the professional phase Peter is in now: making an impact, a contribution to others.

"I found out about the Camino on a poetry retreat with the Irish poet David White," Peter says. "The workshop was in Tuscany and someone there had just walked it. I'd just turned 60 years old and I'm feeling this restlessness. I didn't know what the restlessness was at the time, but I had an impulse to go accomplish something else. I realized later that I'd accomplished everything I wanted to, professionally. Another professional accomplishment just wouldn't cut it. So I walked the Camino, and it was wonderfully informative. For me it confirmed that I didn't need to accomplish anything else. Now it's about impact and contribution. Just simply give back what you know and continue to learn. But give it back in my role as a Vistage Chair."

Vistage is a 60-year old organization with over 24,000 members worldwide, hundreds of 16 member executive peer groups in 20 countries learning from one another. Peter has been an unmitigated success there since joining as a Chair 16 years ago. Today, he's a Master Chair and leader of six groups. Master Chairs have demonstrated continually high levels of performance.

In addition to becoming a Master Chair, Peter has won several major Vistage awards. In 2020 Peter was presented with the "Don Cope Memorial Award."The Don Cope Memorial Award is the highest honor a Vistage Chair can receive. It acknowledges the Chair who has made the greatest lasting contribution to the Vistage mission and values in word and deed. The recipient is selected from the highest performing nominees worldwide. A four-time "STAR" award winner, Peter was named Vistage Chair of the year in 2016. He's also won the annual Chair Excellence Award a stunning nine times.

Right now, Peter is running two Chief Executive groups, a key executive group, an emerging leaders group, and is co-leading the Vistage/Stanford Executive Leadership program for select Vistage CEO's in the Mid-Atlantic. He's also the Best Practice Chair for the Baltimore-Washington region, helping new chairs build their groups and setting standards. When asked how many companies he's helped, he doesn't have to estimate; he notes that he recently added them up. He's worked with 279 leaders. Among those companies, he ballparks at least a couple hundred thousand employees, and north of a billion in total revenue.

"It's been the privilege of my lifetime to work side-by-side as a participatory companion with the small business owner," Peter nods. "The wonderful thing is I have people who've been with me the entire 16 years. I've seen marriages, divorces, cancers, kids growing up, multiple successful exits, and even a couple of bankruptcies. I've experienced it all."

Peter got his first leadership certification from Georgetown University in the years before he joined Vistage. He continues to invest in his own development for the purpose of being a thought leader in the leadership development space. Recently, he completed a year-long deep dive with a Harvard professor on immunity to change and adult development theory. He notes that he pursues such deep dives every other year. In 2018, he went through the Vistage Executive Leadership Program through Stanford University, which is three modules on strategy, innovation and leading through change. "It's important to me, if I'm going to have maximum impact on my members, to be a thought leader in this space," Peter asserts. "I consider it my obligation to them to be the 'tip of the spear' with respect to all things related to leadership."

"The reason I do what I do is I want others to live an inspired life," he summarizes. "Ultimately, it's an expression of my spiritual impulse. The word 'inspire' and 'inspiration' mean 'in touch with your spirit.' That is your essential life force, your chi, whatever spiritual tradition you have for understanding spirit. It's that center of you that is the energy that propels your life. I want to live an inspired life, and I want to help others live an inspired life."

Growing up, Peter had no idea he'd end up in such rewarding work. He was born and raised in Levittown, Pennsylvania, a place where he jokes that people "kept down with the Joneses." His family was not wealthy; as he grew up, he remembers his parents struggling financially. Seeing that reality, his first priority when he reached college was not spiritual fulfillment, but money. His mother stayed home with Peter and his three younger siblings. His father worked for a wood preserving company, and over the years, the family's financial status began to improve. Peter's father never finished college and started as a clerk with the business. But he eventually worked his way up to become President. "It was wonderful to watch my father do that," Peter reflects.

Both of Peter's parents were tough and had high expectations of their children. Even though at times they could be unreasonable and angry, Peter loved and admired them. The family always joined together for dinner each evening. He recalls his father's integrity and the respect the workers had for him as he developed into a great leader. His mother, he recalls, had an artistic nature and an eye for beauty. Each Christmas, she made it her business to give the children a holiday wonderland. She didn't have much interest in blinking lights around the garage; instead she gravitated toward more unique décor, like beautiful bells in the windows.

Peter always did well in school. Although neither of his parents had finished college, they made it clear that all four of their children would attend. Additionally, he developed a love for athletics at an early age. He excelled in baseball and believes that his early success in sports contributed to his successes later in life. "I'm very kinesthetic, and I played every sport I could play," he smiles. "I won a lot; I remember being in swimming and winning over and over. In baseball, I was a great hitter and pitcher. I had this experience in my childhood of winning, and I really believe that that's how I came to expect winning of myself. I wanted to win and I wanted to excel, so I set that standard for myself." In middle school, Peter's eyesight suddenly worsened, and he struggled to deal with the loss of baseball. However, he leaned into his training on the swim team, quickly becoming a star there as well.

Also from an early age, Peter had the instincts of an entrepreneur. As an altar boy, he cannily got himself into a leadership role where he could determine assignments. Knowing the big events like weddings, Christenings and funerals usually brought in tips, he began assigning himself all the good shifts. "Finally one of the nuns intervened to tell me, 'Hey, spread the wealth'," laughs Peter. "So I began to learn management while I was learning how to make money."

His first job was shoveling snow in the neighborhood. Then he got a paper route. Finally, in high school, he began working at the wood preservation company alongside his dad. "It was fun to work at the plant even if it was physical labor," Peter recalls. "That experience instilled in me a sense of respect for the working man. They had dignity; this was the best way they had to make a buck."

After high school, Peter went off to college as planned. He began at Temple University, but when his parents moved to Norfolk, Virginia, he transferred to Old Dominion University. His parents still didn't have much money, and Peter was paying his own way through school by working. Transferring meant he qualified for in-state tuition.

Throughout school he maintained a hectic schedule of studies and jobs. He worked in construction building tennis courts. He loaded trucks for Nabisco and brought home free broken cookies to eat for dinner. He was a lifeguard at the beach and a bartender in local establishments. Through it all he earned decent grades, hitting his self-imposed goal of maintaining a 3.0 GPA through graduation.

The rigorous schedule wasn't the only difficulty Peter encountered in college. When he was a junior, his mother committed suicide. It was a crushing blow. "It numbed me," he reflects. "It took me a while to find joy again. The loss of a parent at a young age shapes a person. My siblings were also hugely devastated by it." And to make matters worse, his father quickly remarried a mere six months later. He wanted the kids to accept a new stepmother but that was difficult to do so shortly after their mother's death. Although his father was doubtless mourning in his own way, the decision was deeply offensive to Peter. For a long time, Peter could not find the power to forgive his father.

Ultimately, Peter and his father were able to work through their differences during the last three days of his father's life. "It was all forgotten during that time," he says soberly. "I was running Vistage meetings that week and at the end of each meeting, I would drive three hours to my father's hospital and spend the night. I did that for three nights in a row, and on the last night he passed. When I drove back home, I had my eyes set on the road in front of me, and I realized that I don't need to look back and regret a thing. I'm really grateful for the time I was able to spend with my father during those three days."

Originally, Peter had considered a pre-med major, but quickly found it wasn't for him. By chance, he discovered the mythology course that became so influential on his journey. Ultimately, he majored in psychology and minored in mythology. But upon graduating, he knew mythology wasn't where he'd be able to make a buck. He was still focused on securing his financial future before looking to feed his spirit. At a party, he ran into a girl who was working for C&P Telephone. He learned that she was making pretty good money at her job. Shortly thereafter, he happened to read an article in the *Wall Street Journal* about emerging industries: one was telecom. Peter reached a decision. He went out and got a job selling telephone systems for a start-up.

At first, it was rough going. But after a manager pulled him aside and assured him that successful people involve others in their sales, Peter learned to value help from others. He learned that working with others yields tremendous dividends. And soon after, he was named Rookie of the Year at his Fortune 500 start-up. "That was an eye-opening moment for me," he declares. "It taught me the importance of a change mindset."

From there, the sky was the limit. Peter climbed the ladder, eventually moving into VP and Senior VP roles at various telecom companies. After several years, he went out on his own, reselling long-distance with a good number of contractors on staff. Then he took a position as a Principal in a consulting business. Finally, in his last role before joining Vistage, he was VP of Strategic Alliances at another start-up. The business went from four employees to 400 in the space of a few years and raised $75 million in venture funds. Ultimately though, the new business was a casualty of the dotcom boom. "I liked being in start-ups," Peter reflects. "I was able to sell a brand-new product in a market that's never been sold before. I developed my capacity to take an early stage concept or company to maturity."

By the time the last business went under, Peter had already taken his first few leadership training courses. Although he enjoyed many of his previous roles, he began to realize that his real passion lay in guiding others. "I say I get two paychecks," he smiles. "I get the financial paycheck from Vistage, and I get an emotional paycheck from the work I do. And most months the emotional paycheck is larger than the financial paycheck. That's a fact. The joy in it for me is that I don't have a bad day. There are days that are more difficult than others, but I never have a bad day. I may have five 1-to-1 meetings with members and come home exhausted, but emotionally I feel privileged."

For the past five years, Peter has also had the emotional support of his wife Elaine. Elaine is an artist, with an ambition to excel in her chosen second career. Peter finds a great deal to admire in this. "The passion we have for our work is very additive to our relationship," he affirms. "She's a wonderful person, and the list of reasons I admire her is just too long to list. We're the best of friends, and we make great travelling companions. But I really admire her so much for her commitment to her craft."

As a "leadership journeyman", Peter has reflected long and hard about the nature of leadership. Some of the lessons he took from the Camino de Santiago were to "learn to travel light", to "find the joy in the walking" and to learn to respect and love the imperfect and impermanence of all things. It's no surprise he has an elegant answer to the question of the meaning of leadership. "It's nothing more than the deployment of self into circumstance to create a desired outcome," he articulates. "That's the most beautiful and simple definition of leadership to me. First of all, it says you know what your desired outcome is. And the self is the version of you that you bring into that context to create that outcome. So to be able to self-assess before you enter a situation: How do I need to be experienced? What impact do I want to have in this context? That's leadership."

To young adults entering the working world today, he advises discipline. "Set a high bar for yourself and be willing to pay the price," he instructs. "That means get out of bed in the morning, put one foot in front of the other, and move toward your goal no matter what. Enjoy it. But set the bar high."

Mehul S. Shah

Whatever It Takes

Mehul Shah was born in Mumbai, India, the only child of parents who, in spite of their limited financial circumstances, always prioritized his education. Although he went to one of the best schools in the area—surrounded by wealthy kids living completely alien lives—Mehul didn't grow up with a silver spoon. In fact, he cracks, "I didn't even grow up with a spoon!"

But Mehul's parents' decision to invest what little savings they had in private school paid off. He was able to complete an engineering degree and secure a good job after graduation. Then, at a conference, he fatefully met an American businessman. The two hit it off, and the businessman told Mehul he could look him up if he ever made it to the U.S. "I think he forgot about it most likely," smiles Mehul. "He probably thought I would never show up. But I actually appeared on his doorstep and said, 'Hey, you told me to look you up. I'm here!' I'd taken all my savings and sold everything to buy my tickets and get my visa." The businessman was shocked by Mehul's commitment and offered him a job. Mehul didn't plan to stay long-term, but he converted his visa to a business visa and became an employee.

It was 1994 when he arrived, and the next few years passed in a haze of work and study. He found a place he could afford to life in Herndon, Virginia, but his new job was all the way up in Shady Grove, Maryland. Mehul would wake up at 4 o'clock in the morning, head out by 5:00, walk a mile to the bus stop, catch a bus to Vienna to get on the metro, and arrive at work by 8:00. He'd work straight through lunch so he'd be able to head out by 4:00 PM, but his day was far from over. Instead, he took a bus to Silver Spring to his second job at a high school, teaching calculus and physics until 6:00. Still, his workday wasn't over. Next, he headed across the street to the 7-11, where he'd start his shift driving a delivery truck for four hours. He'd arrive home before midnight and would spend a couple of hours preparing for his classes the following day and practicing his English language skills. "I would stand in front of the mirror practicing my diction for hours," Mehul recalls. "I would focus on people talking, the way their lips moved. I couldn't say 'embarrassing' to save my life; instead, I'd say 'embracing.' It was embarrassing! I know I'll always have an accent, but I wanted to feel like I belonged. I worked hard at it."

Before long, Mehul's tireless work ethic and commitment began to pay off. In 1996, his new wife Ketki came back with him from India, where the two young people's families had arranged their marriage. "Her name is a purple flower," Mehul explains lovingly of his wife of 23 years. By then, he had become a Project Manager at his company, and the young couple was prospering. A couple years after that, in 1998, Mehul began discussing the prospect of launching a business with a couple of partners. It was the height of the dotcom boom, and the horizon was wide open. With about $50,000 in savings, Mehul and his partners launched their content management business, helping other businesses with their websites and branding.

At first, everything went smoothly. Mehul and Ketki moved to Washington, and within a few months, she was pregnant with their first child. The firm had an interesting model. Rather than taking direct payment, they instead asked for equity in the businesses they worked with. This structure meant that 29-year-old Mehul was quickly on a path to make tens of millions of dollars. But abruptly, everything fell apart. It was 2001, and the dotcom bubble had burst. Suddenly, all of that equity was worthless, and the business owed almost $2.2 million when the dust cleared.

Mehul and his partners split the debt which meant that he was left with $712,000 of debt. Mehul immediately fell into a depression. Between January and May of that year, he says, "I didn't know what was happening. We were in such bad shape that we lost everything. I had to let go of the houses, cars, and anything of value. Everything was gone. I'd wake up in the morning every day and stare out the window wondering how I was going to feed my children the next day. We were even thinking about moving back to India. If it wasn't for my mother and my wife, I don't know how I would've gotten through it."

Again and again, Mehul reaffirms that his wife, Ketki, and his mother, were the twin pillars that supported him through everything—the good times and the bad. As he dealt with the nearly three-quarters of a million dollars in debt, they advised him against declaring bankruptcy. "They said, don't do it. If you want to sleep peacefully at night, pay it off. I still remember that statement," Mehul reflects. "Until my dying day, I'll be proud that I made the decision to pay it off. I consolidated the debt and found a job at a company called Wipro in California. I became an enterprise architect for them." It wasn't the first time that Mehul went from nothing to something. In fact, he describes himself as "a cat," noting that no matter what, he lands on his feet.

The next four years were a whirlwind. At Wipro, Mehul once again began quickly rising through the ranks as he demonstrated his talent and work ethic. Wipro moved him to Kansas to work with H&R Block and later to Michigan to work on their GM account. While there, Mehul was part of the team that won a $650 million contract. "That got me super famous at the company," he recalls. "It was a $15 billion company, so it's not a small company, but at the time this was the largest deal they'd ever won."

Mehul was promoted again. This time he was sent to Minnesota to take over the region with giant clients including Best Buy and Target. Finally, they asked Mehul to run their global pharmaceutical practice through Johnson & Johnson and moved the family to New Jersey. At this point, Mehul, Ketki and their two daughters had moved from Washington to California to Kansas to Michigan to Minnesota to New Jersey in a space of eight years. Fortunately, his girls were adventurous. "The family was happy and the kids were loving it. Every year, my girls would ask, 'Where next!" laughs Mehul. "It took a lot of effort and hard work, but I was happy they were happy."

Finally, in 2006, Mehul and Ketki decided to have a party to celebrate their 10th wedding anniversary. Mehul called up his old boss—the same businessman who he'd met at the long-ago conference in India and who'd given him his first job in the U.S.—and invited him to the party. The two got to talking at the anniversary party, and Mehul's old boss was shocked and impressed by how high Mehul had climbed in less than a decade since he'd left. Then he shared some news of his own. "He told me, Mehul, 'I have been diagnosed with congestive heart failure. I need somebody I can trust and who I know has done well,'" remembers Mehul. "'Would you mind coming over and taking over my company for me?'" And that's how Mehul, an immigrant raised in a poor home in Mumbai, ended up becoming President of the company he'd come to the U.S. to work for a decade earlier.

Today, Mehul is his own boss. He and his wife Ketki chose to launch Cognizance Technologies after a lifetime of learning in various roles and in various industries after identifying a gap in the health marketplace. Cognizance is a government contractor (with some commercial contracts) that works to put the right data, in the right hands, at the right time, and in the right place. "When data gets into the hands of the right person, it becomes information," says Mehul. "When it gets to the right person at the right time, it becomes knowledge. And when it falls to the right person, at the right place, at the right time, that's cognizance; that's where we get our name. It saves lives because now the doctor is able to make informed decisions. Cognizance collects anything and everything about individuals, about patients, about diseases, about drugs, about everything. We're a 360-degree data company."

Mehul has long worked with computers on the engineering side, and Ketki got into health during the family's time in New Jersey. Previously, she'd been focused on raising the couple's young daughters, but as the girls got older and their youngest went off to first grade, Ketki knew she wanted to develop her own interests and career. She began with a job as a teller at a bank. Then, she began working at a doctor's office, a decision that would turn out to be fateful. "She became a coder," explains Mehul. "Every time you are diagnosed or receive any treatment, you have to code your care to the insurance company. That knowledge has helped us tremendously. Now she trains a team of four people on medical billing and coding work."

Cognizance was founded in early 2016, and Ketki was actually the one who first conceptualized and launched the firm. It took Mehul a little more time to be convinced. However, a tragic event helped make up his mind about the rightness of taking the risk. Mehul's mother, who had come to the U.S. to live with them after his father passed away years earlier, passed away leaving Mehul with one less pillar of support. "Those two pillars have kept me stable, kept me straight, and made sure I didn't stumble," relates Mehul soberly. "The death of my mom took such a huge toll on me because I had two support pillars, and now one of them was gone." Her passing brought some things into focus for Mehul; he reflected on how short life was, and how important working on medical data was for patients and their loving families. He followed Ketki's lead and joined Cognizance as the CEO. Today, Cognizance has over 20 employees.

Mehul's goal for Cognizance is simple: it's about serving the community. Six of his aunts died of cancer, as did his grandmother and mother-in-law. Both his mother and father died of cardiac arrests. "I realized I can help address these issues even without being a doctor," Mehul points out. "I've been very, very lucky, and I've been somebody who has had the opportunity to make a difference. Even though I'm an engineer by education, I'm still able to contribute to the medical field. One program we were a part of was a partnership between the National Cancer Institute (NCI) and Bristol Myers. They produced a blockbuster breast cancer drug called Paxil. I was managing the system and that basically told me that we can make a difference. I'm so blessed to be able to make a difference in this field."

It's no surprise that Mehul felt such a close affinity with both his parents. As mentioned, he was their only child, and they invested what little they had in him whenever they could.

His mother stayed at home taking care of him; her whole life, Mehul notes, was basically about caring for him. His father was a day trader and would buy and sell stocks but never managed to make much more than what the family needed to survive. They both doted on him. His father had had a job that required a good deal of travel around India, but when Mehul reached grade school, that changed. His father reorganized his life to make sure he wouldn't miss the joys of his son growing up. Unlike the other kids at his school who were dropped off by chauffeurs, Mehul's father dropped him off every single day. It was something so unusual that his classmates still remember it to this day.

Outside of school, Mehul rarely studied. His school didn't have a lot of homework, and he was more interested in playing sports with the neighborhood kids. He particularly enjoyed cricket, which was wildly popular in India. But in the 9th grade his mother insisted he focus on his studies. "My father never graduated," says Mehul. "He got lured into the family business. My dad always made sure I was happy and getting whatever I needed, but my mom was the person who made sure I studied. Over time, I started to appreciate it. I realized that the only thing in your control is the effort you expend. The outcome is out of your control but can be influenced if you make an effort. The importance of education and the company you keep was instilled in me."

In India, after the 9th and 10th grade, students typically chose to specialize in a certain field and go off to junior colleges. They pursue a degree in either the arts, teaching, law, finance and accounting, or science. Mehul picked the science area and studied computer engineering. "I always wanted to be an engineer and was always enamored by computers," states Mehul. "I didn't know exactly what I wanted to be, but even in the fourth and fifth grade, I would say I wanted to be a computer science guy."

In junior college, Mehul first began to encounter English. At first, he could barely speak, knowing only the words for 'bye', 'thank you' and 'okay.' But as his classes went on, he acquired the basics. From there, he continued to a university and received admission to a very competitive program. "They only look at your physics, math and chemistry scores, and I had a 93.33%," describes Mehul. "I was the last person admitted in my college in the computer science stream. It was very, very competitive with thousands and thousands of kids gaining entrance. With a score of 93.33%, I barely made it." After getting his degree and landing an internship, he was sent to the conference where he met the American businessman, and began his decade's long trip-turned-move to the U.S.

Mehul had not initially planned to stay in the U.S. In fact, he had told his parents he would stay for only five years. This was why, in

2008, while serving as President of the business he'd immigrated to work at, he encountered a difficulty with his visa. It could no longer be renewed and was due to expire. He would have to leave the country. Fortunately, Mehul had some heavyweights on his side, thanks to the lasting impression his competence had made. Two respected doctors at the NCI and NAID wrote letters directly to the President of the United States to request that he be allowed to stay. Mehul became one of only 2,000 awardees to date of something called the "O" visa, exempting him from the tedious renewal process. Four months later, he finally got his green card.

One of Mehul's only regrets is not bringing his father to the U.S. after it became clear he wouldn't be moving back to India anytime soon. "I grew up in a 464 square foot home," he explains. "I wish I had brought my dad to see the car and see the house. He made so many sacrifices for me. I wish he could see the results of his hard work and the successes I have achieved." Mehul's father passed in 1998.

After his father's death, he knew he needed to bring his mother to the U.S. She missed her extended family in India and never grew accustomed to our winters so she would return to India during the winter. Nevertheless, Mehul feels blessed that he was able to spend so much time with her every summer. His mother was deeply religious so Mehul moved his home office into the basement so his mother could set up a temple as a private area of worship. There, she would pray for hours each morning. Having such a temple is a large responsibility in Hinduism. When his mother passed, Mehul and Ketki could have donated her temple and the small idol of Krishna inside to a bigger temple. Instead, they choose to keep the temple and Krishna idol and take on the duty of completing the rituals each day. On the day she died, Mehul's mother asked Ketki to watch over Mehul and her temple; this is their way of obeying her final wish. Today, it is the family's most deeply cherished possession.

For Mehul, honoring family and community is paramount. That's why as a leader, he feels the most important quality is attitude. "Every time I hire somebody, I look for attitude," he affirms. "Skills in my book can be taught. Attitude cannot be not taught. As long as you have the integrity, the ethos, the drive, and the willingness to learn and go the extra mile, I will invest in him or her. As long as I can see that attitude, I am willing to bet on that person."

He encourages young people to follow their dreams and to do what they believe in. Today, his youngest daughter is becoming a teacher, and he couldn't be prouder. "I had wanted her to become a lawyer or a CPA or something, because she's very good with numbers," he admits. "But her passion is with children. She wants to teach special needs students from grades 1 through 3, and I fully support her passion. I know she can use her talents to accomplish her dreams. So if you have a dream, chase it and do whatever it takes."

Elizabeth Shea

Making Connections

Elizabeth Shea's parents always taught her independence from the time she was a little girl.

When she was 12, Elizabeth's family left Vermont to move to Oregon, driving cross-country in a camper with an "Oregon or Bust" bumper sticker. "My dad always tells me this story about that trip," Elizabeth laughs. "Every Sunday he would go out and get us a half-dozen donuts. There were five of us and six donuts, so we'd always argue over who got the last one. Finally, my dad said to me, 'Beth, when you grow up, you better marry a millionaire because you always want, want, want!' And I said, 'Dad, I'm not going to marry a millionaire, I'm going to be a millionaire!'"

Now the Executive Vice President at REQ and previously the CEO of the public relations (PR) and marketing firm SpeakerBox for 21 years, Elizabeth's self-reliant nature has served her well. From a young age, she knew she'd like to own her own business, though she had no idea she'd end up working in PR. "SpeakerBox evolved to be a PR firm," Elizabeth notes. "I didn't even have a background in public relations, I was more of a technology geek.

Before the founding of SpeakerBox, Elizabeth had worked extensively in marketing. PR was something of a different beast but one she took to immediately. "I get joy in connecting people," reflects Elizabeth. "It's the core of who I am. Being a connector is what I love about what I do because it's all about connecting clients to reporters or to customers. PR is relationship building, and I quickly found that I loved it."

Originally founded as Magellan Marketing, Elizabeth decided to launch the company after witnessing firsthand the lack of PR and marketing options in the technology space. At the time, almost every major PR firm in the region focused on public affairs. "There was only one firm in town that could even spell 'technology,'" deadpans Elizabeth. "I was working as a director of marketing at the time, and we invited that one firm to our office to discuss tech PR. It quickly became obvious that they didn't understand our business or the technology landscape at all. I decided, if there aren't any marketing firms that know tech, I could launch a marketing firm that does."

That was 1997. In 1999, Elizabeth brought on a partner, Kristi Hedges, who was a PR expert working as an independent contractor at the time. Kristi joined Elizabeth's firm of four people, and the small business rebranded as SheaHedges.

SheaHedges quickly began to grow. The firm was one of the first in town to offer marketing and PR for the burgeoning tech industry, and the late 90s were a boom time. Retainers were running higher than $20,000 a month and newly funded operations were looking for publicity every day. When that bubble eventually burst; SheaHedges was able to outlast its competitors with its diversified client base. The firm had been representing the public sector sales side of many large businesses, and it was these business-to-government clients that held them over through the downturn. "We had focused on building those business-to-government clients, and that carried us through," nods Elizabeth. "I'm not saying we didn't have a dip, but those companies still sold to government during the dotcom bust. A lot of our competition didn't make it because their firms were primarily dotcom tech—we were more like half and half, so we were fortunate."

In 2006, Kristi chose to make an exit from the firm, pursuing her passion of becoming a leadership coach and author. On her tenth anniversary, Elizabeth decided to rebrand again. With typical transparency, Elizabeth brought the whole staff together to come up with options and then make the final decision. It was then that a staff member came up with the name "SpeakerBox" during a company-wide brainstorming session.

By this time, Elizabeth had decided to really lean in on the firm's capabilities in PR and content development. "I wanted to be laser-focused in doing what we do best," she explains, "and in the tech sector in this region, be the best at it." The firm continued to grow, expanding its client base and stressing its company values—scrappiness, caring, drive for high performance, and commitment to the team.

Finally, in 2017, Elizabeth began shopping for a partner or buyer for the company. She still wanted to remain in management and didn't want to be absorbed into a giant firm. She wanted to be part of a larger organization that could offer a broader range of services. Times were changing, and it made sense for businesses to hire agencies for all their marketing needs under one roof. "There's a spectrum of services called PESO," explains Elizabeth, "paid media, earned media, social and shared media, and owned media. Those four areas drive different services. Paid media would be any kind of advertising, on or offline. Shared and social media is what people are sharing through different channels. Owned media would be what you create, your blog, your website for example. Earned media is anything that's not controlled by you; in effect, what other third-parties are writing about you. So, that usually covers media relationships, analyst relations, award recognition, etc. And that was SpeakerBox before we merged with REQ. We helped people gain third party validation through other people talking about them."

REQ, a leading digital marketing and brand management firm, was well equipped to offer the paid, social, and owned media services, but they sought a partner to get the earned media piece. "As the market has evolved, we found the same thing REQ found," says Elizabeth. "Everything is so much more interconnected now that we found ourselves increasingly working with other agencies, and we couldn't control the work those other agencies did. I had to figure out how to grow into the next generation." It took her two years of searching, but eventually, REQ CEO Tripp Donnelly and Elizabeth worked out a deal, with REQ acquiring SpeakerBox in January 2019. Today, REQ is set to surpass 110 employees.

Although she was raised to believe in herself, becoming a powerful executive in the Nation's Capital was far from Elizabeth's mind while she was growing up in rural, picturesque Vermont. The family lived not in downtown Burlington, but in South Burlington, a suburb. "I wanted to be Dorothy Hamill when I grew up," smiles Elizabeth. The town was small, and the kids walked to school, the park, their sports games, and everywhere they wanted to go. Elizabeth dropped dance classes, but she excelled at running cross country and track, and studied piano and guitar through high school.

Elizabeth had been shy in elementary school, but a big move to Oregon from Vermont helped build her self-confidence. In five years, Elizabeth attended five different schools. She believes making so many changes so quickly taught her to become more extroverted, learning how to make friends quickly over and over again.

The big move was brought on by her father's desire to attend graduate school. He had been a school guidance counselor and was looking to move into administration. The family moved to Oregon so her father could pursue a Master's in Education and Administration. Initially, they only planned to stay until his degree was completed, but after graduation, he was offered a job in nearby Albany, Oregon, as a school principal, and the Sheas decided to stay.

After several years of upheaval, Elizabeth began to feel like she belonged to her community as she entered high school. She loved playing softball and running cross country, and outside of class she also joined the cheerleading squad and the Future Business Leaders of America Club. As a senior, she was voted onto the Homecoming Court, alongside her sister. She showed an interest in computers, although, at the time, girls were not always encouraged to pursue coding. Her strongest subjects were math and science, and today, Elizabeth is a strong advocate for STEM education for young women.

Elizabeth's father was the principal of her high school, which meant she always had an eye or two on her. She remembers her parents as strict, making certain she came home at reasonable hours and emphasizing education. The family worked hard to make ends meet; Elizabeth took to sewing her own clothes and cutting her own hair, even cutting classmates' hair for money once she got the hang of it.

Elizabeth had been planning to attend community college, but instead, based on the good fortune of finding a scholarship through Knights of Columbus, she applied to and received admission to Santa Clara University, where she studied business and marketing. While there, she took on odd jobs to cover her expenses, delivering the San Jose Mercury News every morning, and even selling books door-to-door one summer. After graduation in 1987, she was recruited by a then not well-known company called Apple to provide marketing geared toward distributors. At first, she was assigned to the higher education channel, but later, she transitioned to commercial and then government distributors.

During her three years there, she came into contact with a company called Falcon which down the road would become her employer when she relocated to the Washington, DC area. She worked at Apple for three years, then left for a marketing manager role for a start-up called SuperMac, and then another startup called Momenta Computer. It was a time of recession, however, and after a year, the start-up went under, and Elizabeth was in the market for a new role.

Around this same time, she went to Washington DC to visit her then-boyfriend and scope out the East Coast. It was while she was visiting him that she reconnected with friends at Falcon and was offered a job there. For two years she worked as a marketing manager for Falcon, before deciding she'd like to strike out on her own. For the first time, she was her own boss, working as an independent consultant for several clients including her former employer, a firm called EdgeMark, and a third company called Institutional Shareholder Services. Elizabeth was new to the consulting game and had a lot to learn about managing multiple clients while not getting burned out. After a couple years of working days, nights and weekend, she decided to accept a full-time role with her client EdgeMark, where mentor Lee Raesly brought her on.

After two and a half years with EdgeMark, in 1997, Elizabeth was ready to try her hand at independence again. It was at EdgeMark that she noted the lack of PR services offered to tech firms, and set out to establish Magellan Marketing, the company that would later flourish into SpeakerBox. Her first client was Craig Abod, the CEO of a government reseller, and she built out her team subletting space in his office. He has served as a mentor, friend and client to this day.

Elizabeth's story is full of names of those who helped her along the way. But her first mentors, of course, were her parents, whom she considers to be role models in their own right. From her mother, Elizabeth says she got her independence. From her father, his sociability and outgoing nature. "My parents are like the Mayors of DC," laughs Elizabeth. "My dad can't walk into a restaurant without chatting somebody up. He's a friendly, funny, charismatic guy. He had a lot of success in his career, going into schools and turning them around by really engaging with the community. As an English major, my mom inspired me to become the writer and reader that I am today. She worked in community relations for years and inspired the connectedness I take pride in delivering."

As a leader, Elizabeth considers herself to be transparent, authentic, and focused on the community. She believes in sharing financial statements and balance sheets with the staff, explaining what they mean and offering context where needed, noting that this type of communication has led the staff to become far more engaged. When she hires, she focuses on hiring not so much for a specific skill set, but for intelligence, warmth and positivity, noting that her ideal employees are 'smart and happy'.

"We're all in this together," she affirms, "I think that's empowering for people to feel that. One of the things I've been told about myself is, even if I don't agree, I'll at least listen. I'm very open door minded, I'm willing to hear what you have to say. I've always had a coach, through Vistage, EO, or my own business coach. I think it's important to continue to listen and better yourself. I've been told that's very empowering for people, because they feel they can give feedback."

Along those same lines, Elizabeth's advice to young people graduating college today revolves around asking questions and listening to others. "Seek advice and counsel from anyone you can," she encourages. "It can be frustrating when you don't see younger people doing that as much today. I would encourage people to seek out help from all generations and to find a mentor. The people around you can help!"

Jennifer W. Siciliano

In the Thick of Things

Jennifer Siciliano didn't have any idea what she'd like to be when she left for college at Marymount University in Virginia. Both of her parents were educators, but she wasn't so sure she wanted to follow in their footsteps. Armed with a desire to have her car at school and a requirement by her parents to independently fund that desire, led her to what would be the first step in her career journey. Jen headed over to the career center one fateful day to flip through a three-ring binder full of local job opportunities. By chance, a call for interns—unpaid, of course—in the office of Alaska Representative Don Young had been stuffed into the wrong binder. Jen hadn't been looking for an internship in the U.S. House of Representatives but the letter intrigued her. Maybe being on Capitol Hill in the thick of things would be a worthwhile experience.

She made her way to Rep. Young's office where she was quickly brought on in a volunteer capacity. She did it all—opening mail, answering phones, running errands for the staff two days a week. By her junior year, the volunteer position turned into a formal paid internship and during the second semester of her senior year a life-changing opportunity took place. Rep. Young's front desk staffer left the position, and the Congressman offered it to her. Jen had a light course-load that semester, but even so, she wasn't sure how a full-time job would fit into her college schedule. Rep. Young asked her to speak with her professors about finishing the semester remotely. She talked to them and was able to successfully complete her education and work full-time. Jen smoothly transitioned from college into a career on Capitol Hill where she quickly climbed the ranks. She ultimately ended up as the Communications Director for the Senate Appropriations Committee before leaving Capitol Hill 13 years after she started as a volunteer.

After several intervening years as a lobbyist, Jen landed at Inova Health System (Inova) where she currently serves as the Chief External Affairs and Communications Officer. Although she left her days on Capitol Hill behind, she never left her passion for positive change, or her enjoyment of being in the thick of things. "My job is a lot of different things to a lot of different people," she explains. "It's government relations, it's community relations, it's marketing; I have all those teams alongside me. I think my entire career has been about being in the middle of things, being where things happen. I think I'd be bored if I didn't have something different to do every day. That's one of the beauties of this job; no day is ever the same, and I wouldn't have it any other way."

Inova is a respected non-profit healthcare provider serving over two million patients a year at five major hospitals—four in Fairfax County and one in Loudon County. It employs around 19,000 people in the region and is constantly working to expand its services and level of care. It boasts a heart and vascular institute, a cancer institute, and a neuroscience and spine institute, as well as Northern Virginia's only Level 1 Trauma Center and Level 4 Neonatal Intensive Care Unit. It also enjoys a stellar reputation, with all of their hospitals earning the top grade of 5 stars from the Center for Medicare & Medicaid Services. Their Inova Fairfax Hospital was recently listed as number 1 in the region by US News and World Report.

"I love our mission because it's simple, easy to understand, and all our employees live by it every single day. Our mission is to provide world-class healthcare, every time, every touch, to each person in every community we have the privilege to serve," affirms Jen. "The history of Inova is that it was created by the community, for the community, because it was what they needed. Way before my time, when Fairfax County was very rural, a group of community leaders recognized the need for health care and as the story goes, came together around someone's kitchen table and made it happen. We've always been a really large part of this community. The marketing team makes fun of me because I always bring up that kitchen table where the idea was born. Personally, I want to find that kitchen table! It would be a great historical item to have!"

Jen previously worked for Inova as a consultant when they were one of her clients, but she became a full-time employee in 2007. In her 13 years with the team, she's seen a fair amount of growth and a lot of change. The constantly changing regulatory environment is the main reason for the change, but Jen emphasizes that the core focus on patient care has always been strong. Most recently, Inova completed the Schar Cancer Center and seeing the transformation there has been a joy. "I remember when we acquired the property, an elected official said to me that the (former Exxon Mobil) building looked 'like Darth Vader's summer home'," laughs Jen. "The challenge was turning that into the beautiful clinical space it is now." And it's not only the aesthetics and design that set the Schar Cancer Center apart. "In the past, when you had a cancer diagnosis, you would have to travel to many different places—for appointments with various physicians, for tests, etc.—in order to receive your care, but now we have everything in one space, in one building thanks to the feedback from doctors, nurses, and patients," explains Jen. "After you park, you can access all of your care in one place. At a very difficult time in people's lives, being able to provide that service is gratifying."

As much as Jen loves being at the pulse of things today, she grew up feeling far from the center of anything in the little town of Marbury in rural Charles County, Maryland. Her father had grown up across the road, and early on, her grandmother lived in the same house where he was raised. Jen's father lost his dad when he was young and his Aunt Margie and Uncle Bob had a big hand in raising him. They lived next door, and Jen's father was very close to them.

Jen was an only child but she often spent time at Aunt Margie and Uncle Bob's feeding the chickens or helping with their corn and kale crops. Family was always close by.

The community was close, too. When Jen was about six years old, she got involved with the local church youth group, and ever since, faith has been an important part of her life.

She also became very involved with the local 4-H club and participated in photography, the fashion revue, and public speaking. She thrived with public speaking. Around the age of 11, she made it to the State-level public speaking finals and went home with the top prize. Jen also loved music and attended summer camps at Deep Creek Lake every year. After camp, she would travel to nearby Western Maryland to spend two weeks with her maternal grandparents, with whom she was also very close. "I would go to camp for 2 weeks, my grandparents would pick me up from camp, and I'd spend another 2 weeks with them," Jen recalls. "I literally was gone for a month of the summer."

Academically, Jen did well. Her father was a middle school principal for 44 years, while her mother spent 38 as a math teacher in the county. When Jen entered high school, her mother became her Algebra I teacher, an arrangement that didn't always go swimmingly. "I'm not the most math inclined person you'll ever meet," smiles Jen. "I think that's why I was attracted to communications! In that math class, my father will tell you, I got no special treatment from my mother. My father would often be the one waving the white flag at home and trying to make peace between us."

With her mother teaching at the high school, Jen didn't get into much trouble. In fact, she ended up having a perfect attendance record from kindergarten through 12th grade. "I remember intentionally going to the office one day during middle school and telling them I felt sick and needed to go home," grins Jen. "I told them to call my dad!" Instead, her mother got wind of it and sent her back to class with her tail between her legs. "As much as I laugh about that, I will say that there are days when you just don't feel like getting up and going, but you know you're capable of it," reflects Jen. "My mother gave me that discipline to follow through regardless of how I felt."

Both of Jen's parents demonstrated the importance of giving back to the community. They were active volunteers with several organizations. From her mother, Jen says she got her drive and competitive side; from her father, she got his empathy and compassion. In his free time, her father was a private pilot and would often take Jen out flying. Today, her father is suffering from Alzheimer's, but he still recalls their annual tradition of traveling to see the Blue Angels flying in Ocean City, Maryland. "He has good days and bad," says Jen. "The last time we were there to see the Blue Angels, we decided to take the bus to the viewing area. He was worried we were going to be late to see the planes. All of a sudden we heard a jet, and he told me what kind of jet it was by the sound it made. I pulled up the schedule on my phone, and sure enough, he was right. Alzheimer's is a terrible disease, but we are rewarded when he has those amazing moments of clarity."

Thanks in part to her parents' lifelong emphasis on education, Jen finished high school with a strong resume. She had been involved in student government, had done well in class, and played Varsity Field Hockey all 4 years wearing jersey number 17. Jen notes that her youngest daughter. Ryleigh, also plays high school field hockey; when it came time to choose her jersey, she chose 17 to match mom.

Jen applied to several colleges and decided on Marymount University thinking it was a good mixture of close-enough-to-visit and far-enough-mom-and-dad-won't-drop-in. On her college visit day, she remembers being so nervous she burst into tears and said to her father that she didn't want to go to college. Her mother told her to, basically, get it together.

With a little tough love, Jen was out the door and soon thriving. She decided to major in Communications and Politics and ended up becoming President of the Student body. "I remember one of the big issues when I was in office was that the bookstore was carrying *Cosmo* magazine and the nuns did not want it," says Jen. In the end, we worked out a compromise. We got to keep our *Cosmo*, but it had to have a cover over it just as if it were a *Playboy*. My first successful campaign!"

By the time she graduated, Jen was already set up in her job at Congressman Young's office, where she worked at the front desk for a year before being promoted to Scheduler. Meanwhile, she decided to go back to school at American University to get her Master's in Public Communication, through a program for Capitol Hill staffers. While completing the program, she was offered another promotion—the Press Secretary role which was a perfect fit for the skill set she was cultivating.

Jen stayed in Congressman Young's office for three more years before briefly jumping over to the House Science Committee. Right away, she felt the role wasn't the right fit and began working on an exit strategy. However, before she could even plan her next role, she received a call from Senator Ted Stevens.

"I was maybe two months into my job on the Science Committee when my phone rang," recalls Jen. "A voice just said, 'Jen? Ted Stevens. My press secretary is leaving—Thursday 1:30, come see me.' I said 'ok,' and on Thursday, I headed over. The first thing he asks me when he sees me is, 'did you make a decision?' I was confused and asked, 'make a decision about what?' He goes, 'The job!'" It turned out Ted wanted to hire her on as Communications Director for the Senate Appropriations Committee. Jen jokingly said she would think it over, but she knew right away it was a great opportunity.

In fact, Jen loved the job and the leadership example Senator Stevens exuded but her years there were not without some difficult times. Her maternal grandparents, with whom she was very close, passed away during her tenure, and she recalls it as a defining moment. "It was one of the first times I'd really had to deal with death," she recalls. "My grandfather was an incredibly dignified gentleman." During his last few days at the hospital she was able to be there with him. She particularly remembers an incident where he sent her out for some butter pecan ice cream. Upon returning, she found that the nurse refused to let him have the ice cream. "My grandfather was dying, and I was determined to give him some butter pecan ice cream if that is what he wanted," says Jen. "I requested to see a supervisor, and the supervisor had no problem with him having some ice cream. So we sat there and ate the ice cream." As she left the hospital, her grandfather told her, "I'll see your blue eyes in heaven," a touching farewell, and the last words he spoke to her.

Another life-changing event took place on 9/11, which was obviously particularly affecting as a staffer at the Capitol. "All I wanted to do was shut down," remembers Jen. "But luckily we were surrounded by many great leaders including Senator Stevens. He helped us understand why we needed to keep going forward. The day after 9/11, we had to come back to the office and keep the government going. I had a very small role in that, but it was a defining moment. I learned, no matter how bad it gets, you've got to move forward."

By this time Jen had had her oldest daughter, Maggie, and the crazy schedule of Capitol Hill was wearing on her. She decided to try her hand at consulting and took a position at The Podesta Group in 2003. She remained with the firm for four years. It was there that she began representing Inova as one of her clients. Over time she began to think about how she'd like to develop a deeper knowledge of healthcare and Inova, rather than continuing to cultivate the broad range of clients she had at The Podesta Group.

All of these experiences contributed to making Jen the leader she is today. "I feel I have this really unique perspective on things," she muses. "I spent time in the House of Representatives, first as just a casual observer, then in a lot of different positions. I then went to the Senate and got that perspective while working with some of the most amazing legislators of my time. The main lesson for me was that Senator Stevens and Senator Byrd, who ran that committee as co-chairmen for a long time, really epitomized bipartisanship. I have the lobbying perspective and now at Inova have had the non-profit and state and local government experience—all in all, I feel I have a pretty good world view."

As a leader, Jen notes that her style is "incredibly inclusive." "My expectations for my team are very high," she acknowledges. "But I am also flexible and try to make work fun, too. It's easy for people to interpret a strong leader as just tough and lacking empathy. But for me demonstrating kindness and compassion with the folks you're leading speaks to a confidence in yourself and in your people. When you build a foundation of trust with people, they want to be a partner with you."

To young people entering the working world for the first time, she advises self-compassion, too. "Forgive yourself when you don't get it right," encourages Jen, "especially when you're new in your career and growing professionally. You're not perfect, and that's okay." She also emphasizes the importance of making connections with others, and not being afraid to do the dirty work. "I try to learn something from every person I meet, and I try to give them something as well," Jen affirms. "That's important, because it's all about relationships. I feel incredibly lucky, the way that my path has taken me. I've worked really hard to get here. I especially worked really hard in my early days. You have to be willing to do the non-glamorous, non-sexy stuff. That only adds to a well-rounded perspective and lays the foundation of who you are, your leadership style, and your success."

Julie Simmons

Adapt to Win

Julie Simmons never planned to start her own business. After years of hard work, things were falling into place for her professionally. She was leaving a stable, comfortable job for a promotion and additional responsibilities at a larger corporation for which she had been recruited. She was thrilled to begin working with a government contractor, a "brass ring" she notes that she's been chasing for years. And personally, life was going swimmingly as well; after trying to get pregnant for some time, she and her husband, Greg, were finally expecting twins.

Then, life threw Julie a curveball. She had had her last day of work on a Wednesday and was scheduled to start her new job the following Monday. She called her new employer to disclose her pregnancy to them before she started at the office. That Friday, her new employer retracted her job offer. Two weeks before Christmas, Julie found herself pregnant with twins, unemployed, and uncertain of what to do next.

She immediately called Greg who was concerned and upset, but also supportive and encouraging. "From the minute it happened, he always said that we were going to be fine," remembers Julie. "I gave myself a little bit of time to wallow in my feelings, and then it became clear to me that I can't just sit at home and wait for the kids to come." The following week, Julie got up early to attend a 7:00 AM networking meeting in Arlington with the hope of obtaining a lead. While networking she ran into a former professor of hers who had taught at Marymount where Julie had attended graduate school. "She was so gracious and kind and told me she was transitioning out of a role," explains Julie. "She offered to talk to the executive director about me taking on an interim role for about four months as a 1099 contractor."

It was Julie's first independent consulting gig, and she quickly found she enjoyed the flexibility of working for herself. Four days a week, she brought in income at her interim job, and in her free time she began networking for other clients and contracts. "I quickly figured out there were people who really valued my skills," Julie recalls. "The combination of uncertainty with employment and carrying twins made my life challenging, but it also gave me purpose. It reinforced my self-esteem and confidence that there is value in the marketplace for my talents." At the end of four months, her interim employer offered her a full-time position, but by that time, Julie had been bitten by the entrepreneurial bug. She leaned into her new life as an independent contractor, learned how to navigate the market, set her fees for services, and made more and more contacts. She founded Human Capital Strategic Consulting (HCSC) and never looked back.

That was nine years ago. Today, HCSC is a successful HR firm helping small- and medium-size businesses improve individual and organization-wide performance. Julie works with between 12 to 15 consultants at a time and carefully matches the right consultant with the right clients based on expertise and needs. "The first thing I do when working with a consultant is find out what they want to do, what their priority areas are, what they enjoy doing, and what types of people they enjoy working with in terms of leadership style," Julie describes. "Then when I have an opportunity that comes across my desk, I can match the right consultant with the client. When you can align personality types, interests, and expertise with client needs, it goes very smoothly."

Julie is similarly thorough when it comes to vetting her clients. She conducts a prospective client evaluation to assess the organization's leadership structure and style, what the culture and team looks like, and whether her team is a fit for the client. During the interview process she may not accept an engagement if she doesn't think it is a good match with HCSC's values. Approximately 60% of their client base is composed of government contractors with the remaining 40% split between non-profit organizations, higher education institutions, professional services firms, and healthcare firms.

Most of our clients have between 25 to 75 employees. "That's our sweet spot," elaborates Julie. "Once you hit 25, you usually can start to afford a luxury resource like an HR consultant. I like working with evolved leaders. And building business around referrals is great because I find that those leaders attract other leaders with similar thinking."

Julie has always emphasized such relationships throughout her career so it stands to reason that she considers them a cornerstone of her company's success. "I love helping people," she affirms. "Professionally, what that looks like is solving problems for clients. I love to bridge the gap between a need that a client has and the skills that my team has. Understanding the puzzle to solve and matching the right person to the client is what makes work fun every day."

Julie is no stranger to adapting to changing circumstances. Her father was a Naval officer which meant her family moved every few years while she was growing up. Born in a Naval hospital in Bremerton, Washington, Julie was only six weeks old when her parents and 2-and-a-half-year-old sister moved to Japan. A couple of years after that the family transferred to the Philippines, then back to the Seattle area for

2 years before moving to San Diego. Julie's first memories are of idyllic Coronado Island, where she attended first through third grade. She and her sister spent those years biking around in the beautiful sunshine.

With her father often at sea, her mother kept busy as an administrative professional for the government. She loved having her own work to keep her busy, and in addition to her career, she also ran women's clubs for military spouses. Because both of their parents worked, Julie and her sister had a lot of freedom. Julie describes she and her sister as "latchkey kids" who played outside, watched TV, read books, and basically did whatever they liked. Thanks to their constant relocating, the girls were very close and have remained so.

When Julie was entering fourth grade, the family moved to Ocean Springs, Mississippi on the Gulf Coast. For the first time, her father was no longer at sea; he was put in charge of ship repair. Three years later, the family returned to the Seattle area where Julie attended 7th through 9th grade. Academically, she did all right as a basically A/B student although she admits she probably wasn't living up to her full potential. At the age of 13 she got her first job working at a little diner called The Varsity Inn for $3.25 an hour. Each Saturday and Sunday her day started at 5:30 in the morning and ended at 2:30 PM. "I was bussing tables, but I loved that job," she smiles. "I had to get up early and figure out how to balance work with everything else in my life. It was a great learning experience." In her free time, she attended church, learned to ski and loved taking ski trips with friends whenever she could.

Initially, her dad had expected the post in Seattle to be his last duty station, and the family was expecting to settle there for good. But he was offered a position too good to refuse. He was given a post as the Ship Repair Officer for the 7th Fleet in Ukaska, Japan. It was a major role and a big promotion. At 15 years of age and in the middle of high school, Julie was starting over again in Japan. And this time, her best friend and her older sister wouldn't be going with them. She was starting college in Washington, and Julie was truly alone.

Japan was a huge adjustment. Previously, Julie had always attended public and parochial schools, but now, for the first time, she attended the military school on the base. The school was cliquey, and oddly, she found her father's position as a respected officer was more of a liability than anything. Other students resented her when their own fathers were reprimanded or ordered around by her dad. On top of that, there were very few other white students in the school; Julie notes that having the experience of being a racial minority was an important one for her. "Having an opportunity to feel what it felt like to be different was transformative," she nods. "It was a very fundamental lesson, and it enabled me to have an empathy on a level that I think I otherwise would never have had."

Just before Julie entered college, the family relocated for the final time in her father's military career. He was offered a position as Dean of the Department of Engineering and Weaponry at the Naval Academy in Annapolis, MD. Receiving this role was especially poignant for Julie's father. By returning to the Naval Academy, his career had made a full circle by returning to the place where had begun his Naval career as an 18-year-old kid. It was a fitting and fulfilling conclusion to a successful career.

"My dad was born in Eau Clair, Wisconsin, and had no money to go to college," relates Julie. "When he got to the Naval Academy, he thought, the Navy was just a way for him to get an education. But the values and skills that he learned in those four years propelled him forward. He started a life of service and constant learning. He has three master's degrees today, and I am still benefitting from his example. I have a reverence for education and the military." In fact, Julie considers one of her most prized possessions to be a copy of a moving and affecting poem called "The Sacred Dixie Cup," by James W. Conte. The title is a reference to the special hat worn by plebes during their first summer at the Naval Academy. The poem was even read out at the final church service attended by her parents in Annapolis. "It's not about the hat," elaborates Julie. "It's about how people are willing to make those sacrifices for someone they don't even know. I can't imagine being 18 years old and signing up to make a sacrifice for your country. It represents the sacrifices, hard work, camaraderie, leadership, teamwork, and commitment—the values I try to espouse every day."

Julie reflects that she inherited her ability to persevere from her father and credits him with raising her with the military values that got him so far in life. Her mother, meanwhile, was independent and strong in her own right, and she inspired Julie to make the best of every situation. "To marry someone and build a life around the unknown is a challenge," she points out. "There are plenty of people who shy away from change and who may even find it offensive. And then there are people like my mom, and like me, who can lean in and say, 'Okay, this isn't necessarily my choice, but I'm going to make this work.' I think her ability to navigate change successfully over a large part of her life is definitely something she demonstrated for me."

With the whole family on the East Coast for the first time, Julie began looking at colleges nearby. She decided to attend George Mason University mostly for its proximity to home and its good reputation. It turned out to be a perfect fit for her. She loved her time there, made friends easily, and got very involved in her sorority. She ended up being elected to sorority leadership and to a Panhellenic council. She stacked her schedule so that she'd be able to take on a part-time job at a local bank as a teller, a job she enjoyed. By her junior year, she started at the business school and graduated with a business degree. And while at George Mason, she also met Greg, her future husband.

After graduation, Julie spent an additional year working with her sorority in what she jokingly refers to as her "fifth year". Her parents had relocated to Seattle after her father's retirement from the military so she made Seattle her home base but spent the year travelling from campus to campus working with different chapters as a consultant. Between August and June of that academic year, she visited 52 campuses and helped the various chapters figure out recruiting strategy, interviewing their officer boards, and providing leadership advice.

The job was a lot of fun, but hardly a long-term career. After a year of touring college campuses, Julie was ready to settle down. She picked the DC area over Seattle and once again packed up her car for the cross-country drive. In DC, she quickly landed a gig on Arthur Andersen's HR and Recruiting team, where she helped run an audit program for their interns. She remained there for about two and a half years before getting restless. Her job was stable and secure, but Arthur Andersen was huge, and she didn't want to be pigeonholed into a role so early on. She departed and took a job at a small non-profit, where she took on all the HR work.

This was also a great learning opportunity, but ultimately Julie decided she was a bit too fast-paced for the relative calm of the non-profit world. By then it was the late 1990s and she jumped to a technology company when the dot com boom was at its zenith. "It was an employee-owned company so it was fascinating to get experience with a company like that," Julie describes. "After that, I spent seven years at Grant Thornton which was the last in-house job I had."

Julie was a Human Resources Manager at Grant Thornton, an accounting, audit, and tax advisory firm. It was stable and was a great job, but she was ambitious for more. "I didn't have the upward mobility I wanted," she explains. "I felt like having a government contractor on my resume would really help since there are so many government contractors in the DC area. I was being recruited by a large government contractor and felt like it was time to check that box. But the universe had a way of checking me!"

On September 22, 2001, just two weeks after the 9/11 tragedies, Julie and Greg were married. "He's been my biggest supporter through everything," Julie glows. "He always sees the bright side of things; when we found out we were having twins he was the one who had the attitude that 'this is the best thing ever; two for one!' My feeling was one of that 'you have no idea what you're talking about.' But I would never have had the courage to start my business without his support and encouragement."

Julie has come a long way since she accepted the phone call that would change the course of her life. Showcasing the trademark resilience and flexibility passed down to her by her mother, today she's a successful business owner with the confidence and leadership skills to guide an entire team. As a leader, she emphasizes collaboration. "I like to understand where someone's coming from when I'm leading," she says. "I also feel like I'm very intuitive, and I appreciate the importance of servant leadership. We need to make sure we're walking with our team and giving them the respect and admiration they deserve. I always give my consultants the opportunity to meet the clients before any engagement is considered. I want them to have buy-in. That's the type of leader I am."

To young people entering the working world today, her advice is simple: "Put the phone down!" she laughs. "Have conversations with people. Getting business done is very relationship based, and I've built my business by making it a priority to go out and meet people who are different and who do different things than I do. Find your commonalities but be able to enter a room and meet someone—a future friend who you don't know yet."

She also advises taking risks and surrounding yourself with people who have your back. "Find those five or six people who will be your champions," she encourages. "My former professor at Marymount University and some of my former bosses are people that were all instrumental to my success. Find your network and the people who are going to rally around you because this is certainly not a solo journey."

Sunny Singh

Hungry for More

Sunny Singh's father was granted asylum in the U.S. in 1988, a few years after religious riots threw parts of India into chaos, parts that were traditionally peaceful. In order to pursue a better, less volatile life for their family, the Singhs decided to find a safer place to raise their young son.

Sunny's father began driving a cab in DC, and it took him five more years to raise the money to bring over his family. By then, Sunny was eight, and his new younger brother was only about nine months old. The family rented an apartment in Alexandria, Virginia, where the boys quickly began to learn the American dialect and accent and make friends in their diverse neighborhood.

A few years after that, Sunny's mother finally got her driver's license, and the family went to pick out a used car for her. The occasion turned out to be a memorable and motivating one for Sunny. "We ended up settling on this 1993 Ford Escort station wagon," he recalls. "They paid about $1,200 for it, and the look of excitement on their face was incredible. Even though my parents felt excitement, I felt sadness. It was a bittersweet moment for me because I knew the car was a piece of crap. It had around 180,000 miles on it. And I said to myself, 'I want more, I don't want to settle.'"

From then on, Sunny was never satisfied with his lot in life. Upon graduation, when other kids went to college, he was focused on making money. Now, he sees the value in education, but at the time, he was hellbent on getting a full-time job and beginning to climb the corporate ladder and achieve financial success. His first job was an entry-level gig at Chevy Chase Bank as a service associate selling bank accounts to customers. He had immediate success and began attracting attention from his superiors. He set his mind to attaining the branch manager position, and before long, he rose to Assistant Branch Manager, and then Branch Manager at the age of 20.

But then something funny happened. After working so hard to achieve his goal, his dissatisfaction returned with a vengeance. "I got the promotion, and immediately, it was just a big dud," he remembers. "My first thought was, 'So what? What's next? Am I going to be branch manager here for the next ten years? No!' It made me realize that I needed to become an entrepreneur. And immediately I started looking at different businesses to buy. I was hungry for more."

Sunny had a decent amount in savings, but nothing close to what he'd need to buy a large, successful business. Instead, after looking around for some time, he ended up buying a tiny moving company from a man he met through his future father-in-law. In early 2007, Sunny's parents got a home equity loan to help him finance the purchase, and for his money, he got a moving truck and a mere $10,000 a month in revenue. "We were lucky to get five jobs each month," Sunny recalls. "It was that slow. All of the jobs were local moves and did not include any long-distance moves. In my mind, I knew it was something that

I could really grow. But since it was the only thing I could afford, I jumped in headfirst."

Within four years, Sunny had grown the tiny company from around $100,000 annually to over $4 million in annual revenue. Through it all, he never lifted a piece of furniture. He focused on business development, management, and leadership. "I was ambitious, and I was driven," says Sunny. "There was so much room to grow. They didn't have a website when I started so I created a website. I did Basic 101 for Beginners stuff. I reached out to everybody I possibly could including all of the storage companies. I didn't have an employee in the office so I sent all the calls to my cell phone. It was just me, going out, and doing everything I possibly could; and slowly, it just started clicking."

In 2011, with $4 million in annual revenue, Sunny was still looking to expand. As always, success was a motivator to work harder than an invitation to rest. He set his sights on winning government work and applied for a highly competitive Department of Defense contract. "You can't be a prime contractor with the government until they choose to request applications. And there is no set schedule when that will happen," explains Sunny. "So it had been closed for around ten years and they hadn't let anybody into the program when we applied for it. There were over 360 companies who applied, 49 were pre-approved, and 12 actually got the contract. We were one of the 12."

The win was fateful. The contract took effect in 2013, and the business quickly doubled again, rising to about $8 million and then continued to rise. Two years into the DoD work, Waste Management approached Sunny with an offer. They were impressed with his operation and had been hemorrhaging money through their own 1-800-Packrat division. "They decided they were either going to close that division or double down," says Sunny. "I met with the CEO and had some great conversations. He really wanted me to join them. They wanted to buy my company so they could add me to their team. They basically brought me on to turn this division around for them. They were great people, and I'm still in touch with them today."

Over the next three years, Sunny took the division from $1 million to $30 million in revenue as the VP of Government Services. "We went from losing a lot of money to making a lot of money," smiles Sunny. "Then in 2018, my employment contract ended, and Waste Management sold their shares in the logistics division. From the start, I had been upfront with them and told them I was an entrepreneur. They knew that I wasn't there for the long run. They just wanted me to fix that division. So I went from owning a moving company with $12-an-hour movers, to winning a prime DoD contract, to growing significantly, to selling to a publicly traded company, and to running a division that was larger than my company. I had a lot of different experiences for a young person under the age of 30. Now it was time for a new challenge."

This time, Sunny chose carefully. He had had success, he had made money, and he could afford to be picky about where he next invested his energy and expertise. He knew he wanted to get out of moving and more into government contracting. He knew he didn't want to acquire a staffing company; he preferred to run a company with a real mission, a passion, and a culture of dedication. The particular field of the business, however, was less important to Sunny.

"I wanted to buy something that was sustainable, was affordable to an extent, had a leadership team, and had good people in place. I knew I wasn't going to be the subject matter expert," he details. "It had to be a perfect fit and one that would allow me to exercise leadership. Most buyers bring in their own team with them, they clean house, and they identify synergies. I wasn't doing that. In reality, I was a CEO replacement. I wanted to promote and develop from within. I wanted people working there who wanted to be there. I wanted a business that was working to accomplish something special and didn't want to just make money. I wanted to invest in people and grow it from within. And so I bought a company specializing in acquisition strategy and data—Artlin Consulting."

Sunny bought Artlin in November of 2018, a then-seven-year-old company that had grown to $20 million in revenue and 80 employees by its founder, a former VP at IBM. She was brilliant and had done great work taking Artlin as far as she could, but didn't want continue to deal with the headaches. And growth, organization, and management were Sunny's specialties. "They had a very immature infrastructure," observes Sunny. "There was no structure in the organization, just a very flat organization. We were a $20 million company without our own office space. Our address was a UPS box in Fairfax. Today, we're moving into new office space. Financially, we're also in a great position. We've experienced significant growth in the past year and are where I hoped we would be at this time."

Artlin is a government contractor specializing in data and acquisition support. Their primary customer is the Office of the Secretary of Defense (OSD).

Although the staff at Artlin was nervous about the buyout at first, Sunny hopes he's won over their trust by demonstrating his commitment to running the business for the long haul. Right away, he introduced new benefits, provided raises, quadrupled the training budget, and began meeting every one of his new employees. "My goal was to shake the hand of every single employee and get to know them within the first 90 days," nods Sunny. "I did it within 60. There was no central office and all employees worked from a client site so it was tricky to get it done. It took a huge commitment on my part to do that, but it was important to me to make it happen. I did a lot of one-on-ones and meet-and-greets with groups of six to eight people. And today, we have strong communications from top to bottom within the Artlin team."

Developing future leaders has a personal resonance for Sunny who, as an Indian immigrant from a poor family, has had a truly impressive career trajectory. Back in India, his father was gone for years at a time working on a Naval vessel before returning home to his humble farming work. In the U.S., he began driving a cab, which he still does to this day. Sunny loved India and would visit each summer. Sunny and his brother were very close to their maternal grandparents and would stay with them when they visited. Sunny's grandmother passed away when he was 13, and his grandfather five years later while visiting them in DC. Both left a lifelong legacy of love and respect. In fact, their picture is Sunny's most prized possession. "I've carried this picture in my wallet for 15 years," he shares. "It's their house in India. Those are two amazing people who really meant a lot to me."

In Alexandria, Sunny and his brother began making friends in their very diverse, new neighborhood. There was a large Indian community, which helped make the transition easier. However, when Sunny turned 12, the family was finally able to afford a house and moved to more remote Springfield, VA. Unlike Alexandria, Springfield was far from diverse. Sunny's family was Sikh which meant he wore a turban growing up. "Kids can be cruel," he acknowledges. "Things got a lot more challenging at that point. I remember being spit upon while riding the school bus for no reason whatsoever other than I was wearing a turban. So those parts were hard. But they did make me stronger."

In the long run, Sunny overcame the bullying and racism, but in high school, his grades suffered as he continued to feel alienated. Looking for something to do and a way to earn money he got a job at a local CVS when he was 15. His family's financial circumstances only added to his difficulties in high school. "The other kids had Air Jordans," he laughs. "I had Hakeem Olajuwons which were $25 from Wal-Mart. So I felt really out of place. My parents couldn't afford to spend the money on nicer clothes so my money allowed me the ability to fit in a little bit more."

By the end of high school, Sunny's GPA was awful. He guesses it may have been something like a 1.6. He didn't have many friends, but he'd already started dating his future wife. Unlike Sunny, she had great academic success and was going on to college. But Sunny remained focused on finding work. His first job after high school was working in the lady's shoe department at Nordstrom. "I was so unsure what I wanted to do," he says. "I had a lot of ambition and envisioned being an entrepreneur at some point. But I didn't know how I was going to get there? I didn't have any guidance or mentors."

After selling lady's shoes for a little while, Sunny had the sales experience to get him in the door at Chevy Chase Bank. Unbeknownst to him, he had set himself on the road that would lead him to the fateful purchase of the moving company and an eventual sale to Waste Management. He ended up getting a college degree online. And while working for Waste Management, he went back to school to get an MBA. "When I went back, I was like, 'Holy cow, if I had only known all this stuff back when I bought my business!' I was such an idiot," Sunny laughs. "I can't believe some of the stuff I did. But in a way, it's a good thing I didn't have the MBA back then because I took risks that I didn't realize were risky. I took risks that I might not take today. But I really got the degree for my son. He hadn't been born yet, but I knew I wanted to set a standard for my future son or daughter. My wife has a Master's degree and works for Northrup Grumman as a CPA. I had to keep up with her!"

Sunny says family is ultimately the reason he does what he does. His wife, Neha, has been a constant source of support and strength through the ups and downs of entrepreneurship. "We grew up together," he smiles. "We're best friends. We know each other well. It's crazy, but we were actually just talking the other day about the fact that we've been together for 17 years. And we still love being together. I couldn't have asked for a better soulmate. She's incredible, and she's always been there for me as I have pursued different opportunities. She's smarter than I am and even passed all four parts of the CPA exam on her first attempt which is very rate. I'm very fortunate." The two have a six-month-old son together.

Sunny's still close with his parents as well, literally. "We have an *Everybody Loves Raymond* situation," he grins. "We bought the house next door to them. My dad's in better shape than I am. The work ethic that guy has is incredible. And my mom, she's a superstar and an overall great person. She's been my primary motivation and drive and was there for me in tough times and good times."

As a leader, Sunny emphasizes the importance of believing in people and in helping them develop and grow. "If somebody's not performing well, it could be just the situation they're in," he points out. "Getting the most out of people means believing in them, talking to them, and putting them in the right situation. I think that goes a long way toward being a good leader. You need to dig in and take the time to invest in people."

To young people entering the working world today, Sunny advises going for what you want in life. "People have dreams ideas, but they don't often pursue them," he says. "When people are on their deathbeds, one of the top regrets they have is that they didn't take that risk. Well, do it! Live in the moment, do it, take that risk. Don't just do something because society thinks you should. Do something because you want to do it, and go through with it, whatever that may be. I was 21 when I bought a moving company, having never worked at a moving company. I'm so glad I did. If I were to kick the bucket tomorrow, I wouldn't have any regrets. How many people can say that?"

Dondi Strong

Things Happen For Us, Not To Us

In early 2018, Dondi Strong was at work when news of the Matt Lauer sexual harassment scandal broke. In that moment, an idea struck her: "What if there was a recruiting firm dedicated to placing women in executive positions and on corporate boards?"

The following Monday, she attended a book launch event for Gretchen Carlson, where the conversation turned to Carlson's experiences being harassed by Roger Ailes at Fox News. After Gretchen spoke, she invited questions and comments. It was there Dondi first vocalized what would become a personal mission: "This isn't just relegated to corporate environments; this harassment is in the same vein as domestic violence," Dondi told the crowd. "I also talked about my experience of being a professional woman getting out of an abusive situation, and how, just like what Gretchen went through at Fox, there's often no support network. So many women of all backgrounds live through abuse and harassment, but oftentimes it gets brushed under the rug. It's important to break the silence."

In what surely felt like fate, that same day, #MeToo began trending on social media worldwide, and Dondi felt the signs could not be clearer; the service she had imagined providing was sorely needed in the corporate world. She knew about a variety of organizations offering networking and mentoring; but nothing like what she knew was needed. She wanted to make sure there was a company whose focus on placing women and other diverse candidates on Boards and in C-Suites across the nation was solid. On April 1, 2018, she founded Levia Partners.

The name "Levia" is particularly meaningful; an anglicization of האיבל or "lioness" in Hebrew. It is also a reference to a book called *Lioness Arising* by Lisa Bevere, a close friend and mentor of Dondi's, and the name of the first female team of Marines special forces sent into Iraq in 2006.

Today, Levia Partners is an executive and board search firm that partners with companies and private equity firms. It focuses on providing authentic diversity; that is, diversity that does more than simply check a box or provide a token candidate. Women are a special focus of Levia, but its services are not strictly limited to women; all forms of diversity are honored, and all those who celebrate inclusion and diversity.

"Many traditional recruiting firms that are highly commission-based put pressure on how many placements should be made each week or month," notes Dondi, "which makes it hard to spend time on quality searches and prime candidates." Because of the flexible nature of owning her own company, she appreciates having the time to do those things with diligence and integrity. Levia Partners has made many successful placements since it started but most notably are the two women, they were able to place on publicly traded boards.

Dondi's specialty is her gift for meaningful relationships, noting that her skill for networking and connecting people is what made recruiting a natural choice for her.

As a young child, Dondi didn't know what type of business she would run, but she did have a specific vision in mind; when asked what she'd like to be when she grew up, she'd reply, "a powerful businesswoman." She had her mother to look up to, who ran a men's wig company along with her father; both of her parents were entrepreneurs with little time for anything but business. Dondi was expected to help whenever it was needed.

Dondi's father taught her many facets of entrepreneurship with the businesses he started and required her to work in all of them. Dondi reflects, "He was all about work, teaching me how to work hard and make money and be responsible. He hoped I would take over the family business at some point."

Her parents also owned one of the only private nightclubs in Salt Lake City, Utah. She remembers, "Every Friday night my parents would get dressed up and go out. My mom was so glamorous, and looked like a model. They smoked, drank, and had a party lifestyle; diamonds and cars and the club, The Gatsby."

The Mormon community she grew up in was strict, and because of her parents' lifestyle, Dondi faced exclusion and harassment, almost to the point of ostracism.

When Dondi was eight years old, her parents took her to a different type of church than the Mormon services she had previously attended. "It was a non-denominational Christian church and after the service, I asked my parents if we could come back," she said. "These people are nice to me."

Thus began Dondi's close relationship with Jesus Christ. Her newfound faith did little to reduce the mistreatment she suffered in her neighborhood and at school. In fact, it worsened the isolation as the family was no longer Mormon. But Dondi focused on prayer, hard work, and Bible study to help get her through her childhood.

When she turned 14, Dondi was required to get her first job. Her father told her he would no longer cover her clothing expenses and that she needed to pull her own weight. Dondi objected that she had to be 16 to get a job, but her father told her to "figure it out," and Dondi did. A friend helped her get a job at a local fast food chain, and from there she tried her hand at a couple of other food service jobs. She joined the family business during her senior year of high school, where she worked long hours answering phones, filing, stacking boxes, stuffing envelopes, and helping fill orders.

When Dondi was in college she met an artist and at the young age of 20, she decided to get married. "My dad was worried we wouldn't have enough money," remembers Dondi. "So, while he was on a trip to Hawaii, he bought the licensing rights to start coffee shops in Utah called Badass Coffee. He enjoyed the implicit irony in doing so, especially since Mormons don't drink coffee."

Dondi and her husband began scoping out sites for the new coffee shops. As they worked to get their stores up and running, Dondi had their daughter, Olivia, and then their son, Michael, in less than 2 years. They moved to Park City to open the second shop, and, despite the two small children, Dondi found herself in a leadership role. "I had been raised in this entrepreneurial environment, so I was able to handle many things with a baby on each hip," smiled Dondi.

After five years of running the coffee shops, Dondi and her husband decided they wanted out of the family business, preferring to make their own way, and decided to move to Seattle, Washington. Her husband had several interviews scheduled with graphic design firms and the couple was immediately greeted with several signs that they'd done the right thing. Among the most poignant was upon walking into the first interview where on the wall was framed a photo of the logo of none other than Badass Coffee. That graphic design firm had done the logo and marketing for the original store in Hawaii. During their brief visit they also checked out a local church, and, feeling at home right away, made the decision to accept a job offer and move in late 1999.

For a while, everything went smoothly, but after 9/11, the economy suffered and her husband's paychecks began bouncing. The couple then decided to strike out on their own and, launched a graphic design business—Serious Design. Her husband was the creative director, handling the artistic side of the work, while Dondi took over the rest, handling everything from operations, to finances, to taxes, to business development. It was the school of hard knocks, but Dondi learned quickly. "I remember calling my dad and telling him that I had been interviewing with attorneys about how to incorporate, and what they wanted to charge me," says Dondi. "He told me, 'What the hell are you thinking? You don't need to pay that! Go figure it out yourself!' and hung up. I almost cried, but when I went and looked it up, I figured it out. That was eye-opening for me, realizing how much I could accomplish if I just tried. I was handling the books, the payroll, the banking—all of it. My dad's tough love moved me to find a way." During this time, Dondi also decided that her children's education was of equal, if not more, importance. Along with a few friends, she started homeschooling their kids in what is known as the Classical Tradition, a methodology she still regards to this day.

In 2006, after seven years in Seattle, Dondi and her husband felt called to help their church start a new location in the Washington, DC area. Their pastor was looking for folks to step up and help, and after six months of prayer, the couple decided they were ready for the move. During their first year in DC, through aggressive business development and with the children now in well-funded public schools, Dondi was able to grow the firm by 100%.

Things went well for a while, but in 2008 a major life-changing event took place: the financial crash, and later bankruptcy. Their firm had done a significant amount of its business with residential and property development companies, and the housing crisis dried up most of their client list. This, among other things, had taken a toll on their marriage as well, causing the couple to divorce shortly after.

But Dondi found a way to thrive. She accepted a job in business development at a local law firm, where she stayed for several years, before being asked to do business development at a national accounting firm. From there she continued climbing the ladder, later securing the position of Regional Director of Client Development at a national law firm. She also remarried and had another son.

Throughout her life and her experiences, she recognizes that many adversities have taught her resilience. "Things happen for us, not to us," encourages Dondi. "My childhood and living through a surprisingly abusive relationship after my first divorce, were like bootcamp for what I do now. I am not afraid. God put this calling on my life, to promote and change the personal and professional landscape for women. Not just to talk about it, but to have the courage to stand up and do something significant to create change."

Beyond her business, Dondi has a history of investing her personal time in women. Along with her work with Levia Partners, she was the chair of Heroines of Washington for many years, a group that highlights the professional and philanthropic successes of women across the D.C. area. She strives to lead by example and follow through even when it gets difficult. "I would say I'm intentional and aggressive," reflects Dondi. "If I say I am going to do something, I go at it 150%. One mistake people in my life have made has been underestimating me. Those who know me understand what I can accomplish. I tell my kids; the definition of leadership is doing what other people are unwilling to do. It is not about success or having people under you; it's about doing what needs to be done, period. Leadership is an inverted pyramid, it's not you on the top." Her kids are now leading themselves. Olivia has graduated college and off on her own with over 10 published poems and looking to pursue a master's degree soon. Her son, Michael, is serving as a United States Marine. A future she had not yet considered when naming her company after one of their missions. And her 11 year old son is a young leader in sports, and especially golf, which he has been competing in events since he was 5 years old.

So what's next for Dondi and her undertaking? She's hoping to launch a woman-owned private equity firm in the coming years. "There is still a huge gap with women leaders, not just in Corporate America but also in private equity and start-ups. Women are significantly under-represented among the investment decision-makers at private equity and venture capital firms, as well as in the leadership of companies that receive this investment capital. Women hold only 10 percent of all senior positions in private equity and venture capital firms globally, and women-led enterprises collected less than three percent of global venture capital in 2017 (Preqin 2017; Zarya, 2018). Without a vision, people will perish," she advises. "Look out at that horizon. Surround yourself with the right people; seek out relationships that make you a better person; and work harder than everyone else."

Dondi still sits on the board of her family's business and helped her father negotiate and successfully sell Badass Coffee to a private equity firm in the summer of 2019. She also sits on the board of the Mid-Atlantic PGA Reach Foundation.

Tracy L. Tyler

From the Bottom to the Top

In college, Tracy Tyler wasn't certain what she wanted to do yet, but she knew she wanted to graduate in four years. She became a business major and after graduation her journey in business started. After a brief stint at a bank, she fell into selling custom accounting software. It was her first sales job, and she was anything but a success.

"I don't know why, but I was terrible at selling software," she laughs now. "It just wasn't the right fit—maybe because I didn't believe in the product." She then moved to selling ads at a radio station, and it was here that she began to connect with her natural talent for selling and helping businesses. "I liked being creative," she reflects. "I liked being able to help businesses by getting to know them and creating an ad campaign that could help their business grow. I realized I'd always had some pre-conceptions of what salespeople were like, and it was typically the stereotype of a slimy used-car salesman. I knew I would never be like that. I was able to factually approach sales with real features and benefits and connect with people in a way that created value and was truly helpful."

Tracy thrived at the radio station for two years and knew she was ready for something more. Friends had suggested that she look into becoming a pharmaceutical sales rep, and the idea appealed to her. However, it had been years since she'd gone on an interview, and she knew the process to become a rep was highly competitive. She decided to prepare by applying to random jobs out of the local paper so she could practice her interview skills. It was then that fate intervened.

For the first practice interview, she picked a metal belt manufacturer. She knew little about the business and never planned to actually accept a job there. "I go into this factory and am instantly fascinated by all the mechanical stuff they're making,"Tracy smiles. "They invited me back for several more interviews, and ultimately, they extended an offer that I accepted. I spent over 25 years there. I started as an entry-level salesperson and spent my last ten years there as the CEO." Thus, Tracy's practice interview launched her on a career through the business, then known as Maryland Wire Belts, which later merged with Cambridge Inc. to form Cambridge International.

Today, Tracy is a Vistage Chair and the founder of TiLT Business Advisors, which she started in March 2018. TiLT offers a broad range of business consulting services to a client list of businesses ranging in size from $1 million to $150 million in annual revenue. Her clients are both U.S. based and global. During her time at Cambridge International, she was able to make connections throughout the world that have been eager to work with her again.

TiLT's focus is fourfold. First, she helps with strategic planning. "Our approach to strategic planning centers around keeping it simple. By understanding where a business is and where they want to go, we work to develop a values driven strategy and action plan. We engage the leadership team by leveraging a 7-step process to point the business and keep it headed in the right direction," says Tracy. Second, she advises clients on merger and acquisition integration. Having been part of multiple mergers and acquisitions—she learned some powerful lessons that she shares in a structured way. By consistently focusing the team from beginning to end, she helps create specific objectives and actions that support the vision," she explains. The key is to not be aligned with a certain way or culture. That mistake usually stands in the way of creating something new by combining the best of each entity. Third, she helps business owners develop engaged and winning cultures. "Making sure that there are good, clear objectives that can cascade through the organization so that everyone knows what they're doing to help the overall success of the company gives people a sense of purpose," she asserts. "As a CEO, culture was very important to me. My team and I worked intentionally to create an environment where people felt valued and enjoyed coming to work. Today I like to use my practical experience to make value driven culture a competitive advantage for the businesses I work with." Lastly, she coaches CEO's, business owners, and executives. This is where Vistage fits in to her focus.

Tracy has always been committed to building a workplace with values and attributes her passion for helping others to the parenting of her mother and step-father. "My step-dad would always say, 'Rich is about being happy,'" she recalls. "'It's not about money. We were rich in love and happiness.' That has stuck with me ever since. My Mom taught me to "meet people where they are". I have considered that a strength of mine throughout my career and life."

Tracy was born in Akron, Ohio, where her father, a surgeon, was stationed as a medical officer in the Air Force. She was the middle child of three girls, each two years apart. Shortly after her younger sister was born, the family moved to California. A year later, her mother made the difficult decision to leave her father and return to her hometown of Preston on the Eastern Shore of Maryland with three little girls in tow who were ages five, three, and one. They rented the place across the street from Tracy's maternal grandmother, who pitched in to help with the girls whenever she could.

Three years later, Tracy's mother married her stepdad, Don, and gained a 10-year-old brother named Bill. While integrating two families wasn't easy at first, the family figured it out and eventually all got along swimmingly. Although they weren't biological siblings, they became just as close. "My brother became our ringleader," laughs Tracy. "We worshipped the ground he walked on. Anything he said, we would do. We loved him, and he loved us."

The happily blended family moved to Cambridge, Maryland, where Tracy spent the remainder of her childhood. She remembers it very fondly and reminisces about the big old houses in her neighborhood. They would go outside and play with the neighborhood kids, climb trees, play kickball and tag, and create their own adventures. Her sisters Kim and Terri have been consistent sources of strength and support throughout all the stages of her life.

The family wasn't rich by any means. Her stepdad was an electronics salesman, and her mother worked some odd jobs but mostly stayed at home with the kids. Her parents were very strict, but loving. They found the right combination of discipline and love. Tracy and her sisters spent time each summer with their biological father, Marc, in California.

The Holidays were a particularly wonderful time of the year. The family rarely went on vacations or received extravagant presents. But Tracy's mom tried to ensure that each year they'd have an exciting Christmas. "It was huge for them,"Tracy smiles. "We always had a lot of presents at Christmas." She also recalls that for years her brother would carefully unwrap the packages in their parents' room whenever they left the house to learn what they bought. The three girls would be on the lookout on the stairways and by the door. It was an annual tradition until one year they all got caught!

Occasionally, they would all travel to Ocean City with their Aunt Aileen, with whom the girls were very close. She generously treated the family to several days there from time to time. "My aunt and my mom would play bingo all night and give us each $5," remembers Tracy. "We would walk on the boardwalk and play skee-ball and pinball throughout the evening. It was a tradition we always looked forward to."

At school, Tracy was a good student, though she remembers that she didn't work particularly hard or study much. It came easy to her, which had its pluses and minuses. She remembers that she had to develop real study habits once she went to college. She and her sisters all got jobs at an early age at the local Dairy Queen. She thinks that starting work at an early age instilled a good work ethic.

While Tracy was still in high school, tragedy struck. Her step-father was diagnosed with cancer, and he passed away when she was only 17. "That was a tough time for the family," remembers Tracy. "The house got very quiet for a while. After my stepdad died, we got a lot visitors but no one really knew what to say or do. And she learned that being there was support enough. No one typically remembers the words that you say, they just remember that you were there. Going through that made me realize that you have to enjoy life while you can. My mom lost her father as a result of a car accident when she was 16. She helped me develop that perspective since you never know what can happen. In her case, he left for work one day and never came home. If you want to find the hidden blessing of someone getting sick, it's having the chance to say good-bye." It has always been important in her family to never leave anything unsaid.

A year after her tragic loss, Tracy enrolled at the University of Maryland. She was excited for the change of scenery and eager to get out of Cambridge which had become stifling. "One night a friend asked me, 'Why do you want to go to Maryland where you're only a number?'" My response was basically that I wanted that anonymity for now."

At Maryland, her grades were average, but she learned a lot. It was the first time she had to make friends and learn how to study effectively. She went from being a Computer Science Major to a Consumer

Economics major. Before her senior year, however, she transferred to nearby Salisbury University to complete her college education. She graduated in her desired four years and earned a degree in Business Administration.

After graduation, she felt a little lost. "I envied my friends who were nurses or social workers because they had a degree with a career path. With a general business degree in a small community, there really wasn't a defined career path. I had to make one." She accepted the first job she could find as a bank teller. From there you know the rest of the story, she tried several jobs before landing at Maryland Wire Belts where she really came into her own.

Her first job at Maryland Wire Belts was entry level sales over the phone. "It's a true skill to be able to connect with someone over the phone and ask the right questions without being able to see their body language or expressions," explains Tracy. "We were selling a highly complex product at a premium price and had to convince them to trust us. I called people all over the country. A typical customer was a Frito-Lay plant that would use the metal belt when making Doritos. It's a fascinating business, and I learned something new every day."

Maryland Wire Belts encouraged her growth within the company. After one year they promoted her to become Department Sales Manager. She credits her boss, Duane, who saw something in her that she didn't see in herself. Her first role in management was anything but successful. "I took over a team of five people that were floundering a bit in a product line that hadn't grown in five years," she recalls. "Within the first three months, all five people quit. They quit because my leadership style was horrific. I had very high standards for myself, but I did not know how to motivate other people. Luckily, I was in an environment where it was okay to make mistakes, and I was able to hire new people and ultimately refine my style. I realized I didn't have to compromise my high standards, but I needed to lead in a way that motivated other people. Within the first year with my newly formed team, we grew that product line by 25%. It was a big public success and put me in a good spot on management's radar."

Soon after, Tracy's boss approached her with great news. He wanted to give her another promotion, but there was a catch. He wanted to make her Co-Sales Manager along with another employee. Tracy balked at the offer. "I told him that if two people are accountable for the work then there would be no accountability. 'You need to pick one,' I told him. To this day, I still can't believe I did that because it was the best career opportunity I'd had up until that point. But I knew that there was something that wouldn't be right about the situation. I think he was so shocked by it and wasn't quite sure what to do." A couple of days later after careful consideration, he made his decision. "He came back and said, 'Be careful what you wish for. I have picked someone, and it's you.'"

"When I got the job, I wasn't sure what the first steps should be," she laughs. "I was one of very few females in a leadership role and had a lot of obstacles to overcome; I had to spend time with people and show them how I operate. Many in the organization had negative preconceived notions about me, but I stayed true to myself and my core values and ultimately won most of them over."

Later, Maryland Wire Belts merged with Cambridge Incorporated, and Tracy's boss, Duane, became the CEO and brought her over to lead sales for the merged companies. By this time, Tracy was more popular in the business. So much so that her co-workers presented her with a congratulatory gift—a sprocket etched with a message on a handmade wooden stand. She considers the sprocket one of her most prized possessions.

Tracy eventually became the VP of Sales and Marketing and later became a Division General Manager where she was able to learn more about the operational side of the business. She enjoyed the challenge of learning about the plant and developing ways to keep the workers engaged and motivated. She used "open book management" to connect the goals and objectives of the sales team with the plant.

Finally, she was promoted to CEO, but she didn't succeed Duane. An operations guy with a background at GE was serving as the interim CEO. Looking back, Tracy considers that to have been the right call. "I wasn't ready yet," reflects Tracy. "And honestly, I didn't even really have my eye on it, I was just looking at the challenges I had in front of me. By the time I was promoted to CEO, I was as ready as I could be. It was a good choice at that point because I knew the market and the business. I don't think it was purposeful that I was groomed for that role, but that was the way my career unfolded. I think I can serve as an example of what value driven hard work, building successful teams, and never backing down from a challenge can do. What helped me stand out was that I was able to surround myself with people who were smarter than me and that I was able to create an environment where people trusted me. I doubt whether anyone is ever really ready to become CEO until you do it. At least for me, I had to learn on the job!"

For the next ten years, Tracy and her team successfully piloted Cambridge International. She considers an early decision one of the best she ever made, and that was hiring of Tom as the COO. They became partners who had the same values and measures of success. They built a team of competent leaders (many who had worked with her from the early days). After creating unprecedented success and value, their Private Equity owner sold Cambridge to a strategic buyer—Rexnord—in 2016, and she decided to stay. "I went from the bottom to the top of this small company that became a global leader," she says. "I had a lot of fun doing that. The company that bought us was a $2 billion publicly traded company, and I thought it would be interesting to see what happens in a much bigger company with 7,000 employees and 500 locations globally."

Tracy stayed for a year but ultimately decided the big business atmosphere wasn't for her. She stepped away from her role, which was one of the hardest things she had ever done.

For several months, Tracy wasn't sure what she would do next. But in September 2017, her Vistage Chair, Harvey, approached her with the news that he was planning to retire and asked whether she'd be willing to take over the group. "I was thrilled at that possibility," she says. "It checked all my boxes in terms of helping people, staying engaged, and being able to make a difference in the lives of people with my practical knowledge and experience."

Through it all, she's had the unconditional support of her husband and their son. Tracy has been married to Ed for 24 years. "My son, Devon, is 20, and I love being his Mom more than anything in the world," says Tracy. "He's a great kid. He is kind, creative, and generous." Ed has been 100% supportive throughout Tracy's many promotions and, ultimately, her decision to leave Rexnord. "Early in my career there was a bit of good, healthy competition," she laughs. In their free time, the couple plays Pickleball, a tennis-like game involving a wiffle-ball and paddle. "I was never a great athlete but was always on the soccer or baseball sidelines cheering on my son. "But about six months into playing Pickleball, I decided to enter a tournament, which was a big stretch for me," Tracy explains. "I found the right partner who keeps me focused and motivated and so far, in our first year, we have eight medals. But the most recent one is the most important to me because that medal means my partner, Vanessa, and I move into the advanced level. It just showed me I can still challenge myself and rise to the occasion."

As a leader, Tracy considers herself to be authentic and genuine. "I was never afraid to say I made a mistake or that I did something wrong," she says. "There's a persona people put on as leaders sometimes that they have to be perfect, never make mistakes, and never let anyone see you sweat. And that's just not the way I would describe myself. I just wanted to be the best version of me as a person and as a leader. I wanted to focus on helping others grow and achieve success beyond what they could have imagined. There are many who made a difference in my life and career. I am grateful to the many people (too many to name) who worked with me and on my teams throughout my career and to those who took me under their wing and mentored me. I hope I was able to do the same."

To kids entering the working world today, Tracy advises following your heart. "Find something that you're passionate about and that you're happy doing, but be prepared to work hard, make mistakes, and keep learning along the way," she encourages. "Maybe it's not the job where you're going to make the most money. And maybe it's going to take you out of your comfort zone. And, if someone starts off like me, unsure what they are passionate about, or what they love, try new things and don't give up until you find it.

Solon G. Vlasto

Took Many Paths, Found a Way

Putting on a play is a complex production, weaving together the diverse elements of lighting, scenery, costumes, sound, script and talent to tell a complete story in the way it was meant to be told. There is no detail too small and no consideration that can be left to chance, with each aspect contributing to the overall picture.

Solon Vlasto first began grasping the gravity of play production in elementary school when he began helping out behind the scenes. He got more involved each year, to the point that he began missing classes in high school to dedicate as much time as possible to theater. "I was working with a fun group of my friends, and every chance we got, we'd work on the upcoming production," he recounts today. "I had no interest whatsoever in being onstage, but I loved the process of creating something from a blank slate, coordinating diverse elements into a clear narrative and experience that was impactful and meaningful to our audience."

Now a co-owner and Principal at Bernhardt Wealth Management (BWM), an independent wealth management firm serving high net worth clients, Solon is still driven by his passion for distilling complexity to clarity for the benefit of others. "As a Christian, I live in faith that we all have unique talents, and that we're meant to share those talents with the world to the best of our abilities," he says. "In wrapping my mind around complicated ideas and then communicating them to clients, sifting through their situations to provide appropriate solutions and excellent service, I believe I'm utilizing my best talent in that way. I want to know the financial planning industry inside and out, and to share that knowledge for client success."

BWM was founded in 1994 to break the mold of traditional commission-based financial planning services by pledging to uphold the fiduciary standard—always acting in the best interests of clients. From asset investment to estate planning to charitable giving to retirement planning, the firm take a holistic view of each individual client's situation and goals. "Like coordinating the elements of a play, its vital that we understand how all these factors work in tandem, since none exist in a vacuum," Solon points out. "We often work with busy clients who have complex financial lives including significant business assets who want to simplify their financial lives and ensure the financial decisions they are making protect what they have worked so hard to build so that they have the mental freedom to focus on the things that really matter to them."

As a wealth manager, Solon's effectiveness rests on his ability to help clients navigate complicated situations and embrace all the opportunities available to them—something that would not be possible without building a high level of trust. "Our industry is fraught with conflicts of interest, so people are right to be skeptical," he says. "But as a fiduciary, we're required to put the client's best interests ahead of ours and our fee-only model aligns our clients' performance with our compensation."

Solon joined the firm in August of 2014 as a Senior Advisor, and in early 2017 became a partner. Through that time, he has contributed to the development of the 26 underlying fundamentals—The Bernhardt Way—that drive the focus of the firm, like honoring commitments, treating others with respect, and maintaining a standard of honesty and openness. These guidelines are in writing and are shared freely with clients for peace of mind and comfort, and they also apply to the way BWM staff interact with one another, allowing for seamless teamwork in service to clients. "The overriding culture of the firm is to do the right thing always," Solon affirms. "That's both rewarding and freeing, as it guides what we do every day and allows us to focus on what matters in our work."

The seeds of Solon's passion for financial planning were first sown when, as a young boy, his father would talk to him about investing. Whenever he bought an interesting stock, or learned a new investment strategy, he would explain it as his face lit up with excitement. "I remember those conversations well," Solon says. "His passion for these ideas opened my eyes to the industry."

Solon's father was a biology professor at the University of Connecticut, while his mother stayed home when he and his younger brother were small. Money was tight and was sometimes a source of tension, but he didn't think much of it. "I'd get a baseball glove, socks, and toys for Christmas, and that was all I wanted," he recalls. "We loved playing outside with the neighborhood kids, building forts or playing sports in our front yard. We'd ride our bikes all over, free to explore as long as we were back in time for dinner."

Solon has always needed to feel that the challenge at hand was meaningful and worthwhile. As a kid, school felt more like a pointless chore than a purposeful pursuit, so he preferred to invest his energy at the Stamford Farm and Nature Center nearby. The working farm and museum happened to catch his eye when he was young, and he began volunteering entirely of his own initiative. "I'd gather eggs, clean out cages, hose down the raccoon pen, make apple cider and help out with public events," he remembers. "There was nothing official about it, and I didn't get paid, but I loved stepping behind the curtain to help out and learn the inner-workings of the operation."

The farm was just one of Solon's wide-ranging interests through childhood, and his parents were always open-minded and supportive as he explored what the world had to offer. From hiking and camping to minibikes and motorcycles to cars, they never pushed him in one direction or another. "Looking back, it might have been helpful for me to pick a focus and stick with it, but overall it was great that they left me free to try things out," he says.

The Vlasto family couldn't afford fancy vacations, but with a little creativity they were able to take fun family trips during his father's long summer breaks from teaching. They went hiking along the Appalachian Trail and loved to camp at Cape Cod, sometimes pitching their tents for a full month at a site a mile's walk from the beach. "I can still remember waking up each morning to the sound of bacon and eggs sizzling on the skillet," Solon says. "We would bike all over the place, taking the back roads from our camp site to the beach or local yacht club to go sailing."

The rest of Solon's summer days were spent biking to the Italian Center in Stamford, where he'd join friends to swim and try to score food from the snack bar. True to form, he eventually found his way behind the counter to become part of the operation, making his first buck frying burgers. "I'd work a couple hours—enough to cover my food for the day with a few extra quarters for the pinball machine," he laughs.

In his freshman year of high school, Solon faced a defining moment when he joined the football team. The coach was exceptionally tough and was known for barking orders and calling out players when they did something wrong. "It was my first experience with a coach like that, and I wasn't a great player, so I was getting yelled at all the time," he says. "It was so hard that I decided to quit, but I regretted it immediately.

I felt like I let myself down, so I asked the coach to take me back. I didn't think he would, but he did, and it completely changed my attitude. While the other kids complained, I saw it as a privilege. I played harder than I had ever played and earned my way to various starting positions."

When Solon switched from football to track the following year, he applied that same focus to pole vaulting and nailed a personal best of 12.5 feet and a second year of earning a varsity letter. Any time he felt passionately about something, he dedicated himself wholeheartedly to the endeavor, like the haunted maze he would help set up every Halloween in the Community House connected to his church. "Other kids' parents would offer to write letters of recommendation for my work ethic after seeing the time and energy I put into that," he says. "At the time I didn't realize what a compliment that was."

Solon's tenacity came, in part, from watching his mother work her way through a Bachelor's and Master's program. He would come home from school to find her studying at her desk. She'd work late into the evenings after taking a break to make dinner. She became valedictorian of her class, demonstrating to Solon and his brother the power of a strong work ethic. "I have that exact same focus now, and I think my daughter picked up on it as she watched me studying for my CFP and CFA certifications," Solon reflects. "Now she's top in her class, too."

Solon's father, as well, taught him the importance of good humor and a positive attitude through life. He was passionate about staying healthy and, above all else, making his family his top priority. "I am blessed to have grown up in a great family and a safe environment," Solon affirms. "I never felt threatened, worried, or unloved; growing up with my family was the greatest gift I could have received. As a result, fame or money have never been a top priority for me. Having a family, making a difference, and contributing to others are what's important to me."

Though Solon never did take to academics in high school, he began considering his future more concretely when he joined Junior

Achievement in high school, and was particularly drawn to a class on the structure of corporations. "It was my first experience with the mechanics of how a corporation is created and grows," he says. "One semester, we launched a corporation building flashlights. We elected a president, sold stock for capital, bought and assembled parts, and sold the flashlights for a profit. My parents didn't know much about that world, and I found that I was hungry to learn more."

Solon's interest was also piqued when he scored particularly well on the vocational aptitude test for the armed forces. Though his parents both valued advanced education, neither pushed him to pursue college, so he began down the road of enlisting in the Army. "I didn't think I could get into college with my grades, but I decided to apply to the University of Connecticut just in case," he says. "I was accepted, and thanks to my father's tenure there, I got free tuition. With that, I enrolled as a Theater Major in the School of Fine Arts."

With time, however, Solon began to realize that a career in theater would be grueling. With its requisite travel and long hours on nights and weekends, it would not be conducive to the family life he wanted. By his junior year, he decided to take a different route. "I was conflicted because I had always had this image in my head of what I was going to do," he recalls. "Now I had to figure out a new path to take with my life."

After a lot of soul searching and support from his parents, Solon decided to lean into another passion of his, flying and becoming a pilot. He enrolled in the Air Force ROTC program at school. Unfortunately, the need for Air Force pilots began to decline, and he decided to switch to civilian flight school. After graduating from college he commenced work toward the various flying licenses he would need. But expenses were adding up, and the Vlastos began to worry. When Solon's father noticed a job advertisement for a stockbroker with no experience necessary, Solon decided to apply. "The plan was to make some money and return to flying in a year," he says. "But with my career launched in finance, I never turned back."

Solon landed the stockbroker job for Chatfield Dean, a firm in Stamford that trained him for his Series 7 exam. "I loved the material and scored well on the test, but then I got to the sales bullpen, and it was nothing like what I had studied," he says. "Once I did 200 dials in a day, nonstop. It was a horrific experience, and I left after three months searching for a better way to serve clients."

Solon then took a job with TD Ameritrade in New York City, where he worked at a call center at 44 Wall Street, helping clients buy and sell stocks. "I enjoyed that because it was everything I had learned for the Series 7," he explains. "I was figuring out margin, working with options and even bond trading." Before long, Solon was promoted to customer service, handling the problems that couldn't be handled elsewhere in the branch. "There was no internet at the time, so the only way people could get information about the markets was from us," he recounts.

Hoping to advance as quickly as possible, Solon told the firm he was willing to move anywhere in the country. When an Assistant Manager position opened up in Arlington, Virginia, he accepted and quickly worked his way up to Manager of the D.C. branch. All went well, until the firm began shifting the branch from a client service focus to a sales focus. "I became a sales manager instead of a branch manager," Solon says. "I didn't like working only towards sales quotas or making sure people had enough dials each day, but I married my wife Kimberly around that time, and we were starting a family. The job allowed me to provide, and I was grateful for that."

On his 20th anniversary with the TD Ameritrade, Solon chose a grandfather clock as his commemorative gift—something timeless to signify the time he had sacrificed to work his way up and create the life he wanted to build for his family. "I had seen my parents tough it out in jobs they didn't love," he says. "Work was work, so I stuck with it, and it helped that I was working with a great team. We were one of the most successful branches of the firm, and I liked that we were still focused on applying our expertise to solve problems."

Then, in 2011, Solon decided it was time for a change. He began studying for the CFP exam, and though the material was challenging, he recognized that old, familiar thrill of studying subject matter he truly enjoyed. He began applying his CFP training to his clients at TD Ameritrade, noting how their conversations broadened and deepened. "It reenergized me and reignited a passion for helping people by translating complexity into clarity for clients," he says.

Pursuing this passion, Solon took a job with a Maryland wealth management firm that allowed him to learn and grow as a financial planner working with high net worth clients. But many of the clients he was landing lived in Maryland, while he wanted to build a book of business closer to his home in Northern Virginia. "That's when I learned BWM was interviewing for a Senior Advisor," he says. "Their investment strategy and commitment to white-glove service and the fiduciary standard was aligned with my own philosophy. It's been a perfect match."

A lifelong learner, Solon continues to educate himself constantly on cutting-edge wealth management techniques and applies that knowledge for the benefit of his clients. "I am passionate about simplifying my client's financial life so they can focus on the things that matter to them," says Solon. "Things like their business or profession, their family, and the causes that are important to them."

It also reminds him of his flying years. "Financial planning is similar to preparing for a flight," Solon affirms. "You plan your route and prepare for what you may encounter along the way. As the trip progresses and when the unexpected happens you remain calm and react skillfully to navigate safely toward your destination."

As a supportive and encouraging leader, Solon advises young people entering the workforce today to pursue a career that strikes a balance between their interests and strengths. "Your first job doesn't need to be your dream job," he says. "Explore your options so you can figure out what you're good at, and what you actually like. Sometimes, you won't know until you try."

Through the various paths Solon himself has tried over the years, his wife Kimberly has been his constant support, affirming the commitment to family that has driven him all along. "Kimberly has always encouraged me to do what I felt I needed to do along the way," he affirms. "We're so proud of our three kids, who are all so different and exceptional in their own ways. Through the complexity of life, one thing has always been clear to me and that is that family is the most important thing. That will never change."

The importance of family was modeled throughout Solon's life by his parents. "After my father's death, my mother gave me Dad's video files. He was known for capturing his family on film. There are videos of my father's life before he met my mother, so you can see how our family unfolded. And there's always a smile in his voice as he's talking to people in the videos. Those video files are one of my most prized possessions and a constant reminder that family is everything."

BERNHARDT

WEALTH MANAGEMENT

Fred Westerlund

Give Them the Tools to Succeed

Growing up, Fred Westerlund didn't dream about going to West Point. Although his grandfathers had served in the military, he never thought seriously about joining the armed forces. Then, as he finished high school with his mind set on getting a degree in engineering, he began to look into various financing options and started considering ROTC. His guidance counselor told him something he wouldn't soon forget. "He told me I would never get into West Point," remembers Fred. "And that gave me a goal I was determined to achieve. I'm the type of person who is highly motivated by hearing what others think I cannot do. So, I made a commitment to myself to challenge his conclusion."

Fred committed himself fully to the application process. He completed the necessary forms, took the physical fitness test, went on interviews, and travelled to his Congressman's office to meet with the staff there. Fred's father drove him to the interview where a dozen other young people were also competing for Representative Brian Donnelly's coveted recommendation. "After the interview, I got in my dad's car and told him, 'I'm going to West Point! I'm in,'" remembers Fred. "My dad reminded me not to get my hopes up too high, but I had that strong feeling of knowing all your hard work is about to payoff. I knew I would get it." And he did.

At West Point, Fred was challenged beyond what he could have imagined, but the experience gave him confidence and leadership skills he would carry throughout the rest of his career. "That first year was especially hard," he recalls. "You're getting letters from your friends in college talking about the parties they're attending, and I'm here working on weekends. I was balancing a heavy course load with military education and leadership development. Even dinner was preceded by a formation. You have to want it, and I definitely wanted it. I just felt like it was so special to be at West Point. I felt honored and privileged to be accepted there."

When it came time to specialize, Fred chose to go into the ordinance corps—a combat support group responsible for equipment maintenance and ammunition supply. He was ranked relatively high in his class which meant he was able to choose his post early. He selected Fort Hood in Texas. "My logic was that of a young man. I chose Fort Hood at least partly because Miss Texas always seemed to be in the running for Miss America," laughs Fred. "But seriously, it's a huge installation with plenty of opportunity."

While at Fort Hood, Fred took over a platoon in a company and began to make use of his newly honed leadership skills. He loved managing the team, working alongside his people, and earning their respect. "I later learned from my commander's performance evaluation that my platoon had been a recalcitrant group of soldiers, and I had formed them into a productive, high-performing team," says Fred. "Evidently the previous platoon leader liked to sit in the office and complete paperwork. I'm not that kind of person. I thrived at this assignment by being outside, being physically active, and being part of the team." Fred's platoon managed half of the largest ammunition supply point in the United States, and day after day, Fred would first handle any necessary paperwork before going to the bunkers to load and unload ammunition with them. "I guess that's what the platoon needed," Fred reflects, "They needed to see a platoon leader who was in it with them, who understood what they did, and who cared for them."

This is the type of leader Fred has always been, and still is today. He's in the bunker sweating with his team, not sitting on the hill doing paperwork. Throughout his career, Fred has been asked to revitalize teams, processes, and whole businesses. As he's gone about this work, he's always prioritized the happiness and well-being of the team. It's not just soft-heartedness that pushes Fred to carefully consider the needs of his staff; it's just good business sense. "I truly enjoy teaching and coaching people. When someone wants to be coached and is receptive to feedback, it's a really rewarding feeling to watch them grow," Fred asserts. "You want people to be happy. If you give them the tools and a supportive work environment, you will achieve most of your goals."

Fred's methodology has been validated in each role he's held, and in 2017, he brought his proven talents to MBH Settlement Group (MBH) where he was hired as CEO. MBH is a prominent title insurance company in Northern Virginia that has been doing steady business for over 25 years but may have stagnated in the years leading up to Fred's involvement. "MBH was well known in real estate circles, but at that time, there was a lot of room for growth," recounts Fred. "I thought revitalizing such a well-known brand would be a terrific challenge. I thought it would be really special and would impact a lot of people in a positive way."

Since Fred took the helm, MBH has grown by any measure. For example, employee turnover is down significantly—a statistic which, in typical Fred fashion, he proudly cites first. Client satisfaction, meanwhile, is at 96%, a reliable indicator thanks to Fred's strategic switch to new software that automatically sends out client surveys after each transaction. The financials have blossomed as well, with revenue and profits increasing. "All metrics are heading in the right direction," observes Fred. "In the first year, you're laying the groundwork. Now we're really starting to see the impact, and I feel good about what we've done and where we're heading. You give your employees the tools to succeed, ensure they understand what success looks like, help them see that they're part of something bigger, and make sure they're appreciated. The results speak for themselves. Client satisfaction increases when employee satisfaction increases."

Fred's employee-focused approach is aimed at ensuring a positive and inclusive culture at MBH, with an emphasis on meaningful collaboration and strong personal relationships. Under his leadership, MBH's offices are encouraged to work together. Employees engage socially at the company's annual holiday party and summer event, and the company's performance is reviewed and our goals and path forward are discussed at our "all-hands" meeting. Fred believes in sharing the company's plans and getting employees personally invested in the company's success. Fred has also worked to introduce more performance metrics and recognize and reward outstanding individual and team performance.

MBH has 20 offices in Virginia, Maryland, and D.C. By refocusing on employee engagement and satisfaction, Fred has positioned MBH to successfully expand its market share and continue its upward trajectory—but he knows growth cannot come at the expense of the positive changes he's already effected. "Eventually we will pursue more business organic to D.C. and Maryland, but we're going to do it right. We're going to take care of our current clients first and continue investing in our employees."

Fred comes by his passion for teaching and coaching naturally. While growing up in Brockton, Massachusetts, his mother was an elementary school teacher, and his father was a draftsman who coached in his spare time. He has one brother who is six years younger; and the family lived near his maternal grandparents. Every Sunday they would have dinner with their grandparents, aunts, uncles, and cousins and eat the delicious food their grandmother spent all day cooking. Fred's paternal grandparents also lived in the area, however in a town that was a little further away. As a boy, he remembers playing army, cops and robbers, street hockey, and pond hockey with the other neighborhood kids. He also loved football, baseball, and basketball.

In the summer, the family would go to Wareham on Cape Cod where Fred's grandparents had a cottage. "In my memory, that place was huge," smiles Fred. "We drove by there a few years ago, and it's really not big at all. There was a little store that had candy for a penny or gum for a nickel and had other things like superhero comic books and little cowboy figures. My cousins and I would walk into that store with a quarter, get a bunch of cool stuff, and then walk down to the beach. It was a quiet, beautiful community."

Fred's parents were loving and supportive as he grew up. He remembers that his mother had a real, personal investment in her students. "One thing I really admire and respect about my mother is that she cared about her kids," affirms Fred. "She felt responsible for them and wasn't just cashing a paycheck. I think that rubbed off on me. It was easy for me to absorb and incorporate being responsible for your team when we were being taught that at West Point."

His father, meanwhile, coached Fred's sports teams from Little League baseball to football to the church league basketball team. Fred's first job was a paper route, which he would do on his own except when it was snowing heavily, then his father would drive him along the route and stop in front of each house for Fred to jump out and deliver the paper. In retrospect, Fred realizes what a supportive thing it was to do, especially since his father had a bad back and would often be in pain after sitting for long periods of time. Fred is visibly touched as he states, "When I was probably five years old in kindergarten, I made a little sailback dinosaur out of clay. It was three or four inches long," he describes. "Several years ago while visiting my parents, I saw that dinosaur on my father's dresser. I couldn't believe that he'd kept it for all those years. It reminded me of how supportive and loving my parents had been when I was a child."

In his thoughtful way, Fred connects this feeling of love between a parent and child with the respect he shows his employees. "Everybody on my team has a relationship like that outside of work," he reflects. "Every single person is special to someone else. I'm partly responsible for the overall well-being of the people on my team, and that's a responsibility I take seriously."

Fred went to West Point with a good grounding in what it meant to be a leader. He graduated with the ability to apply the values he'd grown up with. After his time as a platoon leader at Fort Hood, he became an Executive Officer in an equipment and automotive supply company and was the second in charge after the company commander. Then as the Berlin Wall came down, the government decided to offer buyouts to officers who wanted to leave the military early. Fred had loved his time there but knew he didn't want to make it a career. He left after four years and headed out to put his engineering degree to work.

His first job was with an engineering consulting firm in Fort Worth that worked on nuclear power plants. He began as an engineer and was working on design modifications and testing safety systems. Over time he began managing projects and making sales to utility companies and plant managers. Fred learned a lot after five years there but since there wasn't much potential for moving up Fred decided he wanted to learn more about business. He left to attend the Wharton School of Business on a full-time basis.

At Wharton, he majored in finance and marketing. "Wharton's known for its finance school so it made sense to major in finance. Plus, as an engineer, I was already comfortable with numbers," explains Fred.

"And I majored in marketing because of its role in helping to drive sales. You must grow revenue to run a business successfully." For two years, Fred lived in Centre City, Philadelphia and would ride his bike to school. He also joined Wharton's rowing crew. "That was a blast. We'd get up at 5 o'clock in the morning and would be out there rowing on the river. We were outdoors and on many mornings it would appear as if we were gliding on glass. It was wonderful," reminisces Fred. "In my second year, we won the World MBA Rowing Championships up in Boston."

While at Wharton Fred met his future wife, Chryssa, who, Fred is quick to note, has been incredibly supportive throughout his career. The couple has four children; three sons, who are 19, 18, and 14 respectively, and a 16-year-old daughter. "Chryssa allowed me to put my career first," Fred says. "She has a great career and is a VP with the Metropolitan Washington Airports Authority. But for many years, she put what she saw as the good of the family first allowing me to prioritize my career."

After Wharton, Fred's first job was with Sprint in Reston where he worked in sales. After 18 months, he landed a deal with France Telecom and was promoted to group manager. He took over a pricing group within Sprint Business Marketing in Dallas. There he helped introduce flexible pricing for the salespeople, and after his new pricing brought increased revenue, he was promoted to Director of Marketing for some new internet data products—a $500 million portfolio. He immediately slashed costs with his trademark efficiency and pulled them out of several trade shows that were costing $4 million annually but producing no revenue. Over his tenure, Fred grew his marketing portfolio 60% to over $800 million.

After eight years with Sprint, the company was planning to transfer him to Kansas City where the family had no connections. Fred began a new job search and was offered a VP role at NVR Mortgage Finance, a division of a large homebuilder in Virginia. "They had a unique business model and weren't hiring leaders from other homebuilders. They wanted to build their bench with leaders from outside the industry," relates Fred. "It was an interesting opportunity since I enjoy learning new things and taking on new challenges." So the family moved to Maryland and Fred took over the Washington/Maryland region.

Fred applied his usual management techniques. He learned how the business operated, learned where the inefficiencies were, and pulled all the parts together to work fluidly. He, once again, ensured the staff knew they were appreciated and gave them the tools to succeed. "By the end of my second year we had the leading gross margin in the company at 69.7%," he remembers. "In order to improve the organization, I first had to understand how everything operated from a loan officer's perspective. That enabled me to apply what I'd learned elsewhere to streamline processes, emphasize customer service, redirect incentives, and provide coaching and additional training." Within a couple of years, Fred was moved to headquarters in a COO role to lead title company operations. He was quickly promoted and in his six years as President, customer satisfaction scores and employee retention reached historic highs, the financials improved dramatically, and the business expanded into three new states.

In 2014, Fred sought a change of scenery and eventually took the COO role at PenFed Credit Union, the third largest credit union in the U.S. It was a great opportunity, but ultimately, Fred was receptive when approached by MBH ownership two years later.

As a leader, Fred always bears in mind his responsibility to his team. "I'm not just responsible for the results," he says. "I'm responsible for the well-being of the team. I strive to give them the best possible environment in which to succeed. To me, that means making sure they understand what success is and then providing the tools and resources to achieve that success."

To young people entering the working world today, Fred advises an open mind and confidence. "When you're first coming out of college, it's not a bad time to experiment," he encourages. "You may not know exactly what you want to do. That first job and that first industry may not be for you. And that's okay; just give every opportunity your best and try to learn and grow every step of the way. West Point was crucial in terms of building my confidence, and that confidence has been a key to my success. I enter every situation believing that I'm going to be a part of something special and knowing, with 100% certainty, that I'm going to make it a better place. If you embrace each new opportunity looking to help others and make a difference, then good things will come your way."

BERNHARDT

WEALTH MANAGEMENT

Adham Yusupov

Looking for the Next Thing

In May of 2012, Adham Yusupov had a map of his future. He'd just graduated from George Mason University, and in April he'd taken the LSAT and scored a 162. The next step was a given—he would apply to law school and begin his career on the business side of law. But just then, two events intervened.

The first was a few chance encounters at a Kentucky Derby party on a rooftop in New York City. His brother, whom Adham describes as a "social butterfly," had invited Adham to meet some friends in the music industry and enjoy a day out. But at the party, Adham encountered not one, but several lawyers all of whom were unhappy in their profession. "They were saying things like, 'If I could, I'd throw myself off this rooftop,'" stresses Adham. "It was highly demotivational!"

The second was the illness of his father—the family breadwinner. Adham's father had long been a successful businessman, working for years with the World Bank and then for a prominent think tank. But that year, he suffered a stroke. Adham and his younger brother worried over the future of their younger sister, as well as the wellbeing of their mother, who had been a stay-at-home mom up until this point.

In 2012, the economy was still reeling from the financial crisis, and jobs—particularly well-paying jobs—were in short supply. Suddenly, Adham knew what he had to do. Pulling in his brother to help, he launched a business, Ecology Mir Group (EMG), and from its humble beginnings in his parents' basement, it has quickly grown into a multi-million-dollar company with an impressive array of services.

Initially, EMG was founded as an IT subcontractor, working with a partner to provide IT products and services to the federal government. But over the seven years of its existence, Adham has kept a close eye out for opportunities for expansion and diversification. The first big one came in 2014.

It was EMG's first experience with logistics, and Adham quickly saw the opportunity for expansion. "From there, we just started blowing up," explains Adham. "We continued our partnership on the IT side, but we started focusing heavily on logistics, on getting things from Point A to Point B for the government. It was through the Department of Defense, but also through the Navy, the Army, the FBI, the State Department, you name it, we worked with them all nonstop. We've acquired 760 prime contracts since then."

Their "secret sauce," as Adham puts it, is their efficiency. They have the systems in place and the infrastructure to offer a tight turnaround, accepting seemingly impossible requests from the government late on a Friday evening and having projects completed by Sunday or even Saturday. "The agencies know who we are, because we're the ones who can get it done," affirms Adham. "If they call another company, they won't even hear back until Monday. Not many businesses can do what we do, especially the big ones where there's a lot of bureaucracy."

The next big expansion came in 2016, when Adham's brother approached him with a proposal—getting into the ammunition industry. Not only did they push into manufacturing ammunition and supplying it to the federal government but they expanded into the commercial side under the EMG Ammo label, selling to gun ranges. "One thing led to another, and some of the agencies we're working with realized, 'Hey, you guys are providing the logistics side, you're providing ammunition, can you move bigger things,'" explains Adham. "'Can you transport these missiles? Can you provide these explosives, or certain other items that regular carriers cannot?' And we could. So we signed contracts, we got our licenses to handle grenades and explosives. It was a pivotal moment in the history of our company."

Today, EMG has 12 employees, and will break $10 million in revenue this year. Their year over year growth has been astonishing, and Adham is looking to bring on more staff as their capabilities continue to expand. "We help the government procure mission critical solutions," says Adham of the business today. "That ranges from logistics to armament, even to construction. The government relies on us heavily to be able to procure these things on a quick turnaround. We're moving equipment, we're moving missiles, we're moving ammunition, we're moving people, we're moving soldiers, and we even provide training as well. We continue to pass off to our partner the IT work that we were doing when the company was created."

Ever keen to improve and sharpen the company's edge, Adham has recently turned his attention to EMG's sales department. From the time the business launched in 2012, this department was the purview of his younger brother. However, about a year and a half ago, his brother chose to bow out, feeling exhausted by the 24/7 schedule of running EMG. Adham took this opportunity to begin restructuring the department. "I'm never the type that sits around and gets comfortable, I'm always looking for optimization," reflects Adham. "Everything my brother had built in the sales department was critical. Some of the things he had built were great and some, I learned, needed improvement. But these were all lessons. I had let him take the reins there and run with it. When he left and I looked more closely at the processes in that department, I realized there were things we could do better. Therefore, I brought the right people into the department to really start growing that part of our business. We had a great foundation that he helped us build, but now we're using that to launch into something even better."

Adham and his siblings come by their ambition honestly. Their father was the second most successful businessman in Uzbekistan before the fall of the Soviet Union in 1991. That year, as it collapsed, Adham's father chose to move Adham and his mother to Chicago, Illinois, where Adham's brother was born. Soon after that, when Adham was about 5 years old, the family moved to a big ten acre property outside the DC area, overlooking the Blue Ridge Mountains.

The area was beautiful, but there wasn't much to do out there. There were no neighborhood kids to play with or shopping malls to get lost in. Instead, Adham and his younger brother, and later his younger sister, spent their days playing outside by the Shenandoah River, or swimming in the Olympic-sized pool that was part of our home. "My first friends were probably the deer in our backyard," jokes Adham. In the summers, the whole family would return to Uzbekistan, where the kids loved to spend time with their cousins, aunts, and uncles. Adham's parents also spent a significant amount of time travelling the world, and Adham and his cousins spent time in Europe, Canada, the Caribbean, and Hawaii.

Adham's father became the Regional Director for Central Asia and Azerbaijan at the World Bank. The position meant non-stop travel so Adham's grandparents moved here from Uzbekistan to help watch over the children. They took them to school and attended basketball games with Adham's mother. In fifth grade, Adham had his first taste, literally, of entrepreneurship when he convinced his grandparents to buy him bulk packages of FunDip from Costco. Adham then sold the

FunDip for a dollar a pop on the playground. He paid his grandparents back and made his first $100 in profit.

Academically, he thrived, earning straight A's during his time in elementary school, and then at Randolph Macon Academy (RMA)—the Junior ROTC Air Force Academy in the area. Adham's older cousins from Uzbekistan were already attending the school; some lived on campus, and some, much to Adham's delight, came and stayed with the family. From 6th grade to 9th grade he continued at RMA, and developed his passion for sports, particularly basketball.

After earning a black belt in karate as a young boy, basketball became something of an obsession for Adham. Rain, snow, or shine, he was out in the driveway shooting hoops much to the chagrin of his always-worried grandmother. By eighth grade he had helped RMA earn a conference championships and was attracting the attention of recruiters at local private high schools. In ninth grade, he met with a representative of Wakefield High School to check it out and liked what he saw. As Wakefield was known for its strong academics, his parents approved, and the Yusupov kids began attending the prestigious private school the following fall.

By this time, Adham was such a strong player that he was named Captain of the Varsity Basketball team as a mere sophomore, inviting a fair amount of anger from the older students who felt entitled to the role. However, Adham took to the captain title quickly, learning lessons about leadership along the way. "That's when I really began to develop as a leader. Prior to that I was more egotistical," admits Adham. "It was 'Hey, I'm this, I'm that, I'm the best.' And I started to realize that leadership isn't about "me." You have to focus on what everyone else is doing. You're only as strong as your weakest link. And I believe those lessons transferred over to the business world."

One summer, Adham had the privilege of playing with the National Basketball team of Uzbekistan. His father had previously worked with the Olympic Committee there and was able to get his son in for practices during the summer. "Some of these guys went on to play in the NBA," marvels Adham. "You have to remember that I was the youngest and the shortest and they're looking at me like, 'Why is this kid even on the court?' But when I came back from training that summer my coaches could see that my skills were greatly enhanced. When I came back I was faster, I could jump higher, and I could even dunk at that point. Everyone wondered how I could improve so much just by playing in the backyard until they realized I had spent the summer with the Uzbekistan Olympic team. I think my coaches wanted to send the other kids overseas, too!"

The schedule at Wakefield was punishing. The school was an hour from home, which meant Adham was up every morning by 6:00 AM, and never home at night until 8:00 PM at the earliest. Between school, studying, basketball, and commuting, Adham barely had a minute to himself and often fell asleep at his desk doing homework late at night. As a sophomore, he was taking AP Calculus, and while he loved his math and science courses, his grades were no longer the straight A's he'd enjoyed back in middle school.

As a high school student, Adham focused on math and science because he was interested in becoming a doctor. His grandfather had been a cardiologist, his grandmother a dentist, his aunt a radiologist, to name just a few. He had observed surgeries at hospitals in Uzbekistan as a teenager so Adham felt medicine was in his blood. This idea persisted right up until he was picking classes at the registrar's office at the start of his freshman year at George Mason University (GMU). He looked at his schedule, heavy with biology and chemistry courses, and said to himself, "This isn't what I want to do."

His mother was surprised since being a doctor had been his goal for some time. But Adham pivoted, ultimately majoring in Sociology with a global concentration and minoring in Business.

Adham tried out for the GMU basketball team and was eventually asked to be part of the practice squad. He was also invited to try out for the NBDL, a minor basketball league. He enjoyed the GMU and NBDL but his father had a father-son talk with him. "He said, 'I appreciate what you do, and I know you're good at basketball,'" recalls Adham, "'but are you really going to be great at basketball at the level you're dreaming about, making it to the NBA, where you can sustain yourself and make a living off of it?' So my dad made it very clear to me that I needed to focus on my education and finish my degree where I would have a lot more potential."

Hoping to encourage his business ambitions, Adham's father began involving him in meetings, allowing him to review documents and contracts, and successfully piqued Adham's interest. He still loved basketball, but he was ready to focus fully on his future.

During his time at George Mason, Adham had another crucial encounter: he met the love of his life. The two met in a 300-level Criminology course, where Adham nervously tapped her on the shoulder and asked if she was from Uzbekistan. In fact, she was half-Japanese and half-Persian, but the question launched a conversation, that became a friendship, that became a romance. Adham admires not only his wife's beauty and intelligence—she has since gotten her PhD—but her love of family. "In our culture, it doesn't matter if you're affluent or if you grew up with a silver spoon or not," explains Adham. "At the end of the day you have a lot of responsibility to your family, to your parents. In our culture, as parents get older, they stay with their children. My father stays with me now, and my wife had the same mentality as me about family, that's what really connected us."

It helps, too, that Adham's wife completely supports the work he does with EMG. "She's so supportive, so understanding," he nods. "We went on a vacation to Cabo recently, and it was the first time I'd taken a week off in three years. I was still working 80% of the time. I was on phone calls addressing very critical things. And guess what? She was super understanding; she never gave me a hard time about it. She understood, this is what has to be done. She's truly seen me rise from nothing to something."

Adham's wife also gets along swimmingly with his mother, who has been on her own journey of growth over the past few years. As mentioned, she had been a stay-at-home mom up until Adham's father's stroke. But a couple of years after he fell ill, she decided to try her hand at the professional world, accepting a job as a sous chef. In only four years, she's had a meteoric professional rise, becoming the Executive Chef at well-known restaurant Chef Geoff. She recently accepted a new Executive Chef position with an even larger restaurant company headquartered in Tampa. "She was always passionate about food," smiles Adham. "Right away, when the executives saw her potential, she was climbing that ladder until she got to the top position. In the past few years, we've seen this new side of her. I really admire how she's been able to excel."

Adham asserts that not only his parents, but also his siblings, share his drive and work ethic. "We're very confident in what we do," Adham notes. "Perhaps bouncing around to different schools and moving a lot as a kid helped us become who we are and developed our drive. It built confidence that no matter where we went, we're going to make it happen, we're going to make it big. I know there are people who are happy to put in their 9-to-5, go home and relax, and enjoy a drink. We're not those people!"

As a leader, Adham says he started to develop his leadership skills when he was the team captain of his basketball team. His coach emphasized that the team was only as good as its weakest link and it was his duty to help his teammates.

Adham says his style is still developing, but stresses the importance of patience, especially in the context of a new business. "You want things to happen right away," he says. "But that's not how it works. Be patient with your first contract, be patient with your team, be patient with everything. That's something I admire about my dad, his patience and his diplomacy."

Most of all, he advises courage. "Go for what you want," Adham encourages. "Don't let anyone else tell you what you can or can't do. A lot of people gave me recommendations, some were right, some were wrong. In my gut, I always had a feeling of the direction I needed to go. I believe in growing, diversifying, and always improving. What drives me to do what I do? I'm always looking for the next thing."

BERNHARDT

WEALTH MANAGEMENT

About the Author

Having grown up on a farm in Nebraska, Gordon Bernhardt left the Midwest in the early 1980s for Washington D.C. to work as an assistant in the U.S. House of Representatives. He left behind the rural lifestyle but he carried with him the values of hard work, a focus on what you can control, and service to others—values that continue to influence his life, today.

After completing a bachelor's degree in Commerce at the University of Virginia, Bernhardt began a successful career in finance at a leading accounting firm and two different brokerage companies. In 1994, in order to make the kind of difference in people's lives that he hoped to make, he established Bernhardt Wealth Management, an independent registered investment advisory firm built on the principle of fiduciary care: providing investment and wealth management guidance, service, and advice that places clients' interests and needs ahead of everything else. By adhering to this higher standard, he removed the conflicts of interest that were prevalent elsewhere. Rather than be restricted by a large company's cookie cutter methodology, he and his team are able to create customized plans that are far more appropriate for individual clients. Today, Bernhardt Wealth Management is recognized as one of the top fee-only wealth management firms in the Washington D.C. region.

In addition to being an entrepreneur and wealth manager, Bernhardt is the author of *Buen Camino: What a Hike through Spain Taught Me about Investing and Life*, a memoir about the 35-day, 618-mile pilgrimage he completed in Spain and the lessons he learned along the way. He also writes a weekly finance blog. Bernhardt writes the *Profiles in Success: Inspiration from Executive Leaders* book series, and hosts a podcast with the same name, to expand the influence of outstanding leaders while inspiring the next generation of executives.

Find out more about Gordon Bernhardt at
www.BernhardtWealth.com and www.ProfilesInSuccess.com.

Pvt. Jonathan Lee Gifford was the first U.S. soldier killed in Iraq. He was killed just two days into the war on March 23, 2003. Spc. David Emanual Hickman was killed by a roadside bomb in Iraq on November 14, 2011. *The Washington Post* on December 17, 2011, said Hickman "may have been the last" U.S. soldier killed in Iraq. After reading an article about Gifford and Hickman my sister, Gloria, was inspired to write the following poem.

From Gifford to Hickman

by Gloria J. Bernhardt

From Gifford to Hickman...and all those in between,
You fought bravely amid chaos and dangers unforeseen.
Twenty-one guns have sounded, the riderless horse walks on.
Fond memories are remaining. A nation's child is gone.

Sons and daughters; fathers, mothers—broken hearts intertwined.
Hugs and kisses; their successes—major milestones left behind.
Your selfless gift—a life laid down; for fellow soldier, family, land.
Duty called—call was answered—no greater love hath man.

"I'm getting taller. I lost a tooth. I got 100 on my test!
Miss your pancakes and your tickles, goodnight kisses were the best.
Who will answer all my questions now? I've important stuff to learn!
You said you had a big surprise on the day that you'd return."

"I talk to you at bedtime—after lights go out at night.
I told Jesus that I miss you...sure wish you could hug me tight.
When Grandpa says I look like you, Grandma starts to cry.
I'm mad that you're not coming home...I need to say goodbye!"

From Gifford, to Hickman, through every soldier who has served,
Liberty's fruits are savored and freedom is preserved.
We live freely due to soldiers, willing to support and defend
Our Constitution, our country—against enemies 'til the end.

Sons and daughters; fathers, mothers—broken hearts intertwined.
Hugs and kisses; their successes—major milestones left behind.
Your selfless gift—a life laid down; for fellow soldier, family, land.
Duty called—call was answered—no greater love hath man.

"I had a dream the night before…you smiled and walked on by.
When I awoke, I thought it odd…it seemed like a 'good-bye'.
I couldn't put my finger on the dark cloud that remained,
When the phone began to ring…I knew my life had changed."

"I questioned God, 'Why MY child? Why do I have to lose?'
I imagined His response would be 'If not your child, then whose?'
Your bright life flashed too briefly… seems He only takes the best.
I'm thankful for the time I had. For that I'm truly blessed."

From Gifford to Hickman and every warrior who has passed,
The price you've paid bought freedom, but will we make it last?
Your last breath drawn for citizens in this country and abroad
Are we worthy of such gifts is known only but to God.

Sons and daughters; fathers, mothers—broken hearts intertwined.
Hugs and kisses; their successes—major milestones left behind.
Your selfless gift—a life laid down; for fellow soldier, family, land.
Duty called—call was answered—no greater love hath man.

"My world stopped spinning...I couldn't breathe! Lord, how can I go on?
My days are all one midnight...but they say it's darkest 'fore the dawn.
I can hear you say, 'I'm proud of you! I know that this is hard.'
What do I do without you here? What dreams do I discard?"

"I miss your laugh. I miss your smell. I even miss our fights.
No more messes. No embraces. It's more 'real' late at night.
I saw you in a crowd today; but you vanished in the throng.
Wishful thinking changes nothing! I know my "rock" is gone."

FOR Gifford, FOR Hickman...FOR all the fallen in between,
You've trudged through shadowed valley and joined heroes' ranks unseen.
Upon freedom's altar, we sacrificed our daughters and our sons.
Empty boots stand at attention. The flag is folded. Your mission's done.

Made in United States
Orlando, FL
04 November 2026

90208345R00226